ROBERT ABERLE

FOURTH EDITION

The ADMINISTRATION OF *Justice*

AN INTRODUCTION TO THE
CRIMINAL JUSTICE SYSTEM IN AMERICA

Kendall Hunt
publishing company

BRIEF CONTENTS

CONTENTS

CHAPTER 4   An Introduction to Criminology   63

CHAPTER 5   The Concept of Laws in America   77

CHAPTER 7   Police Procedures   117

CHAPTER 8   Courts: The System

CHAPTER 9   Pretrial Activities, the Criminal Trial, and Sentencing

*C*HAPTER 12 Juvenile Justice   219

Chapter Overview

The United States Constitution is the basis of all laws in this country, and therefore is the basis of our entire criminal justice system. It is only appropriate that any textbook that is intended to give an overview of the criminal justice system in America begin with a discussion about the U.S. Constitution and its applications to justice. A student of Criminal Justice needs to have a working knowledge of how the government is set up, how this structure directly affects how our laws are made, how society influences our laws, and how our individual rights shape our society.

This chapter provides a summary and analysis of the first ten amendments to the U.S. Constitution, commonly referred to as the Bill of Rights. The majority of citizens are at least familiar with most of the rights afforded to them under these amendments, but this chapter will look at how they are applied to the administration of justice. We will also discover that none of these rights are absolute; there are exceptions and limitations to each of them. One of the primary functions of the United States Supreme Court is to interpret the U.S. Constitution, and over the course of the past 220 years the Court has interpreted it in a variety of ways. These interpretations change with each session of the Court, and criminal justice professionals need to stay abreast with these changes because many of the rulings from this Court have a direct effect on, and constantly change, the procedures for each of the three sub-sections of criminal justice: police, courts, and corrections.

CHAPTER LEARNING OBJECTIVES

After reading this chapter you will be able to:

1. Describe the three branches of government and their relation to the criminal justice system.
2. Understand the system of checks and balances within our system of government.
3. List the individual rights associated with the proper amendments of the Bill of Rights.
4. Understand the function of the United States Supreme Court in the interpretation of the U.S. Constitution and the Bill of Rights.
5. Explain why the rights afforded by the U.S. Constitution are not absolute and why their interpretations change over time.

KEYWORDS

United States Constitution
Legislative Branch
Judicial Branch
Bill of Rights
Capital Crime

Amendment Process
Executive Branch
Checks and Balances
Exceptions and Limitations

THE PREAMBLE TO THE UNITED STATES CONSTITUTION

We the People of the United States, In Order to form a more perfect Union, establish Justice, insure domestic Tranquility, provide for the common defence, promote the general Welfare, and secure the Blessings of Liberty to ourselves and our Posterity, do ordain and establish this Constitution for the United States of America.

© Rich Koele, 2011.
Used under license from
Shutterstock, Inc.

INTRODUCTION

The **United States Constitution** is the basis of criminal justice in America. This remarkable document was completed on September 12, 1787 and was ratified and became the law of the land on June 21, 1788. The U.S. Constitution has become one of the most important and influential government documents ever written.

The original United States Constitution is a hand written document that consists of seven Articles (or sections). Since its ratification, the Constitution has been modified and added to, by the use of the **amendment process**. Article V of the Constitution provides that an amendment may be proposed either by the Congress with a two-thirds majority vote in both the House of Representatives and the Senate or by a constitutional convention called for by two-thirds of the State legislatures. None of the twenty-seven amendments to the Constitution have been proposed by constitutional convention. The Constitution currently contains twenty-seven amendments.

United States Constitution

The United States Constitution is the basis of all laws in the United States and was ratified and became the law of the land on June 21, 1788. The Constitution also set up the framework of our government and defined the roles of the three separate branches.

Amendment process

The amendment process is the procedure used to modify or add to the United States Constitution. The Constitution has been amended twenty-seven times since its inception.

*B*RANCHES OF GOVERNMENT

© Songquan Deng, 2011. Used under license from Shutterstock, Inc.

© kropic1, 2011. Used under license from Shutterstock, Inc.

© Gary Blakeley, 2011. Used under license from Shutterstock, Inc.

CHECKS AND BALANCES

The United States is divided into three branches of government: legislative, executive, and judicial. These branches were set up by the United States Constitution. Article I established the legislative branch, Article II established the executive branch, and Article III established the judicial branch.

The **legislative branch** of government is responsible for making the laws of the country. The legislature of the United States is housed in The United States

Legislative branch

The legislative branch of government is responsible for writing and passing all laws. Each level of government (federal, state, and local) has a legislative branch. The United States Congress makes the laws on the federal level. Each state has a legislature that makes the laws for each state. Local governments have a legislative process which is typically comprised of a city council or county commission.

Executive branch

The executive branch of government is responsible for carrying out or enforcing the laws that have been passed by the legislative branch. Each level of government (federal, state, and local) has an executive branch. The President of the United States heads the executive branch of the federal government. Governors run the executive branch of the states, and mayors run the executive branch of cities.

Judicial branch

The judicial branch of government consists of the courts at each governmental level. The court systems of the federal, state, and local governments are responsible for interpreting the laws passed by the legislative branch and enforced by the executive branch. The United States Supreme Court is the highest court in the country.

Checks and balances

Checks and balances is the system set up by the United States Constitution to ensure that none of the branches becomes too powerful. Each branch holds certain powers that can keep each of the other two branches in check.

Congress, which is made up of the House of Representatives and the Senate. There are 435 members of the House of Representatives and one hundred senators in the Senate. The **executive branch** of government is responsible for carrying out the laws; and the **judicial branch** of government is responsible for interpreting the laws, and the highest court is the United States Supreme Court which has the authority as the interpreter of last resort.

The framers of the Constitution wanted each of these branches to work equally and in concert with each other and did not want any one branch to become more powerful than another. It was for this reason that a system of **checks and balances** was built into the Constitution itself. Each of the independent branches of government has the power and responsibility to keep the other two branches in check.

The legislative branch of government has the power to override any vetoes that the President may place on laws that it has passed (with two-thirds majority). They also have the power to control the spending of the government and, in extreme cases, have the ability to impeach and remove the President from office. The Senate must also approve presidential appointments, which is one of the checks the legislative branch has over the judicial branch since it also approves the appointment of all federal judges.

The executive branch has the power and authority to check the legislative branch by vetoing laws that they have passed. The check of this branch over the judiciary is that they appoint all federal judges, including those who serve on the Supreme Court.

The most powerful check of the judicial branch is the ability to interpret the laws passed by the legislative branch and declare them to be unconstitutional.

APPLICATIONS TO THE CRIMINAL JUSTICE SYSTEM

To put the branches of government into perspective within the Criminal Justice System, the legislature makes the laws that the police and courts must enforce. The police fall under the executive branch and enforce those laws, and the judicial branch tries the cases that the police initiate through arrest.

© Vince Clements, 2011. Used under license from Shutterstock, Inc.

This separation of powers applies to all levels of government: federal, state, and local. On the state level, the governor oversees the executive branch and controls the state public safety functions. The legislative branch makes the state laws; and the judicial branch is responsible for interpretation of the state constitution, and the trial of offenders who violate the laws and are apprehended by the police.

On a local level the legislative function is performed by city councils and county commissions which are responsible for making local laws (or ordinances). The executive branch is headed by a mayor, city or county manager, or other elected official who is responsible to the community for running the government. The judicial role is assumed by the local court system, whether it is city (municipal) or county (justice court or equivalent).

THE BILL OF RIGHTS

The **Bill of Rights** is the common name given to the first ten Amendments to the United States Constitution. These amendments establish the basic rights and liberties that all citizens of the United States enjoy.[1] The Bill of Rights was ratified on December 15, 1791, three years after the U.S. Constitution. The actual amendments contained in the Bill of Rights contain only 462 words, yet thousands of volumes of court decisions over the past 220 years have been based on these words. These decisions make it clear that none of these rights are absolute since the courts have applied many **exceptions and limitations** to them and some of these exceptions are discussed in the following section.

The United States Supreme Court (see Chapter 8 for a comprehensive discussion on the workings of the court) has never applied the rights of the first eight amendments[2] uniformly to the states. When it was ratified, the individual rights afforded by the Bill of Rights (arguably) applied only to the federal courts, not the state courts. To put this simply, this means that a person charged with a federal crime would have been granted all of the rights enumerated in the Bill of Rights while a person charged with a state crime would not necessarily be given the same rights. The person charged in the state court would be granted those rights as adopted by the individual state.

The United States Supreme Court has adopted a process of "selective incorporation" of the rights afforded under the Bill of Rights to the individual states.[3] The dates and the U.S. Supreme Court cases that applied each of the individual rights to the states, and therefore to everyone under every circumstance, are cited in the discussions of the selected amendments which follow. It is important to note that four of the rights stated in the Bill of Rights have never been fully incorporated or specifically applied to the states:

1. The Third Amendment's protection against quartering of soldiers.
2. The Fifth Amendment's grand jury indictment requirement.
3. The Seventh Amendment's right to a jury trial in civil cases.
4. The Eighth Amendment's prohibition on excessive fines.

Bill of Rights

The Bill of Rights is the common name given to the first ten amendments of the United States Constitution. The Bill of Rights was ratified on December 15, 1791, three years after the Constitution was ratified.

Exceptions and limitations

The rights afforded all Americans by the Bill of Rights are not absolute. Over the past 220 years, the United States Supreme Court has recognized the need to apply exceptions and impose certain limitations on the constitutional rights granted by amendments to the United States Constitution. The court has the power to do this through its use of judicial review and its authority to interpret the Constitution.

——————— FIRST AMENDMENT ———————

Congress shall make no law respecting an establishment of religion, or prohibiting the free exercise thereof; or abridging the freedom of speech, or of the press; or the right of the people peaceably to assemble, and to petition the Government for a redress of grievances.

OVERVIEW AND RELEVANCE TO THE CRIMINAL JUSTICE SYSTEM:

The First Amendment contains some of the most basic rights that all persons in the United States enjoy. The rights to express ourselves in our speech, our writings, and our religion are so basic to Americans that we tend to take them for granted.

RIGHTS AFFORDED UNDER THE FIRST AMENDMENT:

1. Establishment of religion and not prohibiting the free exercise of it.
2. Freedom of speech and of the press.
3. Right to peaceably assemble and to petition the government for a redress of grievances.

EXCEPTIONS AND LIMITATIONS OF THE RIGHTS AFFORDED UNDER THE FIRST AMENDMENT:

1. Establishment of religion and not prohibiting the free exercise of it.

© Christy Thompson, 2011. Used under license from Shutterstock, Inc.

The courts have consistently affirmed that the Free Exercise Clause of the First Amendment protects religious beliefs[4]. This means that Americans are free to *maintain* their religious beliefs without interference by state or federal legislation, or other authority. How you think and what you believe is a basic freedom. There are no 'thought' police. This freedom is not always extended to how we act on these thoughts and beliefs. The courts have stepped in and limited some conduct that has been associated with religious beliefs. They have ruled that some religious practices so patently violate the standards of conduct in our society that they have taken action to restrict them.

One of the first and most famous of these restrictions involved the Mormon Church and its practice of polygamy. The U.S. Supreme Court, in the 1890 case of *Davis v. Beason,* stated that "Bigamy and polygamy are crimes by the laws of all civilized and Christian countries." The Court went on to say that "To call their advocacy a tenet of religion is to offend the common sense of mankind."[5]

The 'Establishment Clause' which allowed for the establishment of religions, was applied to the states in 1947.[6] The 'Free Exercise Clause' which gives us the right to worship whatever way we want, was applied in 1940.[7]

2. Freedom of speech and of the press.

The right to express ourselves both orally and in the written word is one of the basic freedoms that separate the United States from much of the rest of the world. Americans can be rightfully proud of their ability to express their feelings without fear of governmental reprisal. Over the years, the U.S. Supreme Court has been very cautious when facing challenges to these basic freedoms. The Court takes many factors into consideration when limiting these rights, including the vagueness of the individual laws and the impact that any restriction will have on our society as a whole. The Court has stated that the government may not restrict speech "because of its message, its ideas, its subject matter, or its content."[8]

There are situations where the courts have imposed restrictions on these basic freedoms. "The most stringent protection of free speech would not protect a man falsely shouting fire in a theatre and causing a panic."[9] The Court has also ruled that a person cannot use "fighting words,"[10] which are "words . . . [which] have a direct tendency to cause acts of violence by the person to whom, individually, the remark was addressed."[11] Restrictions have also been imposed on the use of libelous statements[12] (libel is the making of false or malicious statements published to hurt or damage a person's reputation). The U.S. Supreme Court has also held ". . . that obscenity is not within the area of constitutionally protected free speech or press."[13]

While the United States Supreme Court has ruled that there are compelling exceptions to the First Amendment freedom of expression, it has consistently stated that some acts, even some that offend many people, are not prohibited. "While flag desecration . . . like virulent ethnic and religious epithets, vulgar repudiations of the draft, and scurrilous caricatures . . . is deeply offensive to many, the Government may not prohibit the expression of an idea simply because society finds the idea itself offensive or disagreeable."[14]

Freedom of speech was applied to the states in 1925[15] and the freedom of the press was applied in 1931.[16]

3. Right to peaceably assemble and to petition the government for a redress of grievances.

The rights to peaceably assemble and to petition the government have been merged over the years into the basic First Amendment right to freedom of expression. The courts have not interfered very often in this area except to allow for governmental regulations related to obtaining permits and restricting specific areas that may not be used for demonstrations.[17]

The right to peaceably assemble was applied to the states in 1937.[18]

--------- SECOND AMENDMENT ---------

A well regulated Militia, being necessary to the security of a free State, the right of the people to keep and bear Arms, shall not be infringed.

OVERVIEW AND RELEVANCE TO THE CRIMINAL JUSTICE SYSTEM:

Probably one of the most controversial amendments in recent years has been the Second Amendment right to bear arms. There has been heated debate on both sides of this issue. Gun rights advocates argue that individuals have the absolute right to own guns without restrictions imposed by the federal or individual state governments. Opponents argue that the government has the right to regulate all weapons. The debate has also focused on the wording of the amendment and its reference to "a well regulated Militia" and the implications in a modern society.

This amendment is of particular importance to the police throughout the United States. The police are the ones who must regulate firearm laws in this country and must be thoroughly versed in the laws that govern firearms within their jurisdictions. The police must also be aware at all times that, while law-abiding citizens have a right to possess and carry weapons, so do the not so law-abiding. What makes this even more concerning to police is the fact that, according to the National Rifle Association, there are about 300 million legal firearms in this country and about 100 million of these are handguns.[19]

RIGHTS AFFORDED UNDER THE SECOND AMENDMENT:

1. The right to bear arms.

© patrimonio designs limited, 2011. Used under license from Shutterstock, Inc.

EXCEPTIONS AND LIMITATIONS OF THE RIGHTS AFFORDED UNDER THE SECOND AMENDMENT:

Like most rights, the Second Amendment right is not unlimited. It is not a right to keep and carry any weapon whatsoever in any manner whatsoever and for whatever purpose: For example, concealed weapons prohibitions have been upheld under the Amendment or state analogues. The Court's opinion should not be taken to cast doubt on longstanding prohibitions on the possession of firearms by felons and the mentally ill, or laws forbidding the carrying of firearms in sensitive places such as schools and government buildings, or laws imposing conditions and qualifications on the commercial sale of arms. The U.S. Supreme Court has held that the sorts of weapons protected are those "in common use at the time" and finds support in the historical tradition of prohibiting the carrying of dangerous and unusual weapons.[20] Private citizens may not possess most military weapons such as hand grenades, bombs, and cannons. It has also been well established that the government can regulate such things as fully automatic guns as well as sawed-off shotguns.[21]

The United States Supreme Court did not apply the rights afforded under the Second Amendment to the states until 2010.[22]

FOURTH AMENDMENT

*T*he right of the people to be secure in their persons, houses, papers, and effects, against unreasonable searches and seizures, shall not be violated, and no Warrants shall issue, but upon probable cause, supported by Oath or affirmation, and particularly describing the place to be searched, and the persons or things to be seized.

OVERVIEW AND RELEVANCE TO THE CRIMINAL JUSTICE SYSTEM:

A thorough understanding of the Fourth Amendment is essential to all police officers (as well as prosecutors, judges, criminal defense attorneys, and almost all criminal justice practitioners) in the United States. This is the basis of all searches and seizures conducted by the police and includes the laws of arrest. Police officers at every level receive extensive training concerning this amendment and all of the exceptions that have been associated with it.

This amendment includes the provisions for an arrest. An arrest is a seizure of a person and must be based on probable cause (see Chapter 5 for definitions). An arrest can be made with a warrant or without a warrant if it is based upon probable cause, or if the suspected criminal act occurred in the officer's presence. The Fourth Amendment does not allow warrantless arrests of persons within their own home unless there is some exigent (emergency) circumstance that would make the obtaining of a warrant unreasonable.[23]

RIGHTS AFFORDED UNDER THE FOURTH AMENDMENT:

1. Right against unreasonable searches and seizures.

EXCEPTIONS AND LIMITATIONS OF THE RIGHTS AFFORDED UNDER THE FOURTH AMENDMENT:

1. Right against unreasonable searches and seizures.

There are probably more Supreme Court and other appellate court decisions dealing with the Fourth Amendment than all of the other amendments combined. The United States Supreme Court has decided many cases that have expanded the interpretation of this amendment. Below is a list of some of the exceptions that have been decided (these will be examined in more detail in Chapter 5).

Exceptions to this amendment include:

2. Consent searches
3. Vehicular searches
4. Border searches
5. "Open Fields" searches
6. Abandoned property searches
7. "Plain View" searches
8. Public school searches
9. Prison searches
10. Searches incident to arrest
11. Probation and parole searches
12. Detention and "Stop-and-Frisk"

The United States Supreme Court applied the freedom from unreasonable searches and seizures to the states in 1949[24] and applied the warrant requirement in 1964.[25]

———————————————— FIFTH AMENDMENT ————————————————

No person shall be held to answer for a capital, or otherwise infamous crime, unless on a presentment or indictment of a Grand Jury, except in cases arising in the land or naval forces, or in the Militia, when in actual service in time of War or public danger; nor shall any person be subject for the same offence to be twice put in jeopardy of life or limb; nor shall be compelled in any criminal case to be a witness against himself, nor be deprived of life, liberty, or property, without due process of law; nor shall private property be taken for public use, without just compensation.

OVERVIEW AND RELEVANCE TO THE CRIMINAL JUSTICE SYSTEM:

The Fifth Amendment contains the rights of persons and is broken into several different categories of rights, and includes one that deals with the non-criminal right of the government to take your property for eminent domain[26]. The amendment also contains some language that needs explanation in today's terms.

"No person shall be held to answer for a capital, or otherwise infamous crime . . ." A **capital crime** is a crime for which the accused could get the death penalty if convicted (capital punishment). An "infamous" crime is generally accepted as a crime for which the punishment would be imprisonment in a state prison or penitentiary.[27] Today, this category of crimes is called felonies.

One of the most well known U.S. Supreme Court cases is based, in part, on the Fifth Amendment right against self-incrimination. The *Miranda* decision in 1966[28] has had far-reaching effects on the criminal justice system. One of the foremost changes involves the procedures that police officers use when interrogating suspects and obtaining confessions.[29]

The concept of double jeopardy is also addressed in this amendment. This right is one that prosecutors and the courts must be aware of at all times in criminal cases.

RIGHTS AFFORDED UNDER THE FIFTH AMENDMENT:

1. Right to a Grand Jury hearing.
2. Right against double jeopardy.
3. Right against self-incrimination.

EXCEPTIONS AND LIMITATIONS OF THE RIGHTS AFFORDED UNDER THE FIFTH AMENDMENT:

1. Right to a grand jury hearing.

"The grand jury is an integral part of our constitutional heritage which was brought to this country with the common law. The Framers, most of them trained in English law and traditions, accepted the grand jury as a basic guarantee of individual liberty; notwithstanding periodic criticism, much of which is superficial, overlooking relevant history, the grand jury continues to function as a barrier to reckless or unfounded charges. . . . Its historic office has been to provide a shield against arbitrary or oppressive action, by insuring that serious criminal accusations will be brought only upon the considered judgment of a representative body of citizens acting under oath and under judicial instruction and guidance."[30]

The grand jury is generally comprised of twenty-three citizens who are subpoenaed for jury duty and serve for a designated amount of time on the jury. Unlike a criminal trial jury, these jurors hear evidence presented by witnesses called by the prosecuting attorney to establish whether or not probable cause exists to prosecute a defendant or to issue a warrant of arrest. The actual procedures vary from jurisdiction to jurisdiction but in most cases the defendant is not even present for the hearing.[31]

© kenny1, 2011. Used under license from Shutterstock, Inc.

The right of a defendant to have a grand jury indictment has never been incorporated or applied by the courts to the states. This constitutional right remains a requirement within the Federal Court System but not a requirement for the individual States. Many of the States have adopted the grand jury system of indictments for felony cases; however, some have adopted other procedures in its place (see Chapter 7).

2.   Right against double jeopardy.

". . . nor shall any person be subject for the same offence to be twice put in jeopardy of life or limb;"

The concept of double jeopardy protects individuals from being convicted twice for the same crime. Once an individual is prosecuted for a criminal offence, this Fifth Amendment right guarantees that the government cannot prosecute the person again for the same criminal act.

To put this constitutional right in perspective, if a person is tried for burglary in a state court and found not guilty, the state is barred from prosecuting the person again for that same crime.[32] This would be true even if additional evidence is later discovered that would tend to prove that the person was guilty of that crime.

The right of double jeopardy, like all rights, is for the benefit of the accused, not the prosecution. The prosecution is not permitted to appeal an acquittal (a verdict of not guilty).[33] Once a person is found to be not guilty in a criminal court, the prosecution is barred from appealing the decision. On the other hand, if the defendant is found guilty in court, they have the right to appeal the decision to a higher court. This is true even though one of the results of that appeal could be a retrial on the same charges. This is not double jeopardy because the defendant is the one who initiates the request for appeal and therefore is constructively waiving their right to another trial if they win their appeal.[34]

There have been many instances of a person being found not guilty in a criminal court and then being sued in civil court using the same witnesses and evidence and subsequently having the civil court finding against them.[35] The language of the Amendment states that a person cannot be put in "jeopardy of life or limb." Since a person is not put in jeopardy of criminal punishment (capital punishment, imprisonment, or punitive fines), the courts have held that double jeopardy does not apply in noncriminal proceedings.[36]

The double jeopardy clause was applied to the states in 1969.[37]

© bikeriderlondon/Shutterstock.com

3.   Right against self-incrimination.

". . . nor shall be compelled in any criminal case to be a witness against himself . . ."

The right against self-incrimination means that a person cannot be forced or required to make any statements that could be used against them in any criminal proceeding (present or future) or to be used as a basis to discover any other incriminating evidence against them. This privilege is applicable in criminal court proceedings, as well as while being questioned by the police in an interrogation situation.

A defendant is not required to take the stand and testify in their own behalf in a criminal proceeding or trial and the prosecution is prohibited from commenting to the jury on this lack of testimony.[38] If the defendant does take the stand and testify, they then waive their right against self-incrimination and are required to answer questions under cross-examination. The defendant can be impeached when they take the stand because the courts will then allow the prosecution to introduce any prior criminal record and can comment on the defendant's prior silence during police questioning.[39]

The right does not apply to "routine" booking questions. When a person is arrested, the police (and/or the jail) may ask questions required to properly book the person without asking for a waiver and are not violating this right. Such questions include asking the suspect their name, address, date of birth, and other identifiers.[40] The court has also determined that requiring a person to submit to a blood alcohol test is not a violation of this right, even though refusal to submit to the test may be used as evidence against them.[41]

Probation revocation hearings have also been ruled by the courts to not be criminal proceedings, so a probationer is required to answer questions during the hearing even though the questions may be incriminating in nature and may result in the revocation of probation.[42]

This right is the basis of the *Miranda* decision, where suspects must be advised that they have the right to remain silent (the right against self-incrimination) and that if they do waive this right, that anything they say can be used against them in court.

This right does not, however, apply in civil cases or in situations where a person does not face criminal or other significant penalties (other than just monetary).

The privilege against self-incrimination was applied to the states in 1964.[43]

4. Due process of law in criminal prosecutions.

This right guarantees that a person who is accused of a crime will be given the opportunity to have their case heard in a court of law, and will be afforded all of the constitutional rights that are applicable to their case and situation. The Fifth Amendment originally applied this right to those cases that were in Federal Court and it was applied to everyone in all cases with the adoption of the Fourteenth Amendment.

© Gina Sanders, 2011. Used under license from Shutterstock, Inc.

SIXTH AMENDMENT

In all criminal prosecutions, the accused shall enjoy the right to a speedy and public trial, by an impartial jury of the State and district wherein the crime shall have been committed, which district shall have been previously ascertained by law, and to be informed of the nature and cause of the accusation; to be confronted with the witnesses against him; to have compulsory process for obtaining witnesses in his favor, and to have the Assistance of Counsel for his defence.

OVERVIEW AND RELEVANCE TO THE CRIMINAL JUSTICE SYSTEM:

The Sixth Amendment encompasses those rights that a person has when they are accused of a crime and formally enter the criminal justice system. While all persons in the United States have the rights afforded under this amendment, they do not become applicable until a person is actually accused of a criminal offense. Once accused, a person enters the court system of the United States, whether it is on a federal, state, or local level. The Sixth Amendment protects the accused throughout this process. The amendment guarantees that the process will be fair and impartial and is the basis of due process. The Sixth Amendment rights are read to the accused in court as a part of the arraignment process.[44]

RIGHTS AFFORDED UNDER THE SIXTH AMENDMENT:

1. Right to a speedy trial.
2. Right to a public trial.
3. Right to a trial by an impartial jury.
4. Right to be informed of the charges against you.
5. Right to confront witnesses against you.
6. Right to have compulsory process for obtaining witnesses in your favor.
7. Right to have an attorney.

EXCEPTIONS AND LIMITATIONS OF THE RIGHTS AFFORDED UNDER THE SIXTH AMENDMENT:

1. Right to a speedy trial.

The right to a speedy trial "is one of the most basic rights preserved by our Constitution."[45] The purpose of this guarantee is to prevent long delays before trial for an accused person who may have to remain in custody before going to trial. It also affords the defendant with the opportunity to go to trial without the concern that witnesses may not be available to come to court or that their memory may not be as fresh if there is a long delay.

While the constitution does guarantee a "speedy" trial, it does not specify a specific time frame in which it must take place. Title 1 of the Speedy Trial Act of 1974[46] (amended in 1979) specifies the time restrictions that must be followed in criminal proceedings in Federal Court. This statute states the information (or indictment from the grand jury) must be filed within thirty days from the date of arrest or service of the summons. The trial must then begin within seventy days from the date the information or indictment was filed, or from the date the defendant appears before an officer of the court in which the charge is pending, whichever is later.

States do not have to establish a firm time line; however, most states have adopted time frames that are similar to those established by the federal Speedy Trial Act.

This right was applied to the states in 1967.[47]

2.   Right to a public trial.

With very few exceptions,[48] court hearings and trials are open to the public. The openness of our trial system is a safeguard against any attempt to employ our courts as instruments of persecution.[49] Open trials also assure that the criminal defendant receives a fair and accurate adjudication of guilt or innocence. It also provides a public demonstration of fairness and discourages perjury. The Court has also stated that open trials enable the public to see justice done and the fulfillment of the urge for retribution that people feel upon the commission of some kinds of crimes.[50]

The right to a public trial was applied to the states in 1948.[51]

3.   Right to a trial by an impartial jury.

The Sixth Amendment gives us the right to a trial by an impartial jury. Originally, this meant that a person accused of any crime had the right to have their case heard before a jury comprised of twelve impartial citizens. Over the years, the Court has reexamined this right and has limited the requirement to serious crimes (generally felonies) and has stated that juries can be comprised of less than twelve jurors,[52] but had to be made up of more than five.[53]

While the Court applied this right to the states in 1968,[54] the individual states are still free to limit jury trials to felonies only and can reduce the size of the jury from the traditional twelve to six.

4.   Right to be informed of the charges against you.

Every defendant who is accused of a criminal offense has the Sixth Amendment right to have the charges against them be properly explained and given to them. This allows the defendant to be able to prepare a proper defense to the charges and to protect them once a judgment has been rendered against any additional prosecution on the same charge (double jeopardy).[55]

It is important to note that the charges that the defendant is informed of under this amendment are not necessarily the same charges that the person was arrested for. A person could be arrested by the police and charged with the crime of burglary. After review by the prosecutor, the charge may be reduced prior to trial to the crime of grand larceny. The person would then be informed in court (usually during the arraignment) of the charge of grand larceny, not burglary, and this would meet the Sixth Amendment requirement.

5.   Right to confront witnesses against you.

This constitutional provision was included to give assurance to defendants that they may question anyone who accuses them of a crime. The U.S. Supreme court has said criminal accusations should not be by written affidavits (sworn documents) only. They further stated that an affidavit is not to be used ". . . in lieu of a personal examination and cross-examination of the witness in which the accused has an opportunity not only of testing the recollection and sifting the conscience of the witness, but of compelling him to stand face to face with the jury in order that they may look at him, and judge by his demeanor upon the stand and the manner in which he gives his testimony whether he is worthy of belief."[56]

Most of the exceptions to this right deal with the testimony of child witnesses when the welfare of the child outweighs the right of the defendant to confront them in court.[57] The U.S. Supreme Court has also made exceptions when dealing with child sex crime victims.[58]

The right to confront witnesses was applied to the states in 1965.[59]

6.   Right to have compulsory process for obtaining witnesses in your favor.

Every defendant in a criminal trial has the right to present a defense. Part of this defense may be the presentation of testimony from witnesses who may have evidence favorable for the defendant. Many defendants do not have the money or resources to find and subpoena these witnesses and get them into court. This constitutional right guarantees that these witnesses will be brought to court (if applicable) even when the defendants cannot afford to do so for themselves.[60]

This part of the Sixth Amendment was applied to the states in (1967).[61]

7.   Right to have an attorney.

The Sixth Amendment gives all persons in the United States who are charged with a criminal offense the right to have an attorney represent them at every stage of the criminal process. This premise was solidified in the landmark U.S. Supreme Court decision in *Gideon v. Wainwright*.[62] The Court stated in this case "that in our adversary system of criminal justice, any person haled [sic] into court, who is too poor to hire a lawyer, cannot be assured a fair trial unless counsel is provided

for him." *Gideon v. Wainwright* is also the case that applied this right to the states.

The assistance of counsel applies to all criminal defendants who potentially face imprisonment for the crime they are charged with, even if the charge is a misdemeanor.[63] This right has also been extended to juveniles.[64]

If a person accused of a criminal offense cannot afford to hire an attorney themselves, then the government entity that is prosecuting the case must provide an attorney for them at no cost to the defendant.[65,66] This Court has also gone so far as to say that the counsel appointed must be "effective" counsel.[67]

———————— EIGHTH AMENDMENT ————————

Excessive bail shall not be required, nor excessive fines imposed, nor cruel and unusual punishments inflicted.

OVERVIEW AND RELEVANCE TO THE CRIMINAL JUSTICE SYSTEM:

The Eighth Amendment is a continuation of the rights given to defendants, and subsequently to those convicted of a crime, who become a part of the court and correctional systems. Although this is the shortest Amendment to the U.S. Constitution, it has far-reaching implications, particularly the right against cruel and unusual punishments.

RIGHTS AFFORDED UNDER THE EIGHTH AMENDMENT:

1. Right against excessive bail.
2. Right against excessive fines.
3. Right against cruel and unusual punishments inflicted.

EXCEPTIONS AND LIMITATIONS OF THE RIGHTS AFFORDED UNDER THE EIGHTH AMENDMENT:

1. Right against excessive bail.

One of the most important legal premises in a free society is the presumption of innocence. In our system of justice, just because a person is arrested and brought to trial on a criminal charge does not mean that they are guilty of that crime. The presumption is that the person is innocent of the charge and will be afforded full due process of law. The burden of proof to prove guilt rests firmly on the shoulders of the prosecution. With this in mind, it would be unfair to keep the accused in jail while awaiting trial. We do not incarcerate innocent people. The right to reasonable bail insures that the accused has an opportunity to be free prior to conviction. The Court has said that: "Unless this right to bail before trial is preserved, the presumption of innocence, secured only after centuries of struggle, would lose its meaning."[68]

There are times when the safety of society outweighs the need to offer bail to a suspect. Certain crimes have been deemed to be so serious, that even the presumption of innocence does not allow the person arrested to be granted bail. Murder, sexual assaults, high level drug trafficking, and crimes involving serious bodily injury are all examples of crimes that the courts have determined (on a case by case basis) that the assignment of no bail may be warranted. The courts may also consider such variables as flight risk and possible attempts by the suspect to commit additional serious crimes.

Excessive bail has been held to be an amount that is higher than what would be "reasonable" for the circumstances.[69] The term "reasonable" is one that the courts have intentionally left vague. It would be unreasonable to set a bail of one million dollars for a person who has been arrested for shoplifting, but it may not be considered unreasonable for a person who was arrested for smuggling twenty million dollars' worth of drugs into the United States.

The right against excessive bail was applied to the states in 1971.[70]

2. Right against excessive fines.

The United States Supreme Court has had very little to say about this clause to the Eighth Amendment. The Court has ruled, however, that a person who does not have the ability to pay a fine because they are indigent cannot be given a jail or prison sentence because of this inability.[71] The Court has never applied this constitutional right to the states.

3. Right against cruel and unusual punishments inflicted.

The Court has never given a precise definition of what "cruel and unusual" actually is. In the 1800s the Court did give some insight by stating: ". . . it is safe to affirm that punishments of torture [such as drawing and quartering, embowelling alive, beheading, public dissecting, and burning alive], and all others in the same line of unnecessary cruelty, are forbidden by that amendment to the Constitution"[sic].[72]

© Linda Bucklin, 2011. Used under license from Shutterstock, Inc.

The Court has, over the past two hundred years, ruled that the various techniques used to legally carry out the death penalty in the United States have passed the legal scrutiny and have been ruled not to be cruel and unusual. Firing squads[73] and electrocution[74] are examples of types of executions that have been ruled acceptable. The Court even went so far as to rule that it was not cruel and unusual when the State of Louisiana had to electrocute a man a second time when a mechanical failure during the first execution only injured but did not kill the condemned man.[75]

In 1972 the Court, in the landmark case of *Furman v. Georgia,* looked at the way the death penalty was administered (as opposed to the actual mechanisms of putting a person to death) and ruled that the death penalty violated the cruel and unusual clause of the Eighth Amendment.[76] This decision effectively suspended executions in the United States for several years. Following this ruling, thirty-five states redid their death penalty statutes to conform to the *Furman* decision, and resumed executions in their respective states.

Since the *Furman* decision, the Court has made several rulings that have put limits on who may be executed. In 1977, in *Coker v. Georgia,* the Court held that rapists could not be executed if they did not take the victims life during the commission of the crime.[77] The Court stated that ". . . rape cannot compare with murder in terms of moral depravity and of injury to the person and the public."[78]

The Court has also ruled that the Eighth Amendment prohibits the execution of a person who is insane,[79] but does not specifically prohibit the execution of juveniles who commit crimes when sixteen or seventeen years of age[80] who have been certified as adults (but does prohibit the execution of fifteen year olds[81]).

The cruel and unusual punishment clause of the Eighth Amendment was applied to the states in 1962.[82]

FOURTEENTH AMENDMENT

Section. 1. All persons born or naturalized in the United States and subject to the jurisdiction thereof, are citizens of the United States and of the State wherein they reside. No State shall make or enforce any law which shall abridge the privileges or immunities of citizens of the United States; nor shall any State deprive any person of life, liberty, or property, without due process of law; nor deny to any person within its jurisdiction the equal protection of the laws.

Section. 2. Representatives shall be apportioned among the several States according to their respective numbers, counting the whole number of persons in each State, excluding Indians not taxed. But when the right to vote at any election for the choice of electors for President and Vice President of the United States, Representatives in Congress, the Executive and Judicial officers of a State, or the members of the Legislature thereof, is denied to any of the male inhabitants of such State, being twenty-one years of age, and citizens of the United States, or in any way abridged, except for participation in rebellion, or other crime, the basis of representation therein shall be reduced in the proportion which the number of such male citizens shall bear to the whole number of male citizens twenty-one years of age in such State.

Section. 3. No person shall be a Senator or Representative in Congress, or elector of President and Vice President, or hold any office, civil or military, under the United States, or under any State, who, having previously taken an oath, as a member of Congress, or as an officer of the United States, or as a member of any State legislature, or as an executive or judicial officer of any State, to support the Constitution of the United States, shall have engaged in insurrection or rebellion against the same, or given aid or comfort to the enemies thereof. But Congress may by a vote of two-thirds of each House, remove such disability.

𝒮*ection. 4. The validity of the public debt of the United States, authorized by law, including debts incurred for payment of pensions and bounties for services in suppressing insurrection or rebellion, shall not be questioned. But neither the United States nor any State shall assume or pay any debt or obligation incurred in aid of insurrection or rebellion against the United States, or any claim for the loss or emancipation of any slave; but all such debts, obligations and claims shall be held illegal and void.*

𝒮*ection. 5. The Congress shall have power to enforce, by appropriate legislation, the provisions of this article.*

OVERVIEW AND RELEVANCE TO THE CRIMINAL JUSTICE SYSTEM:

© JustASC, 2011. Used under license from Shutterstock, Inc.

The Fourteenth Amendment to the United States Constitution was ratified on July 9, 1868. The amendment is divided into five sections but Section 1 is the one that is most applicable to the criminal justice system. Together with the Fifth Amendment, the Fourteenth guarantees all persons in the United States the right to due process of law in all criminal proceedings.[83] Section 1 of the Fourteenth Amendment has been commonly referred to as the "due process clause" and the amendment is referred to as the "equal rights amendment."

REVIEW QUESTIONS:

1. The basis of all laws in the United States is the _____.

2. The three branches of government are: _____, _____, and

    _____.

3. The first ten amendments to the U.S. Constitution are commonly called the _____.

4. The system of _____ and _____ within the government keeps each branch from becoming too powerful.

5. The "right of the people to keep and bear arms" is found in the _____ Amendment.

6. The right against self incrimination is found in the _____ Amendment.

7. "Freedom of speech" is found in the _____ Amendment.

8. The right "against unreasonable searches and seizures" is found in the _____ Amendment.

9. The right "to be confronted with the witnesses against him" is found in the _____ Amendment.

10. The right protecting us against "cruel and unusual punishments" is found in the _____ Amendment.

CRITICAL THINKING QUESTIONS:

1. Discuss in your own words the concept of checks and balances, and how it is used in the United States. Make sure you include all three branches of government in your discussion.

2. Explain why there are so many exceptions to the rights that are afforded us by the Bill of Rights. How did these exceptions come about?

3. Select one of the amendments from the Bill of Rights that was NOT discussed in this chapter (see Appendix A) and discuss the rights or guarantees that are presented in it.

4. Discuss the importance of the Fourteenth Amendment and explain how it applies to the criminal justice system.

—————————————— NOTES ——————————————

CHAPTER 1

[1] It should be noted that the Fourteenth Amendment (see later in this chapter) guarantees that all "persons" shall be denied neither due process nor equal protection of the law. There has been some controversy as to whether this includes every person who is in the United States (visitors, persons on visas, and illegal aliens) or to just "citizens" of the country. The practice of our courts has, at least over the recent past, been to grant all of these rights to all persons regardless of their status.

[2] Some scholars attribute the Bill of Rights to the first eight amendments only. The Ninth and Tenth Amendments do not establish any individual rights. See Appendix A for the full text of the U.S. Constitution and all twenty-seven of the amendments.

[3] Gideon v. Wainwright, 372 U.S. 335, 341 (1963).

[4] Findlaw, "Free Excercise of Religion." Accessed 2010 at http://caselaw.lp.findlaw.com/data/constitution/amendment01/05.html#2.

[5] Davis v. Beason, 133 U.S. 333 (1890).

[6] Everson v. Board of Education, 330 U.S. 1 (1947).

[7] Cantwell v. Connecticut, 310 U.S. 296 (1940).

[8] Police Department v. Mosley, 408 U.S. 92, 95 (1972).

[9] Schenck v. U.S., 249 U.S. 47 (1919).

[10] Chaplinsky v. New Hampshire, 315 U.S. 568 (1942).

[11] Ibid. at 573.

[12] Beauharnais v. Illinois, 343 U.S. 250 (1952).

[13] Roth v. United States, 354 U.S. 476 (1957).

[14] United States v. Eichman, 496 U.S. 310, 313–319 (1990).

[15] Gitlow v. New York, 268 U.S. 562 (1925).

[16] Near v. Minnesota ex rel. Olson, 283 U.S. 697 (1931).

[17] Hague v. Committee for Industrial Organization, 307 U.S. 496 (1939).

[18] De Jonge v. York, 299 U.S. 353 (1937).

[19] National Rifle Association, "Firearms Fact Card, 2011." Posted January 20, 2011, accessed July, 18, 2011 at http://www.nraila.org/Issues/FactSheets/Read.aspx?ID583.

[20] District of Columbia et al. v. Heller, 554 U.S. 290 (2008).

[21] United States v. Miller, 307 U.S. 174 (1939).

[22] McDonald et al. v. City of Chicago, Illinois, et al., 561 U.S. _____ (2010).

[23] Payton v. New York, 445 U.S. 573 (1980).

[24] Wolf v. Colorado, 338 U.S. 25 (1949).

[25] Aguilar v. Texas, 378 U.S. 108 (1964).

[26] "*. . . nor shall private property be taken for public use, without just compensation.*" Whenever lands in a State are needed for a public purpose, Congress may authorize that they be taken, either by proceedings in the courts of the State, with its consent, or by proceedings in the courts of the United States, with or without any consent or concurrent act of the State with its consent, or by proceedings in the courts of the United States, with or without any consent or concurrent act of the State (Chappell v. United States, 160 U.S. 499 (1896)). In simple terms, this means that if the government decides that it needs to put a freeway through your home, it can condemn your house and force you to give it up, but they have to give you fair market value for it.

[27] Mackin v. United States, 117 U.S. 348 (1886).

[28] Miranda v. Arizona, 384 U.S. 436 (1966).

[29] A full discussion of the *Miranda* case will be presented in Chapter 5.

[30] United States v. Mandujano, 425 U.S. 564 (1976).

[31] For a more detailed explanation of the grand jury process see Chapter 7.

[32] United States v. Martin Linen Co., 430 U.S. 564 (1977).

[33] Burks v. United States, 437 U.S. 1 (1978).

[34] A full explanation of the possible outcomes of an appeal is explained in Chapter 8.

[35] Probably the most famous case involved O. J. Simpson. On October 3, 1995, O. J. Simpson was found not guilty in a criminal court in Los Angeles, California of two counts of murder. The family of one of the victims then sued Mr. Simpson in civil court for the wrongful death of their son, Ronald Goldman, who was one of the victims that he was found not guilty of killing. The civil jury, hearing the same evidence from the murder trial, found against Mr. Simpson and ordered him to pay $33,500,000 in damages on February 5, 1997.

[36] Helvering v. Mitchell, 303 U.S. 391 (1938).

[37] Benton v. Maryland, 395 U.S. 794 (1969).

[38] Griffin v. California, 380 U.S. 609 (1965).

[39] Jenkins v. Anderson, 447 U.S. 231 (1980).

[40] Pennsylvania v. Muniz, 496 U.S. 582 (1990).

[41] South Dakota v. Neville, 459 U.S. 553 (1983).

[42] Minnesota v. Murphy, 465 U.S. 420 (1984).

[43] Mallory v. Hogan, 378 U.S. 1 (1964).

[44] The arraignment will be discussed in detail in Chapter 8.

[45] Klopfer v. North Carolina, 386 U.S. 213 (1967).

[46] 18 U.S.C. §§ 3161_3174.

[47] Klopfer v. North Carolina, 386 U.S. 213 (1967).

[48] Some of the exceptions include juvenile proceedings, grand jury hearings, and times when the judge may declare the need for closure of the court (child witnesses, confidential information disclosed, etc.).

[49] In re Oliver, 333 U.S. 257 (1948).

[50] Estes v. Texas, 381 U.S. 532, 538 (1965).

[51] In re Oliver, 333 U.S. 257 (1948).

[52] Williams v. Florida, 399 U.S. 78 (1970).

[53] Ballew v. Georgia, 435 U.S. 223 (1978).

[54] Duncan v. Louisiana, 391 U.S. 145 (1968).

[55] United States v. Cruikshank, 92 U.S. 542 (1875).

[56] Mattox v. United States, 156 U.S. 237 (1985).

[57] Maryland v. Craig, 497 U.S. 836 (1990).

[58] Kentucky v. Stincer, 482 U.S. 730 (1987).

[59] Pointer v. Texas, 380 U.S. 400 (1965).

[60] United States v. Cooper, 4 U.S. (4 Dall.) 341 (C. C. Pa. 1800).

[61] Washington v. Texas, 388 U.S. 14 (1967).

[62] Gideon v. Wainwright, 372 U.S. 335 (1963).

[63] Argersinger v. Hamlin, 407 U.S. 25 (1972).

[64] In re Gault, 387 U.S. 1 (1967).

[65] Powell v. Alabama, 287 U.S. 45 (1932).

[66] The standard used by most of the courts in the United States to determine if a person is indigent (lacking the necessities of life and therefore unable to afford an attorney on their own) is based on the poverty level for the circumstances of the individual defendant.

[67] McMann v. Richardson, 397 U.S. 759 (1970).

[68] Stack v. Boyle, 342 U.S. 1 (1951).

[69] Ibid. at 4.

[70] Schilb v. Kuebel, 404 U.S. 357 (1971).

[71] Tate v. Short, 401 U.S. 395 (1971).

[72] Wilkerson v. Utah, 99 U.S. 135 (1878).

[73] Ibid.

[74] In re Kemmler, 136 U.S. 436 (1890).

[75] Louisiana ex rel. Francis v. Resweber, 329 U.S. 459 (1947).

[76] Furman v. Georgia, 408 U.S. 238 (1972).

[77] Coker v. Georgia, 433 U.S. 584 (1977).

[78] Ibid. at 598.

[79] Ford v. Wainwright, 477 U.S. 399 (1986).

[80] Thompson v. Oklahoma, 487 U.S. 815 (1988).

[81] Ibid. at 849.

[82] Robinson v. California, 370 U.S. 660 (1962).

[83] Due process will be discussed in detail in Chapter 2.

CHAPTER OVERVIEW

The criminal justice system in the United States is built upon the concept of justice. The notion of justice will be looked at from several different perspectives. This chapter will discuss justice in terms of the traditional way that it is applied to our overall justice system. We will also look at the concept of social justice and how it affects the different societies that we all live in. The principle of the social contract will also be discussed in this chapter.

There are two models that help explain the differences in ideologies within the criminal justice process in the United States. These models, which were developed in 1964 by Herbert L. Packer,[1] are the due process model and the crime control model. We will see that there are strong advocates and opponents for both of these models and we will look at the positions of both. The chapter will also give a brief overview of the three components of the criminal justice system: the police, corrections, and the courts.

𝒞HAPTER LEARNING OBJECTIVES

After reading this chapter you will be able to:

1. Understand the concept of justice as it applies to the criminal justice system in America.
2. Explain the notion of social justice and how it varies within the different societies in which we live.
3. Explain what the social contract is.
4. Compare and contrast the due process model and the crime control model.
5. List the basic components of the criminal justice system.

--- KEYWORDS ---

Justice	Social Justice
Society	Social Contract
Herbert L. Packer	Crime Control Model
Due Process Model	Police
Law Enforcement	Corrections
Jails	Prisons

𝒯HE CONCEPT OF JUSTICE

Justice

While the term justice can have a variety of meanings, for criminal justice it is best described as fundamental fairness.

A discussion about the criminal justice system must start with a basic understanding of the term **justice**. Justice has come to have different meanings depending on how it is used and what it is associated with. The New Oxford American Dictionary[2] defines justice as "the quality of being fair and reasonable." Justice can also be described as fundamental fairness. Aristotle said that justice is equality for equals and wrote that: "Injustice arises when equals are treated unequally and also when

unequals are treated equally."[3] President Theodore Roosevelt gave a very good summary of the term justice when he said:

"*N*o man is above the law and no man is below it; nor do we ask any man's permission when we require him to obey it."

PRESIDENT THEODORE ROOSEVELT—1903[4]

Theodore Roosevelt

What President Roosevelt was saying was that all persons, regardless of their status in society, are expected to obey all of the laws within our society. In order to have true justice, it must be administered fairly and equally to everyone.

Social justice is more of a concept than an actual occurrence. Social justice varies from **society** to society depending on the perception of what constitutes right from wrong within that society. Social justice can also change over time within the same society as the mores and moral values change. Since social justice deals with the fundamental notion of right and wrong as defined by a society, it can also vary within a society.

We all live in several different societies simultaneously, each with their own set of values. We all live in the global society of the world where the most basic values of right and wrong are universal. This would include such things as murder and the stealing of property that belongs to others. We also live in the society of the United States, which is one of the most multi-cultural societies in the world. Since our country is represented by so many different cultural and ethnic backgrounds, it can arguably be said that we cannot come to a consensus on very many important issues. The federal government, through our legislative branch (the House of Representatives and the Senate), makes the criminal laws that affect everyone in the country. These laws, at least theoretically, reflect a consensus of the moral values of all of our citizens because they are written by elected officials who represent the populace. The moral values of the country change over time and are reflected by changes in our laws. It should be noted that the values of individual political parties have a direct influence on the types of laws that are passed, but again, the party in power changes as the values of the country change and new representatives are elected.

We also live within the society of the individual State that we reside in. Although the

Social Justice

The concept of social justice varies from society to society and deals with the perception of what constitutes right from wrong within that society.

Society

A society is a structured group of people with similar traits (traditions, culture, nationality, moral values). We all live in several different societies at the same time.

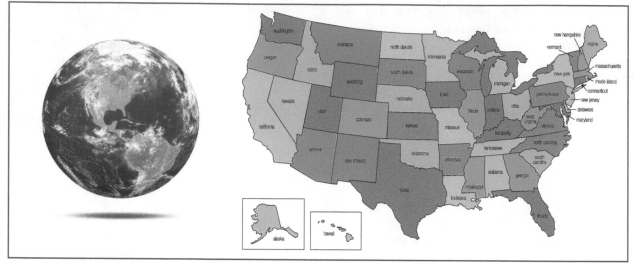

Globe © Alex Staroseltsev, map © jamie cross, 2011. Used under license from Shutterstock, Inc.

overall moral values of each state generally reflect the values of the United States as a whole, there are distinctive differences that can be found. What may be legal in one state may be illegal in another. Marijuana laws are one example of this concept because they vary tremendously in different parts of the country. Recreational use of marijuana has been legislated as legal in several states, a citation offense in some, a misdemeanor in others, and is still a felony in several. The consensus of the citizens within each state is what motivates differences in the laws. Another example of how moral values can vary from state to state would be the State of Nevada. Nevada is the only state that allows for legalized prostitution in the form of brothels in some parts of the state. All of the other forty-nine states have laws making all forms of prostitution illegal.

© jamie cross, 2011. Used under license from Shutterstock, Inc.

The smaller the society that we are a part of, the more agreement there is in relation to our moral values. The society of our local community is more harmonized as to our moral values than the larger societies, and local laws reflect this consistency. The smallest society that we are a part of is the most influential and generally the most cohesive when it comes to our moral values. This is the society of our family. The family is where we shape our individual values and they are influenced by the way we are raised. Our overall perception of what constitutes right and wrong is fashioned and reinforced by our parents or guardians as we grow up. While these values can change over time, they influence the decisions we make throughout our lives and ultimately become an integral part of the larger societies that we become a component of.

To summarize, we can see that the notion of justice in the United States is greatly influenced by the diverse ideals that make up the social justice concepts

© Liv friis-larsen, 2011. Used under license from Shutterstock, Inc.

within the various societies that we live. It is therefore critical that our criminal justice system remain fluid and adaptable to keep up with the changes that take place within the different levels of the societies in which we all live.

© Losevsky Pavel, 2011. Used under license from Shutterstock, Inc.

*S*OCIAL CONTRACT

The term **social contract** refers to an implied agreement between citizens and their government as a way of maintaining social order. The people make a trade-off by giving up some of their rights to a government in return for being able to benefit from a greater social order. The concept of the social contract provides the rationale behind the historically important notion that legitimate state authority must be derived from the consent of the governed.[5] To put this in simple terms, the concept of social justice means that all of the citizens of a society agree to allow the government to represent them and to make the laws of that society. In return, each citizen is expected to obey those laws in order to obtain the benefits provided by the formation of social structures.

Social Contract

The social contract is an implied agreement between citizens and their government as a way of maintaining social order.

The government establishes laws that represent the norms of the society, and any person who violates any of these laws violates the social contract and must be punished in order to restore order.

*D*UE PROCESS VS. CRIME CONTROL

VERSUS

© Onur ERSIN, 2011. Used under license from Shutterstock, Inc.

© Scott Rothstein, 2011. Used under license from Shutterstock, Inc.

Herbert L. Packer

Herbert L. Packer (1925–1972) was a Professor of Law at Stanford University who wrote the paper "Two Models of the Criminal Process" in 1964.

Crime Control Model

This model is based on the proposition that crime must be controlled at all cost in order to have a safe society. In this model the rights of the many (society) outweigh the rights of the few (those who are accused of crime).

Due Process Model

This model is designed to protect the rights of the individual who is accused of a crime and make sure that all legal resources and protections are available and utilized. In this model the rights of the accused outweigh the rights of the many (society).

In 1964, **Herbert L. Packer** published a paper entitled "Two Models of the Criminal Process."[6] This paper has become a standard among criminal justice scholars and students in the debate over the best way to control crime and criminals within our society. The two models are called the "crime control model" and the "due process model." The **crime control model** is based on the proposition that crime must be controlled at all costs in order to have a safe society. Packer says of this model that: "The failure of law enforcement to bring criminal conduct under tight control is viewed as leading to the breakdown of public order and thence to the disappearance of an important condition of human freedom."[7] The **due process model** is designed to protect the rights of the individual who is accused of a crime and make sure that all legal resources and protections are available and utilized. These rights and protections are designed to present a formidable obstacle to the government and the criminal justice system when trying to prosecute those charged with a criminal act.

The basic premise of the crime control model is speed and efficiency. This model says that it is more important to protect society as a whole against the injury caused by criminals than to protect the single person who committed that injury. Society must be able to live in safety and in order to do this we must effectively and efficiently rid the country of those who commit crimes. Packer said that in the crime control model, "all of the components of the criminal justice system must work together to increase the capacity to apprehend, try, convict, and dispose of a high proportion of criminal offenders whose offenses become known."[8]

The crime control model suggests that our system of justice can be sped up, and therefore become more efficient, by determining early in the process who is probably guilty and who is not. If an accused person is determined to be innocent, they can be weeded out of the system early. Those that appear to be guilty can then be pushed through the system with a limited amount of procedural delays. The ultimate goal is to obtain the adjudication of guilt as quickly as possible so that the proper form of punishment can be implemented and society can be made safer.

© Rainer Plendl, 2011. Used under license from Shutterstock, Inc.

The crime control model is likened to an assembly line because speed and efficiency are the key components of this model. The due process model is compared more to an obstacle course because the system is designed to present formidable impediments at every stage of the process. This model says that the individual is more important than the many. It is more important to protect the rights of the accused than to protect the interests of society as a whole. The criminal justice system is a system of man and man is not perfect, mistakes can and are made in the process of justice and the accused must be protected against these mistakes. This model is based on the premise that the constitution guarantees all citizens the right to due process[9] and this and all of the rights enumerated in the Bill of Rights will be fully complied with in every instance.

The due process model says that even if a person appears to be guilty, the system is designed to safeguard the integrity of the justice process. To give explanation to this premise let us look at the following hypothetical scenario. The police are dispatched to a location where shots have been fired. The first officer on the scene sees a body on the ground lying in a pool of blood. There is a man standing over the body with a gun in his hand and several witnesses shouting that the man with

the gun had just shot the victim. The man puts down the gun and tells the officer that he just shot the victim. The officer places the man in handcuffs and arrests him for murder. Witness statements are taken and the man is taken to jail and booked.

The above hypothetical situation could make a reasonable person come to the conclusion that there would be a strong presumption that the man arrested is guilty of the crime of murder. Proponents of the crime control model would say that this is a perfect case for bypassing many of the procedural requirements of the criminal justice system and swiftly adjudicate the accused and apply the appropriate criminal sanctions without any unnecessary delay. Proponents of the due process model, however, would say wait a minute, we need to slow down. The appearance of guilt is not sufficient to speed up the process; there are too many legal variables that have to be considered. Only an impartial tribunal can be trusted to make determinations of legal as opposed to factual guilt. Herbert Packer stated it best when he explained that: "the tribunal that convicts him must have the power to deal with his kind of case ("jurisdiction") and must be geographically appropriate ("venue"); too long a time must not have elapsed since the offense was committed ("statute of limitations"); he must not have been previously convicted or acquitted of the same or a substantially similar offense ("double jeopardy"); he must not fall within a category of persons, such as children or the insane, who are legally immune to conviction ("criminal responsibility"); and so on. None of these requirements has anything to do with the factual question of whether the person did or did not engage in the conduct that is charged as the offense against him; yet favorable answers to any of them will mean that he is legally innocent."[10]

The due process model protects the criminally accused against the overwhelming power of the government that is charged with prosecuting the cases. Due process insures all citizens that this immense power is neutralized so that they can compete fairly within the justice system. The crime control model wants to stream-line the system so that those who deviate from society's norms and values are dealt with swiftly in order to protect those that are law abiding.

It would appear that these two models of justice, each with their seemingly competing ideologies, could never come together to form a consensus system of justice. The reality of this is that they actually do. Our criminal justice system is in a constant state of change, and components of each system manage to influence the philosophy that guides justice within our society.

*T*HE COMPONENTS OF THE CRIMINAL JUSTICE SYSTEM

The criminal justice system of the United States consists of three major compo-nents or functions: the police, corrections, and the courts (judicial). There are nu-merous subcomponents of the system, each of which falls under one of the three main categories. These subcomponents include such things as parole, probation, juvenile justice, and others that will be addressed separately later.

The system also works on three different governmental levels. We have one federal system, fifty different state systems, and thousands of county and munici-pal systems. Local governments spent more on criminal justice direct expenditures than the states or the federal government. Direct expenditures for each of the three major criminal justice functions have increased steadily since 1982. In fiscal year 2012, federal, state, and local governments spent an estimated $264 billion for police protection, corrections, and judicial and legal activities. Local governments account for a majority of the cost of the criminal justice system with expenditures of $132 billion of the $264 billion spent. State government spending accounted for $81 billion, while the federal government spent $52 billion in the same year.[11]

Nationally, there were approximately 2.1 million people employed in the jus-tice system working at the federal, state, and local levels in 2012. The overall growth in the criminal justice system remained relatively stable during the decade between 1997 and 2006. The economy since 2008 has had a slightly negative im-pact on employment in the justice system, but there has been a significant increase in criminal justice employment over the last decade. Overall, employment in the criminal justice system has remained stable even during tough economic times.

POLICE

The largest component of the criminal justice system, both in terms of employment and overall expenditures, is that of the **police**. The United States Department of Justice estimated that there were 891,289 full time law enforcement employees in the United States in 2012.[14] Approximately 76 percent of these employees, which includes both civilian and sworn positions, work for police protection at the local

Police
Police departments (at all levels) are the largest and most visible component of the Criminal Justice System and operate under the Executive Branch of government. Police are tasked with the job of en-forcing the criminal laws within their jurisdiction.

© Anton Prado PHOTO, 2011. Used under license from Shutterstock, Inc.

Law Enforcement

Law enforcement is a term that describes the individuals and agencies responsible for enforcing laws and maintaining public order and public safety.

Corrections

The correctional component of the criminal justice system is responsible for overseeing those individuals who have been arrested and are awaiting trial, as well as those who have been convicted of a crime and are sentenced to serve time. Corrections include both jails and prisons.

Jails

Jails are usually local facilities that serve several different functions including housing people who have been arrested and awaiting trial and those who are serving time for misdemeanor crimes.

level. The federal government accounts for about 14 percent of the employees and the remaining 9.2 percent work for state police protection agencies.

"**Law enforcement**" is the term that describes the individuals and agencies responsible for enforcing laws and maintaining public order and public safety. Law enforcement includes the prevention, detection, and investigation of crime; and the apprehension and detention of individuals suspected of law violation.[16]

There are over 18,000 different law enforcement agencies in the United States. Most of these agencies operate at the local level, which includes cities and counties. There are a wide variety of specialized police agencies which include: school police, campus police, park police, transit police, bailiffs, marshals, and sheriffs, just to name a few. A detailed discussion about law enforcement and the specialties associated with them will be presented in Chapter 6 of this text.

CORRECTIONS

The correctional component of the criminal justice system is responsible for overseeing those individuals who have been arrested and are awaiting trial, as well as those who have been convicted of a crime and are sentenced to serve time. **Corrections** include both jails and prisons. **Jails** are usually local facilities that serve several different functions. When a person is arrested for a crime, they are taken to a jail facility to be processed (booked) and held until they can make bail or see a judge or magistrate. These people have not been convicted of a crime and therefore are presumed innocent; however, they can be held in the jail facility until they are tried for the crime they are accused of. Jails are also used to house those persons who have been found guilty of lesser crimes (misdemeanors and ordinance charges) and have been sentenced to a term of incarceration.

Prisons differ from jails in several respects. Prisons are operated by the various states or by the federal government, not by local governments.[17] Prisons are

© WilleeCole, 2011. Used under license from Shutterstock, Inc.

used to house persons who have been convicted of felonies and are serving a sentence of incarceration of over one year.

The jail population changes constantly as prisoners are released, make bail, or are convicted and transferred to prisons to serve their sentence. New offenders are also arrested and booked and enter the system. Jail facilities in the United States admit and process about thirteen million people a year with almost 800,000 offenders in our jail facilities at any given time. Our state and federal prisons house approximately 1.6 million offenders at any given time.[18] A detailed discussion of the correctional system will be presented in Chapter 10 of this text.

Prisons

Prisons are long term facilities that are operated by state and federal governments and hold prisoners who have been convicted of felony crimes.

COURTS

The judicial component of the criminal justice system is comprised of the courts. Like the other parts of the system, the courts operate on the federal, state, and local levels. The **court** system in the United States is comprised of many different types of courts: criminal, civil, administrative, and a variety of specialized courts. The court system also includes all of the various appellate courts that function on both the federal and state levels.[21]

The criminal courts in the United States handle the most cases within the judicial system, with over 86.2 million criminal cases handled in 2015.[22]

Court

The court system in the United States (part of the judicial system), is comprised of many different types of courts: criminal, civil, administrative, and a variety of specialized courts, as well as our appellate courts.

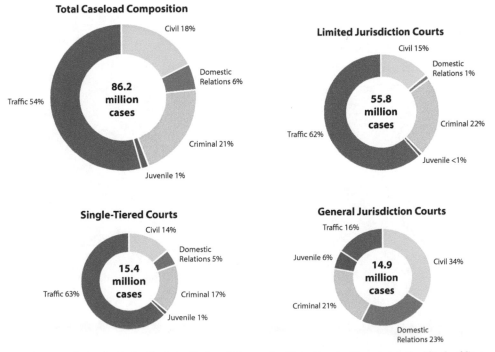

Caseload Composition, Total by Tier, 2015

Source: Court Statistics Project, National Center for State Courts, *Examining the Work of State Courts: An Overview of 2015 State Court Caseloads*.

REVIEW QUESTIONS:

1. _____ can be referred to as fundamental fairness.

2. The concept of _____ _____ changes over time as the moral values of a society change.

3. The implied agreement between citizens and their government as a way of maintaining social order is called the _____ _____.

4. "Two Models of the Criminal Justice Process" was written by _____ _____.

5. The basic premise of the _____ _____ model is speed and efficiency.

6. The _____ _____ model has been compared to an obstacle course.

7. There are _____ main components of the criminal justice system.

8. The _____ component of the criminal justice system has the largest yearly expenditure.

9. Persons housed in a _____ have been convicted of a felony and are serving a sentence of incarceration of over one year.

10. When a person is arrested, they are taken to a _____ to be processed and booked.

CRITICAL THINKING QUESTIONS:

1. How have the moral values in the United States changed over the past two hundred years and how have these changes affected our laws?

2. Discuss how the laws in your local community may be different from those in other communities around the state or the country.

3. Select either the Due Process Model or the Crime Control Model and give the reasons why you think that model should be adopted as the sole basis of the criminal justice system in the United States.

4. Discuss why there are over 86 million court cases processed in the United States every year. Why is this number so high? What can we do to reduce this massive caseload?

CHAPTER 2

[1] 113 U. PA. L. Rev. 1, 1964.

[2] 2nd Edition (New York: Oxford University Press, Inc., 2005).

[3] Connie Ireland and George E. Rush, *The Dictionary of Criminal Justice With Summaries of Supreme Court Cases Affecting Criminal Justice,* 7th Edition (New York: McGraw Hill, 2011).

[4] *Quotations of Theodore Roosevelt* (Bedford, MA: Applewood Books, 2004).

[5] New World Encyclopedia contributors, *New World Encyclopedia,* "Social contract," accessed on February/2011 at http://www.newworldencyclopedia. org/entry/Social_contract?oldid=901448.

[6] U. PA. L. Rev. Op cit.

[7] Ibid.

[8] Ibid.

[9] As stated in the Fifth, Sixth, and Fourteenth Amendments.

[10] U. Pa. L. Rev. Op cit.

[11] Bureau of Justice Statistics, accessed on January 12, 2017 at https://www.bjs.gov/index.cfm?ty=qa&iid=416

[12] Bureau of Justice Statistics, accessed on July/2011 at http://bjs.ojp.usdoj.gov/index.cfm?ty=tp&tid=5.

[13] Ibid.

[14] U.S. Department of Justice, Office of Justice Programs, Bureau of Justice Statistics, *National Sources of Law Enforcement Employment Data*, April 2016.

[15] Bureau of Justice Statistics accessed on January/2011 at http://bjs.ojp.usdoj.gov

[16] It should be noted that there are prisons that are operated under contract with the various states and the federal government. Chapter 10 will discuss private prisons in more detail.

[17] United States Department of Labor, Bureau of Labor Statistics, accessed on February/2011 at http://www. bls.gov/oco/ocos156.htm.

[18] Bureau of Justice Statistics, accessed on February/2011 at http://bjs.ojp.usdoj.gov.

[19] United States Department of Labor, Bureau of Labor Statistics, accessed on February/2011 at http://www. bls.gov/oco/ocos156.htm.

[20] The court system will be discussed in detail in Chapter 8 of this text.

[21] National Center for State Courts, "Court Statistics Project," accessed on January/2017 at http://www. courtstatistics.org/~/media/Microsites/Files/CSP/ EWSC%202015.ashx.

[22] Ibid.

[23] Ibid.

The Extent of Crime in America

Chapter 3

Chapter Overview

© carl ballou, 2011. Used under license from Shutterstock, Inc.

It is important, for a variety of reasons, to know exactly how much crime takes place in the United States. Police departments need to be able to allocate their limited resources in the most efficient manner. Correctional agencies need to know how to utilize the limited available space assigned to them and the judicial system needs to know how to efficiently apportion courtroom schedules. Citizens also want to know where crime takes place so that they may avoid dangerous locations and try to stay safe.

There are three primary sources of crime data in America, the Uniform Crime Report, the National Incident Based Reporting System, and the National Crime Victimization Survey, and we will look at each of these in detail in this chapter. We will see that there are significant discrepancies in the data that is reported by each of these reporting systems, and that these discrepancies can have a dramatic effect on how we look at crime.

We will also examine the current crime picture in the United States. Crime has actually been on the decline throughout the past decade, despite rising unemployment and an uncertain economic situation, a trend that seems to contradict traditional criminological thought. Several possible explanations for this trend will be set forth and examined.

The variables of gender, age, and race have always been the focus of analysis when considering crime rates. This chapter will examine the relationship between these variables and the current crime rates in the United States. An analysis of the extensive use of firearms during the commission of crimes in this country will also be examined.

CHAPTER LEARNING OBJECTIVES

After reading this chapter you will be able to:

1. Identify the three primary sources of crime data in America.
2. Explain how the three primary sources of crime data differ in their methodology.
3. Understand why statistical crime data is not a reliable indicator of actual crime rates.
4. Understand the definitions of Part I crimes.
5. Identify the current trends in crime rates.
6. Explain how crimes are cleared under the Uniform Crime Reporting (UCR) Program.
7. Demonstrate a working knowledge of the relationships between gender, age, race, and crime.
8. Recognize the correlation between guns and crime.

_____ KEYWORDS _____

Adolphe Quetelet   UCR
NIBRS   NCVS
Part I Crimes   Hierarchy Rule
Rate of Crime   Violent Crime
Property Crime   Dark Figure of Crime
Cleared by Arrest   Clearance Rates
Exceptional Clearance   Crime Clock
Gender and Crime   Race and Crime
Firearms

COUNTING CRIME

Crime has been a major concern of societies for thousands of years. There has always been a certain segment within every civilization that has deviated from the accepted social norms and violated the laws of that society. Public fear of crime, both real and perceived, has affected the way people run their day-to-day lives. We lock our doors when we leave or return home, we lock our cars, we avoid walking or driving in certain parts of our communities, and we protect ourselves and our property by a variety of ways. Governments have spent a tremendous amount of time, money, and effort in their attempts to control crime and protect their citizens.

The fundamental questions that have confronted societies have been how much crime actually exists, what types of crimes are taking place, and what causes these crimes to exist. The actual gathering of crime statistics has been a relatively recent activity that has only been around for about two hundred years. Prior that time, governments have been collecting data on population numbers for thousands of years. Ancient Rome and Greece, as well as others, were involved in determining how many citizens were living within their borders. They used these numbers to assess how much money could be collected in taxes and how many males were available for military service.

One of the first people to use statistical analysis in the gathering of crime statistics was **Adolphe Quetelet** (1796–1874). Quetelet was a Belgium astronomer and mathematician who was also one of the founders of the positivist school of criminology (see Chapter 4). In 1831, Quetelet published a summation of his crime research in an essay entitled "Of the Development of the Propensity to Crime."[1] He found a strong relationship between crime rates and such factors as climate, gender, and age. He was the first to analyze these factors and his conclusions, though ground breaking and controversial at the time, are taken for granted today. Quetelet found that there was more property crimes (thefts) committed in colder weather and more violent crimes committed in warmer weather. He also concluded that males committed more crimes than females, and that younger people committed more crimes than older people.

Since the time of Quetelet and the others who followed, the collection of statistical crime data has become more sophisticated and is essential to law enforcement agencies and researchers around the world. Police need these crime statistics in order to know where to effectively allocate their resources so they can try to stop crime before it takes place. Researchers evaluate the statistics in order to come up with causes of crime, which is the first critical step towards preventing future crimes. With this in mind, it only makes sense that the crime data has to be accurate. But is it? The following section will show us that the data we collect today has many inherent flaws that consequently affect how we deal with crime in America.

Adolphe Quetelet

Adolphe Quetelet (1796–1874) was the first person to find a strong relationship between crime rates and such factors as climate, gender, and age.

Adolphe Quetelet
(1796–1874)

SOURCES OF CRIME DATA

There are three primary sources of crime data that are in use in the United States today. The first, and oldest, is the Uniform Crime Report (UCR), which has been the standard for crime statistics for over eighty years. The second is the National Incident Based Reporting System (NIBRS), that is a part of the UCR and collects significantly more data than the original (UCR). The third source is the National Crime Victimization Survey (NCVS) that attempts to collect data on crimes that have never been reported to the police.

UCR

UCR

The Uniform Crime Report (UCR) is a nationwide statistical compilation of reported crime data from more than 18,000 city, county, state, tribal, university and college, and federal law enforcement agencies.

The Uniform Crime Report (**UCR**) is a nationwide statistical compilation of reported crime data from 18,439 city, county, state, tribal, university and college, and federal law enforcement agencies.[2] This data is collected and disseminated by the Federal Bureau of Investigation. The UCR came into existence in 1930 and was tasked with the primary objective of providing reliable crime statistics for use by law enforcement agencies throughout the country. Over time, this data has become one of the country's leading social indicators. Criminologists, sociologists, students, and others have come to rely on this data as a basis for research and planning in the field of criminal justice.[3] In 2015, the UCR collected crime data from law enforcement agencies that represented more than 98 percent of the total population of the United States (more than 321 million people). The submission of data to the FBI is not mandatory for law enforcement and therefore collection of 100 percent of crime data in the country is not possible.[4]

The UCR divides the crimes it collects data on into two parts, and uses different reporting standards for each. **Part I crimes** consist of eight offense classifications that are divided into **violent crimes** and **property crimes**:

Part I Crimes

Part I crimes include the eight most serious crimes: murder, rape, robbery, and aggravated assault.

VIOLENT CRIMES

1. Murder
2. Rape
3. Robbery
4. Aggravated Assault

Violent Crimes

Violent crimes (crimes against persons) include: murder, rape, robbery, and aggravated assault.

PROPERTY CRIMES

5. Burglary
6. Larceny (theft)
7. Motor Vehicle Theft
8. Arson[5]

Property Crimes

Property crimes (crimes against property) include: burglary, larceny (theft), motor vehicle theft, and arson.

The Part I crime classifications were selected because they represent the most serious crimes that are the most likely to be reported and most likely to occur with sufficient frequency to provide an adequate basis for comparison.[6] The data for these crimes is collected from participating law enforcement agencies and includes all of the instances within each category that was reported to the police. It is important to note that some of the data for Part I crimes is distorted by a data collection procedure used by the FBI called the **Hierarchy Rule**. The Hierarchy Rule states that "... when more than one Part I offense is classified, the law enforcement agency must locate the offense that is highest on the hierarchy list and score that offense involved and not the other offense(s) in the multiple-offense situation."[7] The Hierarchy Rule counts only the most serious offense and ignores all others that may have occurred at the same time.

Hierarchy Rule

The Hierarchy Rule counts only the most serious offense and ignores all others that may have occurred at the same time.

To put the Hierarchy Rule into perspective, if a person walks into a bank and pulls a gun and robs the teller, this crime would be correctly reported as one robbery. If that same person walked into that bank and robbed the bank teller, then turned and robbed five customers who were standing in line, and then shot and killed the security officer in the bank, this crime event would only be reported as a murder. The six counts of robbery would not show up as a criminal event in the UCR statistics because only the most serious crime of murder would be reflected. It is important to point out that the Hierarchy Rule applies only to what is reported for purposes of crime statistics. The Rule has no effect on the number of charges for which the defendant may be arrested and prosecuted.[8] There are three exceptions to the Hierarchy Rule: justifiable homicide, motor vehicle theft, and arson.

In addition to the Part I crimes, the UCR compiles data on twenty-one other crime classifications that are called **Part II crimes**. These are less serious crimes and include such offenses as: drunk driving, simple assault, fraud, disorderly conduct, prostitution, and drug-law violations. Unlike the Part I crime data that reports the number of incidents reported to the police, Part II crimes are only reported when an arrest has been made.

Part II Crimes

The UCR compiles data on twenty-one additional crimes not included in Part I. These crimes are only counted when an actual arrest is made.

The UCR reports crime statistics as a **rate of crime** (UCR crime index). Rates of crime are generally expressed as "x number of offenses per 100,000 people." This provides a crime rate that can be compared over time, and from one geographic location to another.

Rate of Crime

Rates of crime are generally expressed as "x number of offenses per 100,000 people." This provides a crime rate that can be compared over time, and from one geographic location to another.

$$\frac{\text{\# of Reported Crimes}}{\text{Total Population}} \; 100{,}000 = \text{rate per } 100{,}000$$

The Federal Bureau of Investigation publishes the compiled data for Part I and Part II crimes every year in their report entitled *"Crime in the United States."* They also publish *"Hate Crime Statistics"* and *"Law Enforcement Officers Killed and Assaulted."* All of these publications are free and are available online at the FBI website www.fbi.gov.

NIBRS

NIBRS

The National Incident-Based Reporting System is an enhanced version of the UCR that collects much more detailed information about each reported crime.

The National Incident-Based Reporting System (**NIBRS**) was developed in the 1980s and was approved in 1988 in response to law enforcements' need for more comprehensive crime data than the UCR was providing. The NIBRS data is collected and disseminated by the FBI and is actually an enhanced version of the UCR. The NIBRS collects data on each single criminal event and arrest within twenty-two offense categories made up of forty-six specific crimes called Group A offenses.[9] The enhanced data that is collected includes much more comprehensive information about each offense than is provided in the UCR. The NIBRS moves beyond just raw counts of crime and arrests and develops an individual record for each reported crime incident and its associated arrest. The data that is collected includes detailed information on the incident itself, the victim, property taken, the suspect, and, if there was an arrest, detailed information on the arrestee (age, sex, race, ethnicity, use of alcohol/drugs, and other specifics).

On February 9, 2016, FBI Director James B. Comey signed a recommendation by the Criminal Justice Services Division's Advisory Board (APB) that will replace the UCR with the NIBRS by January, 2021. Group A crime categories are:

1. Arson
2. Assault Offenses—Aggravated Assault, Simple Assault, Intimidation
3. Bribery
4. Burglary/Breaking and Entering
5. Counterfeiting/Forgery
6. Destruction/Damage/Vandalism of Property
7. Drug/Narcotic Offenses—Drug/Narcotic Violations, Drug Equipment Violations
8. Embezzlement
9. Extortion/Blackmail
10. Fraud Offenses—False Pretenses/Swindle/Confidence Game, Credit Card/Automatic Teller Machine Fraud, Impersonation, Welfare Fraud, Wire Fraud
11. Gambling Offenses—Betting/Wagering, Operating/Promoting/Assisting Gambling, Gambling Equipment Violations, Sports Tampering
12. Homicide Offenses—Murder and Nonnegligent Manslaughter, Negligent Manslaughter, Justifiable Homicide
13. Kidnapping/Abduction
14. Larceny/Theft Offenses—Pocket-Picking, Purse-Snatching, Shoplifting, Theft from Building, Theft from Coin-Operated Machine or Device, Theft from Motor Vehicle, Theft of Motor Vehicle Parts or Accessories, All Other Larceny
15. Motor Vehicle Theft
16. Pornography/Obscene Material
17. Prostitution Offenses—Prostitution, Assisting or Promoting Prostitution
18. Robbery

19. Sex Offenses, Forcible—Forcible Rape, Forcible Sodomy, Sexual Assault with an Object, Forcible Fondling
20. Sex Offenses, Nonforcible—Incest, Statutory Rape
21. Stolen Property Offenses (Receiving, etc.)
22. Weapon Law Violations

In addition to Group A crimes, the NIBRS also collects data on eleven additional crime categories called Group B offenses. Like the Part II crimes under the UCR, only arrest data is collected on these crime categories. The eleven Group B crime categories are:

- Bad Checks
- Curfew/Loitering/Vagrancy Violations
- Disorderly Conduct
- Driving Under the Influence
- Drunkenness
- Family Offenses, Nonviolent
- Liquor Law Violations
- Peeping Tom
- Runaway
- Trespass of Real Property
- All Other Offenses

Because of the amount of data that must be submitted under the criteria of the NIBRS, only law enforcement agencies that use automated data systems are able to submit this enhanced information. Additionally, many agencies have been reluctant to submit such detailed information due to budgetary and other administrative constraints. As of 2015, only 6,648 law enforcement agencies contributed NIBRS data to the UCR.[10] This represents approximately 36.1 percent of all agencies that submit data to the FBI UCR Program. The NIBRS information that is published only represents about 25 percent of the United States population.

NCVS

The third important source of crime data in the United States is the National Crime Victimization Survey (**NCVS**). Unlike the UCR and the NIBRS, which both collect data that has been reported to the police, the NCVS collects information from victims of violent (nonfatal) and property crimes, both reported and not reported, against persons twelve and older. The data is collected from a nationally representative sample of U.S. households. The unreported crime that the NCVS attempts to collect is often referred to as the "**dark figure of crime**" because we do not really know what this number is. The NCVS is sponsored by the U.S. Department of Justice and is implemented by the U.S. Census Bureau.

NCVS
The National Crime Victimization Survey (NCVS) is a statistical survey that attempts to find out how much crime is not reported to the police.

Dark Figure of Crime
The dark figure of crime represents those crimes that are not reported to the police.

The NCVS started collecting data in 1973 and is the nation's primary source of information on criminal victimization. In 2015, representative samples of about 95,760 American households were surveyed. These households are comprised of almost 163,880 people over the age of twelve.[11] The households selected for this survey remain in the sample for three years. The households return surveys that ask about crime that has affected each member of the household who is twelve years of age and older. The surveys are supplemented with a total of seven interviews that are conducted every six months.

Since the households that are selected are a statistically representative sample of the United States, the data can be projected out to give a fairly accurate picture of crime in the entire country.

In 2015 the NCVS found that U.S. residents age twelve and older experienced the following differences in crime victimizations from 2014[12]:

- No statistically significant change occurred in the rate of violent crime from 2014 (20.1 victimizations per 1,000) to 2015 (18.6 per 1,000).••
- No statistically significant change was detected in the percentages of violent crime reported to police from 2014 (46%) to 2015 (47%).
- The rate of property crime decreased from 118.1 victimizations per 1,000 households in 2014 to 110.7 per 1,000 in 2015.
- In 2015, 0.98% of all persons age 12 or older (2.7 million persons) experienced at least one violent victimization.
- The prevalence rate of violent victimization declined from 1.11% of all persons age 12 or older in 2014 to 0.98% in 2015.

Violent crimes measured by the NCVS include rape, sexual assault, robbery, aggravated assault, and simple assault. Property crimes include household burglary, motor vehicle theft, and theft.

PROBLEMS WITH THE DATA

There are many inherent problems associated with the collection of crime data in this country. First and foremost is the fact that the most publicized and relied upon crime statistics come from the UCR. The UCR is a *reporting* system and studies (including the NCVS) have shown us that as much as 50 percent of ALL crimes are not reported to the police. This figure is even higher for some crimes. Since only about half of the crimes in America are even reported, we really do not know the true extent of crime in this country.

There are also problems in what data is actually reported to the UCR, which includes methodological issues:

1. Not all police departments submit data since the reports are voluntary.
2. Federal crimes are not included in the statistics.

3. Only the most serious crime in any criminal event is reported due to the Hierarchy Rule.
4. Incomplete acts (attempts) are included in the statistics the same as completed acts.
5. Part II offenses are only counted when an arrest, not a report, has been made.

Some of the other factors that influence the crime statistics deal with the practices of individual law enforcement agencies:

1. Different police departments use different internal counting procedures.
2. Police also use different departmental statistical procedures when analyzing the crime data within their individual jurisdiction.
3. The definitions for crimes differ from state to state since each is responsible for writing its own laws. These definitions also differ from those of the UCR and the NIBRS. This can cause misinterpretations by law enforcement agencies as to what data they are supposed to submit.

The following are the definitions of rape for each of the three reporting systems:

RAPE:

UCR: penetration, no matter how slight, of the vagina or anus with any body part or object, or oral penetration by a sex organ of another person, without the consent of the victim.

NIBRS: The carnal knowledge of a person, forcibly and/or against the person's will; or not forcibly or against the person's will where the victim is incapable of giving consent because of his/her temporary or permanent mental or physical incapacity, or because of his/her youth.

NCVS: Carnal knowledge through the use of force or the threat of force, including attempts. Statutory rape is excluded—homosexual rape is included.

Each of these definitions requires police departments (UCR and NIBRS) or citizens (NCVS) to submit different data as to the crime of rape. The UCR definition was changed in 2012 because it did not include rapes that were not by force which means that date rapes were not included. It also did not include homosexual or statutory rapes. The new UCR definition now includes homosexual and date rapes; however, it still does not include statutory rape. The NIBRS data also includes date and homosexual rape, but unlike the UCR data, also includes statutory rape. The NCVS includes homosexual rape, but does not include date rape or statutory rape in its reported data. Because of these discrepancies, when we look at the number of rapes that have been committed and reported by the three reporting systems, we will see three different numbers.

DEFINITIONS OF CRIMES

Before an examination of the current crime picture in the United States can be conducted, it is important to have a basic familiarity with definitions of the crimes that will be discussed. The following are the definitions of the Uniform Crime Reporting Program for the eight Part I Crimes[13]:

Criminal homicide: Murder and non-negligent manslaughter: A.) Murder: the willful (non-negligent) killing of one human being by another. Deaths caused by negligence, attempts to kill, assaults to kill, suicides, and accidental deaths are excluded. The program classifies justifiable homicides separately and limits the definition to: (1) the killing of a felon by a law enforcement officer in the line of duty; or (2) the killing of a felon, during the commission of a felony, by a private citizen. B.) Manslaughter by negligence: the killing of another person through gross negligence. Deaths of persons due to their own negligence, accidental deaths not resulting from gross negligence, and traffic fatalities are not included in the category Manslaughter by Negligence.

Rape: penetration, no matter how slight, of the vagina or anus with any body part or object, or oral penetration by a sex organ of another person, without the consent of the victim.

Robbery: The taking or attempting to take anything of value from the care, custody, or control of a person or persons by force or threat of force, or violence and/or by putting the victim in fear.

Aggravated assault: An unlawful attack by one person upon another for the purpose of inflicting severe or aggravated bodily injury. This type of assault usually is accompanied by the use of a weapon or by means likely to produce death or great bodily harm. Simple assaults are excluded.

Burglary (breaking or entering): The unlawful entry of a structure to commit a felony or a theft. Attempted forcible entry is included.

Larceny-theft (except motor vehicle theft): The unlawful taking, carrying, leading, or riding away of property from the possession or constructive possession of another. Examples are thefts of bicycles, motor vehicle parts and accessories, shoplifting, pocket-picking, or the stealing of any property or article that is not taken by force and violence, or by fraud. Attempted larcenies are included. Embezzlement, confidence games, forgery, check fraud, etc., are excluded.

Motor vehicle theft: The theft or attempted theft of a motor vehicle. A motor vehicle is self-propelled and runs on land surface and not on rails. Motorboats, construction equipment, airplanes, and farming equipment are specifically excluded from this category.

Arson: Any willful or malicious burning or attempt to burn, with or without intent to defraud, a dwelling house, public building, motor vehicle or aircraft, personal property of another, etc.

CRIME IN AMERICA

Crime in the United States has been on the decline in almost every category for the past several years since its peak in the 1990's. Violent crime, while showing a slight increase of 3.9% between 2014 1nd 2015, is still 0.7% below the 2011 level and 16.5% below the 2006 level.[14] Property crime has shown a steady decrease since the 1980's. The ten year trend shows a significant decrease of 20.2% since 2006.[15]

The overall continual drop in crime rates seems to defy conventional wisdom. Crime rates have steadily declined even during recent periods of high unemployment and a serious economic recession. It would seem that with these negative variables, the crime rate should be increasing instead of declining. There have been a host of theories put forth in an attempt to explain the recent decline in crime:

1. Increased incarceration rates (see Chapter 10).
2. Stricter sentencing laws (see Chapter 9).
3. Advances in forensic science.
4. Increased and improved training of law enforcement.
5. The "war on drugs."
6. More emphasis on gun control (including the Brady Handgun Violence Prevention Act).

Arguably, one of the most compelling reasons for the decline can be attributed to the fact that our population is getting older. For the first time in United States history, the number of people sixty-five and older outnumbers those who are five and younger. More importantly, the number of people aged eighteen to thirty-four has declined by over 18 percent since the 1990s. As we will see later in this chapter, this is the age group that commits the most crimes.

VIOLENT AND PROPERTY CRIME RATES IN THE UNITED STATES
BY VOLUME AND RATE PER 100,000 INHABITANTS, 1996–2015

YEAR	POPULATION	VIOLENT CRIME RATE	VIOLENT CRIME RATE	MURDER AND NONNEGLIGENT MANSLAUGHTER	MURDER AND NONNEGLIGENT MANSLAUGHTER RATE	PROPERTY CRIME	PROPERTY CRIME RATE
1996	265,228,572	1,688,540	636.6	19,645	7.4	11,805,323	4,451.0
1997	267,783,607	1,636,096	611.0	18,208	6.8	11,558,475	4,316.3
1998	270,248,003	1,533,887	567.6	16,974	6.3	10,951,827	4,052.5
1999	272,690,813	1,426,044	523.0	15,522	5.7	10,208,334	3,743.6
2000	281,421,906	1,425,486	506.5	15,586	5.5	10,182,584	3,618.3
2001	285,317,559	1,439,480	504.5	16,037	5.6	10,437,189	3,658.1
2002	287,973,924	1,423,677	494.4	16,229	5.6	10,455,277	3,630.6
2003	290,788,976	1,383,676	475.8	16,528	5.7	10,442,862	3,591.2
2004	293,656,842	1,360,088	463.2	16,148	5.5	10,319,386	3,514.1
2005	296,507,061	1,390,745	469.0	16,740	5.6	10,174,754	3,431.5
2006	299,398,484	1,435,123	479.3	17,309	5.8	10,019,601	3,346.6
2007	301,621,157	1,422,970	471.8	17,128	5.7	9,882,212	3,276.4
2008	304,059,724	1,394,461	458.6	16,465	5.4	9,774,152	3,214.6
2009	307,006,550	1,325,896	431.9	15,399	5.0	9,337,060	3,041.3
2010	309,330,219	1,251,248	404.5	14,722	4.8	9,112,625	2,945.9
2011	311,587,816	1,206,005	387.1	14,661	4.7	9,052,743	2,905.4
2012	313,873,685	1,217,057	387.8	14,856	4.7	9,001,992	2,868.0
2013	316,497,531	1,168,298	369.1	14,319	4.5	8,651,892	2,733.6
2014	318,907,401	1,153,022	361.6	14,164	4.4	8,209,010	2,574.1
2015	321,418,820	1,197,704	372.6	15,696	4.9	7,993,631	2,487.0

Data from the FBI - UCR 2015

The following chart shows the rate of violent crimes from 1960 to 2015.

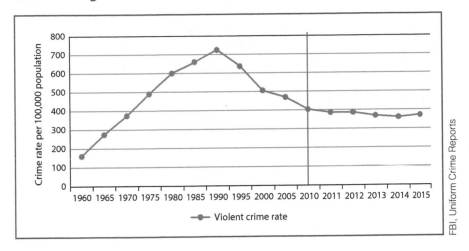

The following chart shows the rate of property crimes from 1960 to 2015.

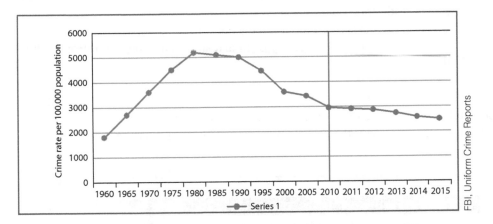

CLEARANCE RATES

When a law enforcement agency clears an offense, it means that it has closed that case. This is the best available data showing how many crimes are solved by the police. The Uniform Crime Reporting (UCR) Program allows law enforcement agencies to clear crimes in one of two ways: by arrest or by exceptional means.

CLEARED BY ARREST

In order for law enforcement to clear an offense by an arrest, three specific conditions must be met. The three conditions are that at least one person has been:

1. Arrested.
2. Charged with the commission of the offense.
3. Turned over to the court for prosecution.

In its clearance calculations, the UCR Program counts the number of offenses that are cleared, not the number of persons arrested. The arrest of one person may clear several crimes, and the arrest of many persons may clear only one offense. In addition, some clearances that an agency records in a particular calendar year, such as in 2015, may pertain to offenses that occurred in previous years.[18]

CLEARED BY EXCEPTIONAL MEANS

There are times when circumstances that are beyond law enforcement's control prevent the actual arrest and charging of an offender. When this occurs, the UCR allows the agency to clear the offence *exceptionally*. In order to clear an offense exceptionally, the agency must meet four conditions:

1. Identify the offender.
2. Gather enough evidence to support an arrest, make a charge, and turn over the offender to the court for prosecution.
3. Identify the offender's exact location so that the suspect could be taken into custody immediately.
4. The agency must have encountered a circumstance outside of law enforcement that prohibits the agency from arresting, charging, and prosecuting the offender.

Examples of exceptional clearances include, but are not limited to, the death of the offender (e.g., suicide or justifiably killed by police or citizen); the victim's refusal to cooperate with the prosecution after the offender has been identified; or

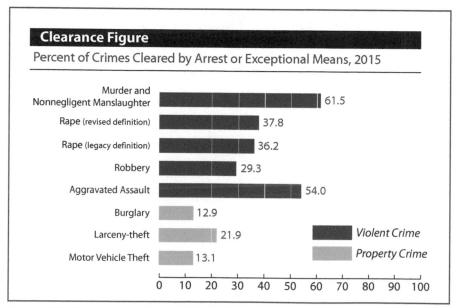

Clearance Figure

Percent of Crimes Cleared by Arrest or Exceptional Means, 2015

Murder and Nonnegligent Manslaughter — 61.5
Rape (revised definition) — 37.8
Rape (legacy definition) — 36.2
Robbery — 29.3
Aggravated Assault — 54.0
Burglary — 12.9
Larceny-theft — 21.9
Motor Vehicle Theft — 13.1

■ *Violent Crime*
■ *Property Crime*

Source: U.S. Department of Justice—Federal Bureau of Investigation, *Crime in the United States, 2015.*[19]

the denial of extradition because the offender committed a crime in another juris-diction and is being prosecuted for that offense. In the UCR Program, the recovery of property alone does not clear an offense.[20]

In the United States in 2015, 46.0 percent of violent crimes and 19.4 percent of property crimes were cleared by arrest or exceptional means.

CRIME CLOCK

The UCR **Crime Clock** is a way of showing the frequency of crime in the United States. It is important to point out that the clock represents the relative frequency of occurrence of Part I offenses. We do not actually have a murder every thirty-three minutes, but if you average every murder that took place in 2015 and divided them into the number of minutes in one year,[21] that would be the frequency of murders in the United States.

Crime Clock
The UCR Crime Clock is a way of showing the frequency of crime in the United States.

2015 CRIME CLOCK STATISTICS

A Violent Crime occurred every	26.3 seconds
One Murder every	33.5 minutes
One Rape every	4.2 minutes
One Robbery every	1.6 minutes
One Aggravated Assault every	41.3 seconds
A Property Crime occurred every	3.9 seconds
One Burglary every	20.0 seconds
One Larceny-theft every	5.5 seconds
One Motor Vehicle Theft every	44.6 seconds

Source: U.S. Department of Justice—Federal Bureau of Investigation, Crime in the United States, 2015.[22]

GENDER AND CRIME

Not surprisingly, males commit the majority of crimes in the United States. In 2015, almost three-fourths (73.1 percent) of all arrests in the United States were male. Males also accounted for 79.7 percent of all violent crime arrests and 87.7 percent of all persons arrested for murder in 2015. The national trend over the past decade 2006 to 2015 has shown that there has been a very significant 25.6 percent decrease in arrests of males while there has been an 11.8 percent increase in arrests of females over the same time period.

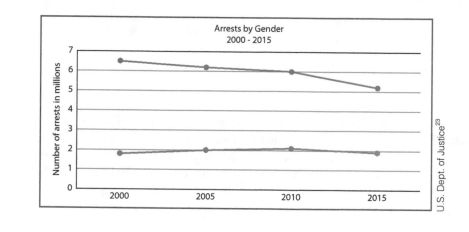

$\mathscr{A}$GE AND CRIME

Earlier in this chapter we have seen that the population in the United States is getting older. This population shift is reflected in the arrest statistics when we look at age as a variable. Juvenile arrests have dropped by 54.8 percent between 2006 and 2015 which is a very significant drop. There was a 16.7 percent decrease in arrests of persons over eighteen during that same time period.

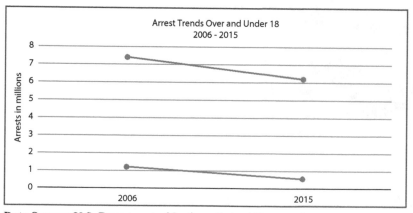

Data Source: U.S. Department of Justice—Federal Bureau of Investigation, Crime in the United States, 2015.[24]

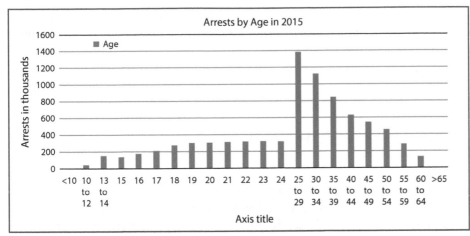

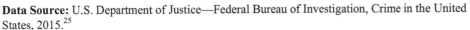

Data Source: U.S. Department of Justice—Federal Bureau of Investigation, Crime in the United States, 2015.[25]

RACE AND CRIME

Race and crime has always been a sensitive issue in criminal justice. There is a disproportionate number of Blacks and other minorities that have been arrested and incarcerated in the United States. Blacks make up approximately 13 percent of

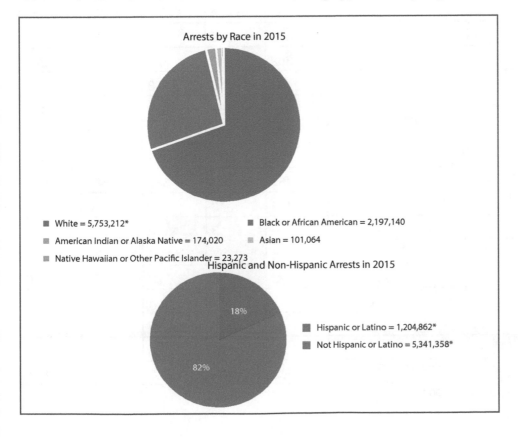

the population of the United States,[26] yet comprised 26.6 percent of all arrests in 2015.[27,28] This disparity has been a major topic of research conducted by criminologists for many years (see Chapter 4).

GUNS AND CRIME

According to some research, there are more privately owned guns in America than there are people.[31] A report in the Washington Post estimates that there were 357 million guns in the United States in 2013[32] These numbers make it easy to see

HOMICIDE DATA BY WEAPON					
MURDER VICTIMS BY WEAPON, 2011–2015					
WEAPONS	2011	2012	2013	2014	2015
Total	**12,795**	**12,888**	**12,253**	**12,270**	**13,455**
Total firearms:	8,653	8,897	8,454	8,312	9,616
Handguns	6,251	6,404	5,782	5,673	6,447
Rifles	332	298	285	258	252
Shotguns	362	310	308	264	269
Other guns	97	116	123	93	171
Firearms, type not stated	1,611	1,769	1,956	2,024	2,477
Knives or cutting instruments	1,716	1,604	1,490	1,595	1,544
Blunt objects (clubs, hammers, etc.)	502	522	428	446	437
Personal weapons (hands, fists, feet, etc.)[1]	751	707	687	682	624
Poison	5	13	11	10	7
Explosives	6	8	2	7	1
Fire	76	87	94	71	82
Narcotics	33	38	53	70	70
Drowning	15	14	4	14	14
Strangulation	88	90	85	89	96
Asphyxiation	92	106	95	102	120
Other weapons or weapons not stated	858	802	850	872	844

[1] Pushed is included in personal weapons.

why this country leads all other developed countries in the world in the number of murders and assaults committed with a firearm. Many countries, such as England and Australia, have extremely strict gun laws that make it very difficult, if not impossible, to own or carry a firearm. In England, only 8 percent of murders were committed with a firearm,[33] compared to 71.5 percent in the United States.[34] It is also important to point out that the murder rate (per 100,000) in England is 1.45 compared to 5 in the United States.[35] Firearms were also used in 40.9 percent of robberies and 24.3 percent of aggravated assaults that occurred in this country.[36]

Among inmates in prison for homicide, sexual assault, robbery, assault, or other violent crime, 30 percent of State offenders and 35 percent of Federal offenders carried a firearm when committing the crime. Almost a fourth of State inmates and almost a third of Federal inmates serving a sentence for a violent crime had carried a handgun during the offense.[37]

The chart below shows the different types of weapons that were used in murders in the United States from 2011 to 2015.

REVIEW QUESTIONS:

1. The three primary sources of crime statistics in the United States are the _____, the

   _____, and the _____.

2. The _____ _____ only counts the most serious offense and ignores all others that may have occurred at the same time.

3. The Uniform Crime Report reports crime statistics as a _____ of _____.

4. When a law enforcement agency clears an offense, it means that it has _____ that case.

5. The UCR allows a law enforcement agency to clear a case _____ when circumstances that are beyond the agency's control prevent the actual arrest and charging of the offender.

6. _____ has the highest clearance rate of all crimes.

7. The _____ _____ is a way of graphically showing the frequency of crime in the United States.

8. The arrest of juveniles (those offenders under the age of eighteen) has declined by _____ percent between 2006 and 2015.

9. _____ make up approximately 13 percent of the population of the United States, yet comprised 26.6 percent of all arrests in 2015.

10. According to some research, there are more _____ in America than there are people.

CRITICAL THINKING QUESTIONS:

1. Discuss the reasons that the crime rate in the United States has been declining over the past several years.

2. Explain some of the flaws in the way the UCR Program permits law enforcement agencies to clear criminal cases.

3. How would you explain the significant difference between the United States and England when it comes to use of firearms during the commission of criminal acts.

4. Discuss the disparity between the number of Blacks who are arrested for crimes and the demographic make-up of the population.

5. Why is there so much more violent crime in the United States than in any other developed country in the world?

—————————————— NOTES ——————————————

CHAPTER 3

[1] Piers Beirne, "Adolphe Quetelet and the Origins of Positivist Criminology," *American Journal of Sociology* **92(5):** pp. 1140–1169 (March, 1987).

[2] U.S. Department of Justice, Federal Bureau of Investigation, "Crime in the United States," accessed January, 2017 at https://ucr.fbi.gov/crime-in-the-u.s/2015/crime-in-the-u.s.-2015/home

[3] Ibid.

[4] Ibid.

[5] Arson was added as the eighth Part I category in 1979 by congressional mandate.

[6] FBI Uniform Crime Reports, accessed January, 2011 at http://www.fbi.gov/about-us/cjis/ucr/frequently-asked-questions/ucr_faqs.

[7] Ibid.

[8] The offenses of justifiable homicide, motor vehicle theft, and arson are exceptions to the Hierarchy Rule.

[9] FBI Uniform Crime Reports, accessed January, 2017 at https://ucr.fbi.gov/crime-in-the-u.s/2015/crime-in-the-u.s.-2015

[10] FBI National Incident Based Reporting System, accessed February, 2017 at https://ucr.fbi.gov/nibrs/2015

[11] Ibid

[12] Bureau of Justice Statistics, accessed January, 2017 at https://www.bjs.gov/index.cfm?ty=pbdetail&iid=5804

[13] Ibid

[14] U.S. Department of Justice—Federal Bureau of Investigation, Crime in the United States, 2009, accessed December, 2010 at http://www2.fbi.gov/ucr/cius2009/about/offense_definitions.html.

[15] U.S. Department of Justice—Federal Bureau of Investigation, Crime in the United States, 2015, accessed January, 2017 at https://ucr.fbi.gov/crime-in-the-u.s/2015/crime-in-the-u.s.-2015

[16] U.S. Department of Justice—Federal Bureau of Investigation, Crime in the United States, 2015, accessed January, 2017 at https://ucr.fbi.gov/crime-in-the-u.s/2015/crime-in-the-u.s.-2015

[17] FBI, Uniform Crime Reports as prepared by the National Archive of Criminal Justice Data, accessed December, 2010 at http://www.ucrdatatool.gov/Search/Crime/State/RunCrimeStatebyState.cfm.

[18] FBI, Uniform Crime Reports as prepared by the National Archive of Criminal Justice Data, accessed December, 2010 at http://www.ucrdatatool.gov/Search/Crime/State/RunCrimeStatebyState.cfm.

[19] Ibid.

[20] U.S. Department of Justice—Federal Bureau of Investigation, Crime in the United States, 2015.

[21] U.S. Department of Justice—Federal Bureau of Investigation, Crime in the United States, 2015, accessed January, 2017 at https://ucr.fbi.gov/crime-in-the-u.s/2015/crime-in-the-u.s.-2015/home

[22] There are 525,600 minutes in a year.

[23] U.S. Department of Justice—Federal Bureau of Investigation, Crime in the United States, 2015, accessed January, 2017 at https://ucr.fbi.gov/crime-in-the-u.s/2015/crime-in-the-u.s.-2015/resource-pages/crime-clock

[24] The actual arrest numbers are: for males in 2000 (6,491,372), in 2009 (6,174,287); and for females in 2000 (1,874,217), in 2009 (2,087,303).

[25] U.S. Department of Justice—Federal Bureau of Investigation, Crime in the United States, 2015, accessed January, 2017 at https://ucr.fbi.gov/crime-in-the-u.s/2015/crime-in-the-u.s.-2015/home

[26] U.S. Department of Justice—Federal Bureau of Investigation, Crime in the United States, 2015, accessed January, 2017 at https://ucr.fbi.gov/crime-in-the-u.s/2015/crime-in-the-u.s.-2015/home

[27] Detailed Tables—American FactFinder; T3–2008. Race (7). *2008 Population Estimates.* U.S. Census Bureau, accessed December, 2010 at http://factfinder.census.gov/servlet/DTTable?_bm=y&-state=dt&-context=dt&-ds_name=PEP_2008_EST&-CONTEXT=dt&-mt_name=PEP_2008_EST_G2008_T003_2008&-tree_id=809&-

redoLog=false&-currentselections=PEP_2006_
EST_G2006_T004_2006&-geo_id=01000US&-
geo_id=02000US1&-geo_id=02000US2&-geo_
id=02000US3&-geo_id=02000US4&-search_
results=01000US&-format=&-_lang=en.

[28] U.S. Department of Justice—Federal Bureau of
Investigation, Crime in the United States, 2015,
accessed January, 2015 at https://ucr.fbi.gov/
crime-in-the-u.s/2015/crime-in-the-u.s.-2015/home

[29] It should be noted that both the FBI's UCR and the
U.S. Census Bureau consider Hispanic as an ethnicity,
not a race and therefore may be considered as any race.

[30] Ibid

[31] Post, W. (2015, October 5). *Washinton Post*. Retrieved
March, 2017 from Washintonpost.com: https://www.
washingtonpost.com/news/wonk/wp/2015/10/05/guns-
in-the-united-states-one-for-every-man-woman-and-
child-and-then-some/?utm_term=.8d9cfce87a52

[32] U.S. Department of Justice—Federal Bureau of
Investigation, Crime in the United States, 2015,
accessed January, 2017 at https://ucr.fbi.gov/
crime-in-the-u.s/2015/crime-in-the-u.s.-2015/home

[33] U.S. Department of Justice, Office of Justice Programs,
National Institute of Justice, "Guns in America:
National Survey on Private Ownership and Use of
Firearms" (May 1997).

[34] United Nations Office on Drugs and Crime (UNODC),
"The Seventh United Nations Survey on Crime Trends
and the Operations of Criminal Justice Systems
(1998–2000)," accessed November, 2010 at http://
www.unodc.org/pdf/crime/seventh_survey/7sc.pdf.

[35] U.S. Department of Justice—Federal Bureau of
Investigation, Crime in the United States, 2015,
accessed January, 2017 at https://ucr.fbi.gov/
crime-in-the-u.s/2015/crime-in-the-u.s.-2015/home

[36] United Nations Office on Drugs and Crime (UNODC),
"The Seventh United Nations Survey on Crime Trends
and the Operations of Criminal Justice Systems
(1998–2000)" at http://www.unodc.org/pdf/crime/
seventh_survey/7sc.pdf

[37] U.S. Department of Justice—Federal Bureau of
Investigation, Crime in the United States, 2015,
accessed January, 2017 at https://ucr.fbi.gov/
crime-in-the-u.s/2015/crime-in-the-u.s.-2015/home

[38] Caroline Wolf Harlow, "Firearm Use by Offenders,"
U.S. Department of Justice, Office of Justice Programs,
November 2001, revised 02/04/2002.

An Introduction to Criminology

Chapter Overview

In the simplest of terms, criminology is the study of crime and its causes. Criminologists are concerned with finding the root causes of crime and criminal behavior. It is important to determine why crime exists in a society, because we cannot really begin to prevent crime until we find out what causes it. Criminology is multi-disciplinary in that it utilizes ideas and concepts from a variety of disciplines, including: criminal justice, sociology, political science, biology, psychology, economics, and others.

Portrait of
Cesare Beccaria

© De Agostini Picture Library/
Contributor/Getty Images

Criminologists have been attempting to answer the basic question of why crime exists for over two centuries. In this chapter we will briefly examine several of the principal criminological theories that have been developed over this time period.

CHAPTER LEARNING OBJECTIVES

After reading the chapter you will be able to:

1. Explain the differences between criminology and criminal justice.
2. Understand what a criminological theory is.
3. List the major categories of criminological theories.

―――――――――――――――――― KEYWORDS ――――――――――――――――――

Criminology	Criminal Justice
Crime	Deviance
Theory	Classical School
General Deterrence	Cesare Beccaria
Specific Deterrence	Incarceration
Just Deserts	Biological Theories
Positivist School	Scientific method
Phrenology	Cesare Lombroso
Atavism	Supermales
Psychological Theories	Ivan Pavlov
Sigmund Freud	Social Structure Theories
Anomie	Social Process Theories
Edwin Sutherland	Differential Association
Conflict Theories	Karl Marx

CRIMINOLOGY

A discussion about criminology must begin with an understanding of certain basic terms:

Criminology: In the simplest of terms, criminology is the study of crime and its causes. Criminologists are concerned with finding the root causes of crime and criminal behavior. It is important to determine why crime exists in a society, because we cannot really begin to prevent crime until we find out what causes it. Criminology is multi-disciplinary in that it utilizes ideas and concepts from a variety of disciplines, including: criminal justice, sociology, political science, biology, psychology, economics, and others.

Criminal Justice: Criminal justice differs from criminology because it is a system. Criminal justice deals with the agencies that comprise the three broad segments within this system; police, corrections, and the courts.

Researchers who study criminal justice analyze and look at how these agencies operate.

Crime: A crime is a violation of a criminal law. In the United States, all criminal laws must be written. A person cannot commit a criminal act unless they violate one of these written laws.

Deviance: Deviance is an act that violates or departs from social norms. Not all deviant acts are criminal violations, but all criminal violations, by definition, are deviant acts. There are many things that people do that are considered to be deviant, but may not be criminal in nature. Cheating on an exam in college would be a deviant act; however, the person who did the cheating cannot be arrested because it does not violate a criminal law. There may well be other sanctions that can be taken against the cheater such as getting a failing grade or even expulsion, but they will not enter the criminal justice system for their deviant act.

Theory: A theory is the analysis of a set of facts in their relation to one another.[1] Criminologists look at the facts that deal with crime, crime rates, and criminal activity and attempt to develop theories that explain what causes each of these variables and how they relate to each other. In order for a theory to be of value, it must be validated. Validation is the testing of a theory in order to confirm or establish the soundness of it.

Criminologists study crime in order to find its root causes. They attempt to develop theories that help us understand why some people violate the social norms and commit criminal acts. The research that criminologists engage in depends, to a great extent, on reliable crime statistics. As we have seen earlier in this chapter the available statistics are not always reliable, making the job of criminologists a very challenging profession. If we were able to truly find out what causes people to commit crimes, we could apply remedies to control and actually prevent it.

© alekup, 2011. Used under license from Shutterstock, Inc.

*O*VERVIEW OF CRIMINOLOGICAL THEORIES

People and societies have been concerned about crime and its causes for many centuries. Throughout history many different reasons have been advanced in an attempt to explain crime and deviance. Demonic possession, superstition, and witchcraft were among the ways that people have used to explain the existence of criminal behavior within their various societies.

Modern criminological theories have only been around since the 1700s. This section provides a brief overview of several of the wide-ranging areas of criminological theories, and how they have emerged over the past 250 years. We will examine:

Classical and Neo-Classical Theories
Biological and Trait Theories
Psychological Theories
Social Theories
    Social Structure
    Social Process
Conflict Theories

CLASSICAL AND NEO-CLASSICAL THEORIES

Classical School of Criminology

Founded by Cesare Beccaria, the Classical School of Criminology is based on the notion that all decisions, including those that involve criminal activity, are the result of free will.

Cesare Beccaria

Cesare Beccaria (1738–1794) was an Italian economist and jurist. Beccaria wrote an essay "On Crimes and Punishment" that became the foundation of the classical school of criminology.

The **classical school of criminology** was founded by **Cesare Beccaria** (1738–1794). Beccaria's most noted work was an essay that he published anonymously in 1764 entitled "On Crimes and Punishments." This work has become the foundation which many subsequent criminological theories have used to build and expand upon.[2] Beccaria's theory has three main components. The first states that all individuals have free will and make all of their choices in life based upon this free will. The second is that all individuals look out for their own personal satisfaction. The third states that all humans share a motive of rational self-interest that makes human behavior predictable, and therefore controllable. Beccaria felt that with the proper punishment, the criminal justice system can control the free-willed individual, and consequently control crime and criminal behavior.[3]

Portrait of
Cesare Beccaria

© De Agostini Picture Library/
Contributor/Getty Images

The basis of Beccaria's theory is the idea of free will. Individuals commit crimes because they have made a choice to do so. Since people have free will, they will commit a crime if the pleasure of doing so outweighs the cost. According to Beccaria, the way to prevent crime is to set the punishment for each crime just over the amount of pleasure the individuals receive from the criminal act. Punishments do not have to be too severe because "crimes are more effectively prevented by the certainty than the severity of punishment."[4] He also stated that there should be a set amount of incarceration for each crime. An individual should be punished for attempting to commit a crime and accomplices working together on a crime should be punished equally. The harsher the crime the harsher the punishment should be. He also believed that crimes against persons should result in corporal punishment and persons who committed crimes of theft should be given fines. Beccaria was a strong opponent to the death penalty, for he felt that a lengthy loss of liberty was harsher than a quick death. Beccaria felt that the death penalty, while cruel and excessive, was also an ineffective measure to reduce or punish crime.[5]

One of Cesare Beccaria's followers was an English philosopher named Jeremy Bentham (1738–1832). Bentham expanded on Beccaria's notion of free will and applied it to the concept developed by the Utilitarian's, which is the doctrine that advocates that value is measured in terms of usefulness. Bentham took this a step further and said that mathematics could be used to explain deviant behavior, and he attempted to "reduce our moral judgments to series of problems in moral arithmetic."[6] His mathematical theory became known as "hedonistic calculus" which says that the exercise of free will causes an individual to avoid committing a criminal act if the punishment for committing that crime outweighs the rewards or benefits that are derived from committing it.[7]

Jeremy Bentham
(1738–1832)

Beccaria, Bentham, and the other classical theorists had a tremendous influence on the establishment of the government of the United States. "In our Constitution and Bill of Rights, many of the rights that we, as U.S. citizens, accept as fundamental come from the works of classical criminology. Some of our rights include: rules against vagueness, right to public trial, right to be judged by peers, right to dismiss certain jurors, right against unusual punishments, right to speedy trial, right to examine witnesses, coerced or tortured confessions are considered invalid, right to be informed of accused acts, and the right to bear arms. Our Constitution was greatly influenced by Beccaria, and many of the rights that he advocated were made the foundation of the United States."[8]

The popularity of the classical theories has had resurgence over the past several decades and new theories are emerging that are based on the original classicalists like Beccaria and Bentham. These new theories are classified as neo-classical theories. The foremost of the neo-classical theories is the criminological theory of rational choice which was developed by Derek Cornish and Ronald Clarke, and expanded on by James Q. Wilson and others.[9] The criminological theory of rational choice takes many of the Classical ideas and makes them more relative to today's issues. Rational Choice theory believes in free will and expands it to say that individuals make a rational choice to commit crimes. People use the pleasure/pain concept of the classical theories to make rational choices and people will chose to do things that increase their pleasure. Because of this, the government has the right and duty to preserve the common good by utilizing swift, severe, and certain punishment that will give the government control over the peoples' choices and behavior.

Rational Choice theory also deals with the issues of general and specific deterrence, the use of incarceration and "just deserts."

General deterrence: The concept of general deterrence states that the general public will not commit crimes due to a fear of getting caught, prosecuted, and severely punished.

Specific deterrence: Specific deterrence is using punishments to prevent a known deviant (a specific person) from committing future crime; or that if a criminal receives enough punishment for committing an act, that criminal will not commit that act again.

Charles Darwin
(1809–1882)

© Nicku/Shutterstock.com

Biological Theories

The followers of these theories believe that some criminal behavior could be attributed to a lack of evolutionary development.

Charles Darwin

Charles Darwin (1809–1882) influenced many of the early biological theorists with his famous writing of the *Theory of Evolution.*

Positivist School

The positivist school of thought believed that crime could be eliminated through the systematic application of the scientific method.

Scientific method:

The scientific method uses observation, hypothesis, the testing of the hypothesis, analysis of the data (interpretation), and conclusion as the basis of validating any theory.

Phrenology

Phrenology is the studying of the skull to determine personality traits.

Incarceration: Incarceration is the use of prisons to punish the criminal. By taking a convicted criminal out of society, the criminal is prevented from committing any new harm to society.

"Just deserts": This simply means that if an individual commits a criminal act then they deserve to be punished for that act by the government.

In studying the recent theory of Rational Choice, one can see the large and lasting impact that Beccaria had on the field of criminology.[10]

BIOLOGICAL AND TRAIT THEORIES

Biological theories are based on the belief that criminals are a product of their genetic history. Many of the early biological theorists were influenced by **Charles Darwin** (1809–1882) and his famous *Theory of Evolution.* The early biological theories stated that some criminal behavior can be attributed to a lack of evolutionary development. Some individuals never advanced past the primitive stages of man's evolutionary progress and their criminal behavior, particularly violent behavior, is a reflection of this. In simple terms, the early biological theorists said that criminals were born, not made.

During the late nineteenth century the **positivist school** of criminology emerged. There were several factors that were responsible for the shift from classical to positivist criminology. The primary reason was that during this period of time there was a shift from faith-based beliefs to one of science, which was primarily influenced by the development of the **scientific method**.[11] This in turn inspired the development of empirical research which was now being used to predict whether or not an individual would engage in criminal behavior.[12] The goal of the positivists was the elimination of crime through the systematic application of the scientific method. Positivists believed that all true knowledge is acquired through direct observation and not what we believe, and therefore the scientific method is the only valid way to conduct any research.

Franz Joseph Gall (1758–1828) together with Johann Spurzheim (1776–1832), studied the shape of the skull and its relationship to criminal behavior. Gall suggested that different parts of the brain were responsible for different mental functions and therefore a person's character could be read by examining their skull. This studying of the skull to determine personality traits was called **phrenology**. Gall carried out numerous experiments, taking measurements of the skulls of many people and making note of their characteristics. He developed detailed topological maps of the brain in the belief that his work had practical applications that would allow for the analysis of a person's character (including a propensity for criminal activity) through external examination of the cranium (cranioscopy).[13]

Franz Joseph Gall
(1758–1828)

© Science and Society Picture Library/Contributor/Getty Images

Another follower of the positivist school was **Cesare Lombroso** (1835–1909). Lombroso gained much attention in the field of criminology during the end of the nineteenth century and has been referred to as "the father of modern criminology."[14] Lombroso was a physician who spent a great deal of time studying the cadavers of executed criminals. Lombroso used the scientific method in an attempt to determine whether law violators were physically different from law abiding people.[15] Lombroso developed the criminological theory of **atavism**. Atavism states that some people are born criminals because they are throwbacks to a more primitive stage of development. Lombroso's theory was greatly influenced by the work of Charles Darwin.

Lombroso concluded that there were many different types of criminals, each of which has its own distinct characteristics. His primary categories of criminals included the insane criminal, the criminaloid, and the born criminal.[16] The criminally insane individuals, according to Lombroso, were not born criminals. This category included those people afflicted with dementia, idiots, and imbeciles. The criminaloid was responsible for about a third of all criminals. Lombroso concluded that these people had many similar characteristics as the born criminal, but did not have the same skeletal similarities. This category of criminal was thought to commit their offenses later in life and committed crimes of a lower intensity.[17]

The born criminal was considered to be the most dangerous. "Born criminals form about one third of the mass of offenders, but, though inferior in numbers, they constitute the most important part of the whole criminal army, partly because they are constantly appearing before the public and also because the crimes committed by them are of a peculiarly monstrous character."[18]

Many of the biological theories have been dismissed over the years with advances in medical science and a much better understanding of how the brain functions. There are, however, some modern biological theories that have attempted to explain the criminality of some offenders. One of the theories was based on the chromosome research that emerged in the 1950s. Patricia Jacobs (born 1934), a noted British geneticist, was the first person to discover an abnormal chromosomal makeup that is found in some humans. This abnormality was an extra Y chromosome that is found in some males. The normal chromosome makeup of males is one X chromosome and one Y chromosome (females have two X chromosomes). Jacobs discovered that a small percentage of males have an extra male chromosome (XYY) and were labeled "**supermales**." She also found that there is a higher percentage of these "supermales" in prison than there are in the normal population. The extra chromosome was associated with aggression and violent behavior. There has been subsequent research that dismisses these claims.[19]

PSYCHOLOGICAL THEORIES

Psychological theories look at the individual as the focus of study. These theories attempt to dismiss the classical view of free will and rational choice by saying that not all behavior is rational and therefore there must be other reasons that explain deviant behavior. Two of the prominent psychological theories deal with behavioral conditioning and psychoanalytic theory.

Cesare Lombroso

Cesare Lombroso (1835–1909) is considered by many to be the "father of criminology and developed the theory of atavism.

Atavism

Atavism states that some people are born criminals because they are throwbacks to a more primitive stage of development.

Supermales

The British geneticist Patricia Jacobs discovered that a small percentage of males have an extra male chromosome (XYY) and were labeled "supermales."

Psychological Theories

Psychological theories look at the individual as the focus of study.

Ivan Petrovich Pavlov (1849–1936) was a Russian physiologist who experimented with behavioral modification that he called "classical conditioning." Pavlov conducted his experiments with dogs, in which he studied the salivating response they had to various stimuli. Pavlov discovered that a normal unconditioned stimulus (food) produces an instinctive unlearned behavior (salivation). The salivation was called an unconditioned response because it was not learned. By adding a neutral stimulus (in this case ringing a bell in conjunction with giving the dog food) he could eventually condition the dog to salivate by only ringing the bell and not giving food. Pavlov was able to condition the dog and change an unconditioned response into a conditioned response. Pavlov won a Nobel Prize in physiology and medicine in 1904 for his work in this area.[20]

Ivan Petrovich Pavlov
(1849–1936)

© Hulton Deutsch/Contributor/Getty Images

Behavioral psychologists have expanded the work of Pavlov and applied behavioral conditioning to criminal behavior. These modern theorists say that people commit crime because they model their behavior after others that they see have been rewarded for their deviant behavior. This behavioral conditioning could explain a relationship between violence in the media and criminal violence.[21]

Sigmund Freud (1856–1939) is probably the best known theorist in the area of psychology. Freud developed the psychoanalytic theory in which he tried to explain human behavior in terms of the unconscious. Freudian theory is actually very complex but his writings on the development of the personality are the most applicable to criminology. Freud stated that the human mind is comprised of three competing entities: the id, the ego, and the superego.

Sigmund Freud

© Radu Bercan/Shutterstock.com

According to Freud we are born with the id. The id allows us, as newborns, to get our basic needs. Freud says that the id is pleasure based and wants whatever feels good at the time. If a baby is hungry, the id wants food and will cry if it is not satisfied. The id cares only about itself; when the id wants something nothing else is important.[22]

When the child is about three years old, it starts to interact more with the world around it and starts to develop the second part of the personality, called the ego. The ego is reality based and understands that other people have needs and desires also. The ego's function is to meet the needs of the id, but also takes into consideration the reality of the situation.[23]

The next stage of personality development takes place at about age five. This is when the superego develops. The superego is our moral conscience, and it dictates our moral belief of right and wrong. According to Freud, a normal, mentally healthy person has a strong ego. The strong ego can satisfy the id, not upset the superego, while still taking into consideration the reality of the situation.[24]

Freud did not speak directly about the relationship between the personality and criminal behavior, but psychological criminologists have associated criminal behavior with a weak superego. These theorists say that if the superego is not strong enough to keep the id in check, the result could result in antisocial behavior.

SOCIAL THEORIES

The largest segment of modern criminological theories is in the area of sociology. Sociological theories can be divided into two broad categories: social structure and social process. **Social structure theories** are not concerned with the relationship of individuals, but rather with how individuals are influenced by the various social institutions that make up any organized society. Poverty, disorganized neighborhoods, school systems, and gangs are all legitimate areas of study by social structure criminologists.

Social process theories are concerned with the relationship that an individual has with family, peers, peer group associations, the education system, and interactions with authority figures. These theorists see a potential for criminal behavior when these relationships are improperly socialized.

Social Structure Theories: Social structure theories include social disorganization theory and the strain theory (as well as others). Social disorganization theory ties crime rates to the structure of individual neighborhoods. The more disorganized a neighborhood may be, the more likely that there will be high crime rates. Some of the indicators of a disorganized neighborhood are high unemployment, high dropout rates from school, low income levels, and large numbers of single-parent households. When these factors are present, residents become frustrated and experience conflict, which leads to increases in antisocial behavior.[25]

The contemporary theory that has emerged from social disorganization theories is that of social ecology. This more modern criminological view states that living in deteriorated, crime-ridden neighborhoods exerts a powerful influence over the behavior of the residents. This influence is strong enough to neutralize any positive effects that a supportive family and close social ties which the individual living in this environment might have.[26]

The original strain theories were developed from the works of Emile Durkheim (1858–1917) and Robert Merton (1910–2003). Both of these theorists looked at a person's reason for developing criminal behavior in terms of **anomie**. Anomie literally means "normlessness." Durkheim used anomie to refer to a situation in which cultural norms break down because of rapid change. Durkheim implied that strain can occur when people are not able to achieve the goals that they have learned to pursue. Strain can also occur during good times when people do not know how to limit their goals and be satisfied with their achievements.

Merton changed the concept of anomie slightly when he used it to show the disconnection between socially acceptable goals and means in American society. To put Merton's ideas in simple terms, the goals in America could be equated to attaining the American Dream. While it may be quickly becoming an antiquated concept, traditionally the American Dream consists of achieving enough wealth

Social Structure Theories
Social structure theories include social disorganization theory and the strain theory (as well as others). Social disorganization theory ties crime rates to the structure of individual neighborhoods.

Anomie
Emile Durkheim and Robert Merton looked at a person's reason for developing criminal behavior in terms of anomie. Anomie literally means "normlessness."

and stature to live a comfortable life (the two story suburban house with a white picket fence, a family with two and a half children, a dog, and a soccer van in the driveway). The means are the way we achieve the goals. Merton says that a person who believes in achieving these goals and works hard to achieve the means to get or maintain them, would be a conformist. Merton lists four additional categories of people and rates them as to their relationship between these goals and the means to achieve them. If a person rejects one or both of these values, criminal behavior can be the result.[27]

Conformist: Accepts both values and is a law abiding citizen.
Innovator: Accepts the goals but rejects the means, resulting in petty theft type offenses.
Ritualist: Rejects the goals but accepts the means, leading to a very uneventful, mundane life.
Retreatist: Rejects both the means and the goals, which can result in habitual drug use, homelessness, and commission of other "victimless" crimes.
Rebel: Rejects both values and substitutes their own, which can result in political type crimes.

Social Process Theories

The foremost social process theories fall under the broad heading of social learning. Social learning theorists say that crime and criminal behavior is a product of learning the norms and values of criminal behavior.

Edwin H. Sutherland

Edwin H. Sutherland (1883–1950) developed a social learning theory that he called differential association theory.

Differential Association

Differential association states that crime is learned in the same way that lawful activities are learned.

Social Process Theories: The foremost social process theories fall under the broad heading of social learning. Social learning theorists say that crime and criminal behavior is a product of learning the norms and values of criminal behavior. Social learning includes both the actual learning of criminal techniques (how to bypass an alarm system) as well as learning how to cope with the negative aspects of crime (dealing with the guilt and shame associated with crime).[28]

Edwin H. Sutherland (1883–1950) developed a social learning theory that he called **differential association** theory. Sutherland published this theory in 1939 in the third edition of his textbook, *Principles of Criminology*. Sutherland's theory of differential association states that crime is learned in the same way that lawful activities are learned. He sees criminality as a normal process that some individuals turn to, when their associations are primarily with other individuals who can teach them the ways of crime.

Sutherland originated eight basic principles of differential association[29]:

1. Criminal behavior is learned.
2. Learning is a by-product of interaction.
3. Learning occurs within intimate groups.
4. Criminal techniques are learned.
5. Perceptions of legal codes influence motivation and drives.
6. Differential associations may vary in frequency, duration, priority, and intensity.
7. The process of learning criminal behavior by association with criminal and anticriminal patterns involves all of the mechanisms involved in any other learning process.

8. Criminal behavior is an expression of general needs and values, but is not excused by those general needs and values because noncriminal behavior is also an expression of those same needs and values.

CONFLICT THEORIES

Conflict theories are based on the premise that the fundamental causes of crime are the social and economic forces operating within society. The criminal justice system and criminal law are thought to be operating on behalf of the rich and powerful, who develop policies aimed at controlling the poor. The criminal justice establishment goals are imposing standards of morality and good behavior created by the powerful on the whole of society. Emphasis is on separating the powerful from the have not's, who would steal from others. In the process the legal rights of the poor might be ignored. The middle class tend to side with the elites rather the poor, thinking they might themselves rise to the top by supporting the status quo.[30]

Karl Marx
(1818–1883)

These conflict (or critical) criminologists see crime as a political issue and it is different for every individual society. According to many of these theorists, each society gets the amount of crime it deserves, which is dependent on how that society deals with its own citizens. If a society wants to reduce or eliminate crime, it must remove the social conditions that promote crime, such as poverty and the political distinctions between socioeconomic classes. Many of the conflict theories are based on the writings of **Karl Marx** (1818–1883). While Marx never addressed crime in his writings, criminologists who have adopted his philosophies see behaviors' like stealing as an attempt to take away from the rich.

Conflict Theories

Conflict theories are based on the premise that the fundamental causes of crime are the social and economic forces operating within society.

Karl Marx

Many of the conflict theories are based on the writings of Karl Marx (1818–1883).

SUMMARY OF CRIMINOLOGY

We have examined several of the more prominent criminological theories in this section. It needs to be noted that there are many other theories that have emerged over the last 250 years. This overview should have given the reader a basic understanding of how criminologists have attempted to find the root causes of crime from many different perspectives. Criminologists have yet to find a single cause of crime, and will continue to analyze all of the countless variables that influence criminal behavior.

REVIEW QUESTIONS:

1. _____ is the study of crime and its causes.

2. An act that violates or departs from the social norms is called _____.

3. The classical school of criminology was founded by _____ _____.

4. _____ _____ influenced many of the early biological theorists with his famous writing of the *Theory of Evolution.*

5. _____ _____ means that if an individual commits a criminal act, then they deserve to be punished for that act.

6. _____ is the studying of the skull to determine personality.

7. The "Father of Criminology" is _____ _____.

8. Sigmund Freud determined that the human personality is made up of three parts: the _____,

   the _____, and the _____.

9. _____ _____ theories include social disorganization theory and the strain theory (as well as others).

10. _____ literally means "normlessness."

CRITICAL THINKING QUESTIONS:

1. The text gave an example of a deviant act that is not criminal in nature. What other types of deviant acts can you think of that do not violate criminal laws?

2. Using the classical view and the American criminal justice system, explain why we still have such a high crime rate (hint: consider the concept of swift and certain punishment).

3. Which of the criminological theories presented in the text do think is the most valid, and why.

─────────────── NOTES ───────────────

CHAPTER 4

[1] *Merriam-Webster Dictionary,* accessed March, 2011 at http://mirriam-webster.com/dictionary/theory.

[2] Biography of Cesare Beccaria, accessed March, 2011 at http://www.constitution.org/cb/beccaria_bio.htm.

[3] Ibid.

[4] Cesare Beccaria, "On Crimes and Punishments"; Trans. Henry Paolucci (Englewood Cliffs, New Jersey: Englewood Hall, 1963).

[5] Biography of Cesare Beccaria, accessed March, 2011 at http://www.constitution.org/cb/beccaria_bio.htm.

[6] E. Albee, *A History of English Utilitarianism* (New York: The MacMillan Company, 1901).

[7] Kim Swanson, Florida State University, "Jeremy Bentham," accessed March, 2011 at www.criminology.fsu.edu/crimtheory/bentham.htm.

[8] Biography of Cesare Beccaria, accessed March, 2011 at http://www.constitution.org/cb/beccaria_bio.htm.

[9] Kim Swanson, Florida State University, "Jeremy Bentham" at www.criminology.fsu.edu/crimtheory/bentham.htm.

[10] "Biography of Cesare Beccaria," accessed March, 2011 at http://www.constitution.org/cb/beccaria_bio.htm.

[11] D. A. Jones, *History of Criminology: A Philosophical Perspective* (New York: Greenwood Press, 1986).

[12] Mehala Arjunan, "Cesare Lombroso" (2000), accessed March, 2011 at http://www.criminology.fsu.edu/crim-theory/lombroso.htm.

[13] Paula Hellal, "Franz Joseph Gall and Victorian Phrenology—Measuring Personality in the 19th Century" (2009), accessed on February, 2011 at http://www.suite101.com/content/franz-joseph-gall-and-victorian-phrenology-a121971.

[14] H. Mannheim, *Pioneers in Criminology,* 2nd ed., (Montclair, NJ: Patterson Smith, 1972).

[15] Larry J. Siegal, Judy H. Schmidt, and Michael K. Hooper, *Criminology: with Effective Writing* (Mason, Ohio: Centage Learning, 2008).

[16] Lombroso also found two other types of criminals that he identified as the habitual criminal and the political criminal.

[17] Mehala Arjunan, "Cesare Lombroso" (2000), accessed March, 2011 at http://www.criminology.fsu.edu/crimtheory/lombroso.htm.

[18] G. Lombroso-Ferrero, *Criminal Man: According to the Classification of Cesare Lombroso* (Montclair, NJ: Patterson Smith, 1972).

[19] Frank Schmalleger, *Criminal Justice Today,* 10th Edition (Columbus, Ohio: Pearson, Prentice Hall, 2009).

[20] Santrock, "Theories of Learning in Educational Psychology—Pavlov and Classical Conditioning" (1998), accessed December, 2010 at www.lifecircles-inc.com/Learningtheories/behaviorism/Pavlov.html.

[21] Larry J. Siegal, Judy H. Schmidt, and Michael K. Hooper, *Criminology: with Effective Writing* (Mason, Ohio: Centage Learning, 2008).

[22] Christopher L. Heffner, *Psychology 101* (2001); published online, accessed December, 2010 at http://allpsych.com/psychology101/ego.html.

[23] Ibid.

[24] Ibid.

[25] Larry J. Siegal, Judy H. Schmidt, and Michael K. Hooper, *Criminology: with Effective Writing* (Mason, Ohio: Centage Learning, 2008).

[26] Ibid.

[27] Robert Merton, "Anomie Theory" as published online, accessed December, 2010 at www.d.umn.edu/~bmork/2306/Theories/BAManomie.htm.

[28] Larry J. Siegal, Judy H. Schmidt, and Michael K. Hooper, *Criminology: with Effective Writing* (Mason, Ohio: Centage Learning, 2008).

[29] Edwin Sutherland and Donald Cressey, *Criminology,* 8th Edition (Philadelphia, PA: Lippencott, 1970).

[30] "Conflict Theory" (2005); published online, last modified November 22, 2005, accessed December, 2010 at http://www.criminology.fsu.edu/crimtheory/conflict.htm.

CHAPTER OVERVIEW

Laws are the bond that holds a civilized society together. This chapter will examine the various types of laws that we have in the United States with a primary focus on criminal laws. We will look at the three primary components of most criminal laws, which are *actus reus, mens rea,* and concurrence, and also discuss those laws that do not require that all of these components be present. An explanation of the elements of criminal laws will be presented and how each of them must be proven in court in order to obtain a criminal conviction. This chapter will also define the three categories of crimes that are used in the United States.

There are times when a person may commit a criminal act and have a legal reason for doing so. There are a variety of legal defenses that may explain and excuse criminal behavior. This chapter will examine justification defenses and legal excuses, as well as alibis and entrapment. Justification defenses include the concepts of self-defense and necessity. We will also discuss the different defenses that are categorized within the classification of legal excuses.

CHAPTER LEARNING OBJECTIVES

After reading this chapter you will be able to:

1. Identify the different types of laws in the United States.
2. Describe the three components that must be present to have a crime.
3. Understand what strict liability crimes are.
4. Identify the elements of any criminal law.
5. Distinguish between the different levels of crimes.
6. List the various justification defenses and legal excuses.
7. Explain the differences between the insanity standards that are used in the United States.

―――――――――――――――― KEYWORDS ――――――――――――――――

Statutory law
Precedent
Administrative Law
Tort
Compensatory Damages
Criminal Law
Mala prohibita
Mens rea
Strict Liability Crimes
Elements of a Crime
Misdemeanor
Justification Defenses
Deadly Force
Legal Excuses
Infancy
Mistake of Fact
Insanity Plea
Alibi

Case laws
Stare decisis
Civil Law
Breach of Contract
Punitive damages
Mala in se
Actus reus
Concurrence
Corpus delicti
Felony
Offenses and Infractions
Self-Defense Laws
Necessity
Duress
Mistake of Law
Involuntary Intoxication
Entrapment

WHAT IS LAW?

Laws represent the rules of expected conduct among members of a society. Laws are also designed to maintain an orderly society. Laws in the United States are enacted by the legislative branches of government. Federal laws are passed by the

U.S. Congress and affect everyone in the country. State laws are enacted by the individual state legislatures and define the legal conduct within that state. Other laws are written and passed on local levels including counties and municipalities.

All law is man-made, and as such can be modified or repealed as needed. What would happen if all the laws in the United States were suddenly repealed? People could do whatever they wanted without any consequences and the results would be chaotic. Imagine driving your car when the other drivers do not have to obey any traffic laws. Stoplights, speed limits, lane markers and dividers, and all other traffic laws that we take for granted would cease to exist. People would be taking their life in their own hands just taking their car out of the driveway. Taking this hypothetical scenario one step further, imagine what it would be like with no police and no criminal laws? It would be safe to assume that no one would want to live in such a society. Many times we take our laws for granted, in an orderly society such as ours it is easy to do. We expect everyone to obey the laws and we go about our daily lives without giving much conscious thought to the issue. When we are driving our car we expect other drivers to conform to the traffic laws. It is hard to imagine what would happen if no one had to obey these laws, it would be an alternative that would be totally unacceptable.

TYPES OF LAWS

There are many different types of laws that are in place in the United States. These laws regulate everything from murder (criminal law) to the requirement that construction workers wear hard hats on the job (administrative law). This section will look at some of the categories of laws that in one way or another affect everyone in the country.

STATUTORY LAW

Statutory laws are those laws that are enacted by the legislative branch of government (at all levels) and then codified into written statutes. The codification is the accumulation of all statutory laws that are then consolidated and classified according to subject matter. The federal government has codified all of the federal statutes in *the Revised Statutes of the United States* and *A Code of Laws of the United States*. States have also codified their statutes into published codes (e.g., the State of Nevada has codified all of its statutory laws into the *Nevada Revised Statutes*).

Statutory Law
These are the laws that are passed and enacted by the legislative branch of government (at all levels) and then codified into written statutes.

CASE LAW

Case law is the law that is generated by the decisions rendered by the courts. When an appellate court (see Chapter 8) resolves a case, the decision of the judge

Case Law
Law that is generated by the courts.

Precedent

Prior case law that is used as the basis of new court decisions.

Stare decisis

The practice of following precedent when deciding new cases.

or judges who made it is written, and that decision serves as case law. This case law is now referred to as **precedent**. Precedent serves as the basis of authority for other courts to use when deciding similar cases in the future. The practice of following precedent when deciding new cases is referred to as the doctrine of *stare decisis*, which means "let the decision stand." This doctrine holds that judges should look at cases that have been decided in the past for guidance and to answer questions of law that are consistent with precedent. Following precedent gives consistency and predictability to the law.[1]

© Lane V. Erickson, 2011. Used under license from Shutterstock, Inc.

Administrative Law

Laws related to the various regulatory agencies of the United States and the various states.

ADMINISTRATIVE LAW

Administrative law is comprised of the laws related to the various regulatory agencies of the United States and of the various states. Every agency has laws written that enable them to enforce the regulations that they are empowered to enforce. There are hundreds of federal regulatory agencies that regulate a wide variety of activities. Some examples of these agencies and what they regulate are[2]:

1. **Consumer Product Safety Commission (CPSC)** regulates such things as home appliances and children's toys.
2. **National Highway Traffic Safety Administration (NHTSA)** regulates automotive equipment and child safety seats.
3. **Environmental Protection Agency (EPA)** is charged with enforcement of pesticide products and automobile emission control equipment.
4. **Food and Drug Administration (FDA)** regulates a wide range of products including pet foods, cosmetics, drugs (both prescription and non-prescription), food (except meat and poultry), and medical devices.
5. **United States Department of Agriculture (USDA)** is concerned with regulating and establishing standards when it comes to products like meat, poultry, and eggs.

The violation of administrative laws is generally not a criminal matter; rather it is a civil issue (see the following section). There are times, however, when a person could face criminal charges for violation of an administrative law. An example of this would be the violation of certain administrative laws of the Internal Revenue Service (IRS) (e.g., the intentional failure to file income tax).

CIVIL LAW

Civil Laws

Regulate the relationship between people and/or other parties.

Civil laws regulate (or govern) the relationships between people and/or other parties (companies, corporations, and other businesses). These are the laws that regulate the administrative laws and regulations of the various federal and state agencies, as well as other civil concerns like divorce, custody, child support, inheritance issues (wills and estates), and a host of other issues. Violations of civil laws do not result in criminal actions; rather they usually wind up in civil court in the form of a civil lawsuit. When one party sues another, they are seeking monetary or property compensation or some kind of injunctive relief.

The two primary types of civil lawsuits stem from either a **tort** action or a **breach of contract**. A tort is a civil wrong. It is a breach of a duty to an individual that results in damage to the harmed party. If a person is involved in a traffic accident because another driver failed to yield the right-of-way and damaged their car, the person who was hit may have a cause of action and could sue the negligent driver. This would be a tort action. Let's say that a person signs a contract and pays a roofing company to fix their roof and the roof does not get fixed. The homeowner would that have a cause of action to sue the roofing company under a breach of contract.

There are two main categories of civil compensation, **compensatory damages** and **punitive damages**. Damages are the payment that the courts may award for injury done. Compensatory damages are the recovery of the actual loss for injury sustained. Punitive damages are those that are awarded to punish the party who is at fault. This is the type of damages that make the headlines when the courts will occasionally award millions of dollars for seemingly frivolous reasons.

CRIMINAL LAW

Criminal law is the branch of law that deals with crimes and their punishments. A crime is an act that is considered to be an offense against public authority (the government) or a violation of a public duty. Crimes are usually classified as *mala in se* or *mala prohibita*.[3] ***Mala in se*** crimes are those that are immoral or wrong on their face. Murder, rape, and robbery would all be examples of these types of laws. ***Mala prohibita*** crimes are only illegal because the government says they are. Some states restrict the selling of alcohol on Sunday, yet allow the sale the other six days of the week. This would be an example of a *mala prohibita* law. The only reason that you cannot buy that beer on Sunday is because the government says you can't. Many people have argued that laws that prohibit the personal use of marijuana are *mala prohibita*.

Most criminal statutes require that three components be present in order to have a crime: *actus reus, mens rea,* and concurrence.

ACTUS REUS

In order to have a crime, there must first be an overt or intentional act (or omission) that violates a criminal statute. This intentional act is called ***actus reus***, which means "the guilty act." An omission would be when a person does *not* do something that they are required to do. Failing to stop at a stop sign would be an omission since the law requires that driver to stop.

Tort
A civil wrong.

Breach of Contract
Failing to fulfill a contractual obligation that can result in a civil lawsuit.

Compensatory Damages
Recovery of actual out-of-pocket expenses for injury sustained by another party.

Punitive Damages
Money awarded in a civil court intended to punish the party who is at fault and caused the injury.

Criminal Law
The branch of law that deals with crimes and their punishments.

Mala in se
Crimes that are immoral or wrong on their face.

Mala prohibita
Crimes that are only illegal because the government says they are.

Actus reus
The guilty act.

© Dmitriy Shironosov, 2011. Used under license from Shutterstock, Inc.

Mens rea
The guilty mind.

MENS REA

The second feature that must be present in order to have a criminal act is the **mens rea** or "the guilty mind." This describes the state of mind that accompanies the particular act defined as criminal. This is referred to as the intent to commit the criminal act. Having a "guilty mind" is not enough to constitute a crime. People can think bad thoughts, but unless they actually act on them, there is no crime. We do not have 'thought police,' at least not yet. The *mens rea* for each type of crime will be different. For example, in order to have the crime of receiving stolen goods, there must be knowledge that the goods were stolen. In the case of theft, there must be the intention to steal.[4]

CONCURRENCE

Concurrence
The joining of the guilty act *(actus reus)* and the requisite mental state *(mens rea).*

When the guilty act *(actus reus)* and the requisite mental state *(mens rea)* work in conjunction with each other, they are in **concurrence**, and hence a crime. John Doe has decided that he is going to kill his neighbor Bill because he plays his music too loud. John goes to a gun store and buys a handgun. John waits the required three days and returns to the store and picks up the gun. John then goes to Bill's house and hides in the bushes waiting for him to come home. If John shoots and kills Bill when he arrives, John could be charged with murder because the three features required to have that crime have been met. The guilty act was the shooting and killing of Bill. The guilty mind was purchasing the murder weapon and lying in wait for his victim (malice aforethought).

© Lightspring, 2011. Used under license from Shutterstock, Inc.

If John had purchased the gun with the intent to kill Bill but changed his mind prior to completing the act, there would be no concurrence, and therefore there would be no crime. John's original intentions may have been to murder Bill, but since he did not take any substantial step toward committing the unlawful act of shooting or killing Bill, there is no crime.

*S*TRICT LIABILITY CRIMES

Strict Liability Crimes
These are crimes that do not require concurrence between *actus reus* and the *mens rea.*

Strict liability crimes are the exception to the rule that says there must be concurrence between the *actus reus* and the *mens rea.* This category of crimes does not require that there be criminal intent, they only require the criminal act. Most traffic laws, certain drug laws, and statutory rape are all examples of crimes that a person could be charged with and ultimately found guilty of, even if they did not intend to commit the act itself.

When a police officer stops a driver for running a red light, the officer (and the law itself) does not really care why the driver ran the light. The criminal act itself (the violation of the traffic law) is all that is required. The driver may have been distracted and failed to see the light and had no intention of running it, or the driver may have seen the red light and made a conscious and deliberate effort to go through it. In either case, the driver went through the red light and that is all that is required to find the driver guilty.

In some jurisdictions, certain drug laws meet the criteria of being strict liability crimes. Simple possession of a controlled substance (illegal drug) does not require the element of *mens rea*. The prosecution does not have to prove that a person intended to put methamphetamine in their pocket; they only have to prove that it was in fact methamphetamine and that the person did possess it. The element of intent is not required.

Another example of a strict liability crime is that of statutory rape. Statutory rape is the engaging in consensual sexual relations of a person over the age of consent with a person under the legal age of consent.[5] It does not matter if the offender was aware that their victim was under the legal age for sex or not, merely committing the act is sufficient for prosecution.

CORPUS DELICTI

Corpus delicti is a Latin term that means "the body of the crime." It is the facts that prove that a crime has actually taken place. In a murder case, it must be shown that a person was actually killed and that the killing was done by another human. A suicide or accidental death would not satisfy the proof of *corpus delicti*.[6] It is important for the reader to understand the difference between *corpus delicti* and the elements of an individual crime. *Corpus delicti* is the proof necessary to show that a crime has actually taken place, while the elements of each individual crime is what the prosecution must prove in court in order to obtain a conviction (see the following section).

Corpus delicti
The facts that prove that a crime has actually taken place—"the body of the crime."

ELEMENTS OF A CRIME

Every crime consists of specific elements that make up that crime. The elements are the specific conditions that must be met in order to have a criminal act *(actus reus)*. In order to convict an offender of a crime, the prosecution must be able to prove each and every element of that crime beyond a reasonable doubt (see chapter 9).

The following is a typical burglary statute that will be used to illustrate the elements of a crime:

© Gina Sanders, 2011. Used under license from Shutterstock, Inc.

BURGLARY[7]

> A person who, by day or night, enters any house, room, apartment, tenement, shop, warehouse, store, mill, barn, stable, outhouse or other building, tent, vessel, vehicle, vehicle trailer, semitrailer or house trailer, airplane, glider, boat or railroad car, with the intent to commit grand or petit larceny, assault or battery on any person or any felony, or to obtain money or property by false pretenses, is guilty of burglary.

The elements of this crime of burglary would be:

1. A person
2. By day or night
3. Enters any defined dwelling
4. With the ***INTENT*** to commit:
    1. Grand or petit larceny
    2. Assault or battery on any person
    3. Or to commit any felony
    4. Or to obtain money or property under false pretenses

The first three elements of this crime would be relatively easy to establish. The prosecution would only have to prove that a person, at any time of day, entered any of the defined list of dwellings. The fourth element could be more difficult to prove. This element specifically requires that the prosecution prove the 'intent' to commit one of the listed criminal acts. In order to illustrate the concept of proving the elements of this crime, let us look at some scenarios:

SCENARIO #1

A family comes home at night and sees a person inside their home walking around with a flashlight. They call the police and stay outside of the house. A police officer arrives at the home just when the suspect is walking out of the front door carrying a television. The officer arrests the suspect and interviews the family who tell him that they do not know the suspect and that he did not have permission to enter the house or to take away their television. The suspect is charged with burglary.

In this case, the prosecution could prove each of the elements of the crime of burglary. The suspect was a person who entered a home (one of the listed dwellings) during the night (any time by day or night). The prosecution could also show that the suspect entered with the intent to commit larceny because he was in the process of removing the property of the family with the intent to permanently deprive the owner of the property.

SCENARIO #2

A family comes home at night and when they enter their house, they see a man asleep on their sofa in the living room. Without waking the suspect, the family leaves the house and calls the police. A police officer arrives, and after being briefed by the family, enters the house and finds the suspect still sleeping on the sofa. The officer awakens the suspect and takes him into custody. The family members tell the officer that they do not know the suspect and that they had left their front door unlocked. Further investigation reveals that nothing was taken from the home. Given this information, the officer could not arrest the suspect for the crime of burglary because he would not be able to show the suspect's intent to commit any of the crimes identified in the last element. The suspect could be charged with another crime, such as trespassing, but could not be charged with burglary.

CATEGORIES OF CRIMES

Crimes are categorized by the punishments that are associated with them. The federal government and the governments of the various states and local jurisdictions each have their own definition of what a crime is. There are several different levels of crimes: felonies, misdemeanors, and offenses or infractions.

FELONIES

Felonies are the most serious crimes, and include most of the Uniform Crime Reporting Program Part I crimes as well as many others. Murder, rape, aggravated assault, robbery, burglary, and auto theft are all examples of felony crimes.

Felony
A criminal offense that is punishable by death or incarceration in a prison facility for at least one year.

MISDEMEANORS

Misdemeanors are lessor crimes than felonies, and therefore provide for lessor sentences. Misdemeanors include such crimes as: simple assault, simple battery, prostitution, petit larceny (theft of property that is worth under a specified amount of money—usually between $250 and $1,000), and trespassing.

Misdemeanor
An offense that is punishable by incarceration, usually in a jail facility, for a period of time less than one year.

OFFENSES AND INFRACTIONS

Offenses and Infractions

An offense for which the penalty is usually a fine or some other form of non-incarceration punishment; however, limited jail time is an option in most jurisdictions.[8]

Offenses or infractions are minor violations of the law that are categorized as even less than misdemeanors. Many of these types of offenses are written by local jurisdictions (counties and municipalities) and may be referred to by a variety of terms, including city or county ordinances, infractions, or simple offenses. Some states also refer to many of their traffic laws as infractions as well.

*L*EGAL DEFENSES

The law provides for persons charged with criminal offenses to present a defense to the charges against them. There are times when a defendant, who appears to have met all of the requisite elements of a crime, may be able to provide a lawful reason why the criminal act was committed. Legal defenses can be divided into two broad categories: justification defenses and legal excuses. Alibis and entrapment will be looked at as separate categories.

JUSTIFICATION DEFENSES

Justification Defenses

This is a legal defense that states even though the accused person admits to committing a crime, they had a legal justification for doing so and should not be found guilty of the crime. Legal justifications include self-defense and necessity.

In order for a person to use one of the **justification defenses**, they must first admit that they did in fact commit the acts required (the elements) for the crime they are charged with. While the person admits to committing the crime, they proclaim that they had a legal justification for doing so. If they can prove the justification, then they should not be charged with the crime, or should be found not guilty of the crime if they are charged and brought to trial. Justification defenses include self-defense and necessity.

SELF-DEFENSE

Self-Defense Laws

Laws that give a person the right to defend themselves if they are attacked without provocation.

Self-defense laws state that a person has the right to defend themselves if they are attacked without provocation. This right extends to the protection of others, to property, and to the home. Like all 'rights' this one does not come without certain limitations. Any force that is used to protect oneself or property must be reasonable. Reasonable force is that amount of force necessary to overcome the aggression or to protect the property. The force that is used must end when there is no longer a threat of harm. It is important to point out that the courts have generally ruled that if a person can avoid the use of force by safely retreating, the person must take that avenue of escape.

Deadly Force

Any force that could reasonably be expected to cause death.

    Deadly force is any force that could reasonably be expected to produce death. The use of deadly force is restricted to situations where a person has a reasonable belief that imminent death or substantial bodily harm would result if they did not act. If a person is struck in the face with a fist during a fight, he would not be justified in pulling a firearm and shooting the assailant. The normal result of a fistfight is not death or substantial bodily harm. If an assailant is about to attack a person with a knife, deadly force would probably be justified.

© guruXOX/Shuttertock.com

Deadly force is *never* justified to protect personal property (home defense is discussed separately). If someone is stealing your car out of your driveway, you would not be justified in shooting the suspect. It is also not authorized to set "booby traps" on unattended property that could result in serious bodily harm or death. You could not, for instance, set a shotgun to go off if someone breaks into your garage when you are not home.

The protection of your home is generally an exception that allows for the use of deadly force under certain circumstances. It is also an exception to the rule that states you are required to retreat if you can before using force. There is a legal presumption, in most jurisdictions, that if a person invades your home while it is occupied, they are there to commit bodily harm. Your home, whether it is a house, an apartment, a trailer, or a tent, is your ultimate safe haven or 'castle.' You may protect your 'castle' and anyone who is in it, with the use of deadly force in most situations. The home must be occupied at the time of the invasion in order to justify self-defense. If you come home at night and see through a window that someone is in your house, you would not be justified in entering the house and using deadly force against the intruder. In this case there would not be fear of imminent death or great bodily harm. The use of deadly force in this situation would be to protect property, not people, and would not be authorized in most jurisdictions.

NECESSITY

The **necessity** defense is one that recognizes the fact that there are times when a crime needs to be committed in order to prevent some greater evil from occurring. According to the Model Penal Code, the necessity defense would be permissible if "the harm or evil sought to be avoided by such conduct is greater than that sought to be prevented by the law defining the offense charged."[9]

Necessity
A legal justification for when a person commits a crime for the sole reason of preventing a more serious crime.

You are walking down a street when you observe a van pull up next to a woman who is standing on a street corner. Two men get out of the van and grab the woman and drag her into the vehicle. The woman is fighting and screaming for help while the men are forcing her into the van. There is no one else around, but you are standing next to a car that you see has the keys in the ignition. You break into the car and follow the van while calling 9–1–1 and giving the police the location of the van as it speeds down the streets. The police arrive and pull over the van and ask you to stay and give a statement. While you are with the police, the owner of the car that you took arrives on the scene and has the police arrest you for auto theft. In this case, you could raise the defense of necessity. You could argue that you had to break into the car and take it in order to prevent harm to the victim of the abduction. You could show that while you did take the property of another, the circumstances of this situation made your actions justifiable.

LEGAL EXCUSES

Legal Excuses

A legal excuse is applied when a defendant can show that they should not be held criminally liable for a crime because there was no *mens rea* present.

Just like justification defenses, in order for a person to use one of the **legal excuses**, they must first admit that they did in fact commit the acts required (the elements) for the crime they are charged with. A legal excuse is applied when the defendant can show that they should not be held criminally liable for the offense because there was no *mens rea* (criminal intent) present. Legal excuses include duress, infancy, mistake, involuntary intoxication, and insanity.

DURESS

Duress

Making a person do something they do not want to do by the use of force or the threat of force.

Duress is making someone do something they do not want to do by the use of force or the threat of force. Because a person is forced to commit an act, the requisite *mens rea* would not exist. The law generally requires that four conditions be met in order for a person to assert that the legal excuse of duress:

© Edw, 2011. Used under license from Shutterstock, Inc.

1. The threat must be of serious bodily harm.[10]

If a suspect holds your family hostage and tells you that you must commit a criminal act or he will kill your family, then this condition would probably be met.

2. The harm threatened must be greater than the harm caused by the crime.[11]

If the same suspect holds your family hostage and tells you to rob a bank or he will spank your children, then this condition would probably not be met.

3. The threat must be immediate and inescapable.[12]

This condition would probably not be met if the suspect called you on the phone and told you that he was coming over to your house to take your family hostage tomorrow. You would have sufficient time to take your family, escape, and call the police.

4. The defendant must have become involved in the situation through no fault of his or her own.[13]

You and two of your buddies conspire to rob a bank. The three of you have stolen a getaway car and purchased a gun in order to commit the robbery. You decide at the last minute that you are not going to be a part of the crime. Your two friends come to your house and hold your family hostage and threaten to kill them if you do not go and commit the robbery. In this case, you were originally a part of this crime, so duress would not be a valid excuse.

INFANCY

Under a certain age a child cannot be charged with a criminal act (**infancy**). Traditionally, this age was younger than seven years old. Today, each individual state determines what age is appropriate. The reasoning is based on the idea that below a certain age a child cannot form the requisite intent necessary to commit a criminal act. A very young child does not fully realize the consequences of their actions.

Infancy
A person under a certain age (determined by law) cannot be charged with a criminal offense.

© Dmitriy Shironosov, 2011. Used under license from Shutterstock, Inc.

The defense of infancy should not be confused with the fact that we currently have a juvenile justice system that deals with juveniles under the age of eighteen (or other age as specified by individual state law). Juveniles, in some instances, can even be certified as adults and tried and punished as an adult.

MISTAKE

Mistake can be divided into the categories of mistake of law and mistake of fact. **Mistake of law** is a rarely used excuse. The old axiom "ignorance of the law is no excuse" still holds true in most instances. It is the responsibility of all citizens to "know" what the laws of the land are. With that said, there are times when a law is not properly published, or is so vague or unclear that a person cannot be expected to know it. In these rare cases mistake of law may be a valid excuse.

Mistake of Law
This is a legal excuse for committing an act that would constitute a crime when the law is vague or was not properly published.

© Dano Diament, 2011. Used under license from Shutterstock, Inc.

Mistake of Fact

This a legal excuse for committing an act that would constitute a crime but the person did so without the requisite *mens rea*.

Involuntary Intoxication

A person would have a possible legal excuse if they ingest an intoxicating substance without their knowledge and as a consequence of the intoxication commits an act that would constitute a crime.

Insanity Plea

A legal excuse that says a person is not responsible for their illegal actions because of a mental disease or defect.

Mistake of fact is a much more frequently used excuse. You just got off an airplane and are waiting at baggage claim for your suitcase. The carousel starts and there is a suitcase that looks exactly like yours. You pick it up and leave the airport. When you get home you open it and discover that the bag is not yours. If you immediately return the bag to the airport, you could claim that you picked up the wrong suitcase by mistake. You did not have the *mens rea* to commit the crime of theft. If you decided to keep the bag after discovering the mistake, you could then be charged with theft.

INVOLUNTARY INTOXICATION

Voluntary intoxication is rarely or ever allowed to excuse criminal behavior. When a person voluntarily ingests alcohol or drugs; they are responsible for their actions even if they cannot remember what they have done. Involuntary intoxication is a different situation. If someone puts a drug in another person's drink (or by any another method) without the person's knowledge, the victim could claim **involuntary intoxication** if they committed a criminal act they would not normally have done if they were not intoxicated.

INSANITY

If you watch certain television shows or go to the movies, you would think that the insanity plea in criminal cases is one of the most used defenses in our criminal justice system. The reality is, this plea is rarely used and even more rarely is it used successfully. Studies have shown that the insanity plea is used in less than 1 percent of criminal cases, and when it is used it is only successful about 25 percent of the time.[14]

When a defendant enters an **insanity plea**, they are saying that they did commit the criminal act, but cannot be held responsible because of their insanity.[15] They committed

© Danush M, 2011. Used under license from Shutterstock, Inc.

the crime, but because of severe mental disease or defect, they were unable to appreciate the wrongfulness of his or her acts.[16]

M'NAGHTEN RULE

The first successful insanity plea was entered in England in 1843. Sir Robert Peel[17] was the Prime Minister of England when Daniel M'Naghten laid in wait to assassinate him. M'Naghten mistakenly killed Sir Robert Peel's secretary instead. M'Naghten was brought to trial and admitted that he had committed the murder, but claimed that at the time of the offense he had not been of sound state of mind.

The court agreed with him and he was found not guilty by reason of insanity. The result of this criminal case was what we now refer to as the M'Naghten rule, which is the right-from-wrong test of criminal responsibility. "If the accused was possessed of sufficient understanding when he committed the criminal act to know what he was doing and to know that it was wrong, he is responsible therefore, but if he did not know the nature and quality of the act or did know what he was doing but did not know what he was doing was wrong, he is not responsible."[18] The M'Naghten rule is currently the standard for criminal insanity in twenty-two states.

Other states use different standards for determining if a defendant can be held legally not responsible for their criminal actions.

IRRESISTIBLE-IMPULSE TEST

The irresistible-impulse test is based upon the premise that the person's actions were based upon a mental condition that did not allow them to control an urge to do certain acts. The resulting mental condition did not give the person the willpower or reasoning to control their actions.

DURHAM RULE

The Durham rule is less restrictive than the M'Naghten rule and was originally adopted by several states. This rule came out of a 1954 District of Columbia Federal Court of Appeals case that stated "an accused is not responsible if his unlawful act was the product of mental disease or mental defect."[19] Because of the wording of the court decision, this rule is sometimes referred to as the "products test." The Durham rule was very vague in its definition of "mental disease or mental defect" and is not very popular today.

SUBSTANTIAL-CAPACITY TEST

The substantial-capacity test is a combination of the M'Naghten rule and the irresistible-impulse test. This test was developed by the Model Penal Code and states that a person is not responsible for criminal behavior if the commission of the act was "as a result of mental disease or defect he lacks substantial capacity either to appreciate the wrongfulness of his conduct or to conform his conduct to the requirements of the law."[20] This test of criminal insanity is the standard today in many states.

ENTRAPMENT

Entrapment is inducing a person to commit a crime that he or she would not have committed without such inducement. The inducement is usually made by an undercover officer and is done for the sole purpose of prosecuting the offender. The Supreme Court of the United States established the rules that guide entrapment in the 1932 case *Sorrells v. United States*.[21] This case involved federal agents who,

Entrapment
Entrapment is inducing a person to commit a crime that he or she would not have committed without such inducement.

Alibi

An alibi is a defense that establishes the accused could not have committed the crime because they can offer evidence that they were in another place at the time the crime was committed.

after numerous failed attempts, finally convinced a man to sell them bootleg whiskey. The Supreme Court overturned the conviction and said that a person must not be predisposed to commit the offense.

ALIBI

Justification defenses, legal excuses, and entrapment require that the defendant must admit that they committed the acts that constitute the crime they are charged with. When a person says that they have an **alibi**, they are saying that they did not commit the criminal acts. An alibi is a defense that establishes the accused could not have committed the crime because they can offer evidence that they were in another place at the time the crime was committed. The accused can provide witnesses or other proof that can establish their activities at a location other than at the crime scene at the time of the crime.

REVIEW QUESTIONS:

1. The laws that are written by the Internal Revenue Service to regulate the tax regulations would be an example of _____ law.

2. "The guilty act" is called _____ _____.

3. "The guilty mind" is called _____ _____.

4. Crimes that do not require that criminal intent be present are called _____ _____ crimes.

5. _____ _____ is the Latin term that means "the body of the crime."

6. A criminal offense that is punishable by death or incarceration in a prison facility for at least one year is called a _____.

7. Self-defense and _____ are both justifications defenses.

8. A _____ _____ can be used when the defendant can show that they should not be held criminally liable for an offense because there was no criminal intent present.

9. The inducement of a person by a government agent to commit a crime that they were not predisposed to commit is called _____.

10. When an accused person can provide evidence that they were at a location other than at the crime scene at the time of the crime, they have an _____.

CRITICAL THINKING QUESTIONS:

1. How many *mala prohibita* laws can you identify? Discuss why they are designated as such and whether you agree with the fact that they are prohibited.

2. Using the definition of the crime of burglary that was referred to in this chapter, answer the questions that follow this scenario.

    > An undercover police officer is standing outside of a convenience store when two men walk up and stand close enough to the officer so that he can hear their conversation. The two men check their pockets and discuss the fact that neither of them have any money or credit cards. The officer then hears one suspect tell the other that he was going to enter the store and steal a six-pack of beer. He further states that he is going to grab the beer and run out of the store and run to a nearby park and drink the beer. The suspect then opens the door to the convenience store and takes a step inside.

    In this scenario, when can the officer arrest and charge the suspect? Does he have to wait for the suspect to leave the store with the beer, or could he arrest him when he enters the store? When have all of the elements of the crime of burglary been met?

3. Look up and discuss some of the offenses/infractions that are laws in your local jurisdiction.

4. Discuss why deadly force cannot be used when protecting personal property, other than the exception dealing with the home.

5. Explain way 'voluntary' intoxication is not a valid defense in a criminal case.

_____ NOTES _____

CHAPTER 5

[1] *The Oxford Companion to the Supreme Court of the United States* edited by Kermit L. Hall (New York: Oxford University Press, Inc., 1992).

[2] Answers.USA.gov at http://answers.usa. gov/system/selfservice.controller?CM-D=VIEW_ARTICLE&EXPANDED_ TOPIC_TREE_NODES=&ARTICLE_IN_ NEW_WINDOW_FLAG=&ARTICLE_ ID=9732&CONFIGURATION=1000&PARTITION_ ID=1&TIMEZONE_OFFSET=25200000.

[3] Connie Estrada Ireland and George E. Rush, *The Dictionary of Criminal Justice With Summaries of Supreme Court Cases Affecting Criminal Justice,* 7th Edition (New York: McGraw-Hill Companies, Inc., 2011).

[4] Ibid.

[5] The age of consent varies depending on the jurisdiction, but is usually sixteen years of age or younger.

[6] Ireland, *Dictionary of Criminal Justice.*

[7] This is the Nevada definition of burglary found at NRS 205.060 Burglary: Definition; penalties; venue.

[8] Usually the jail time is for sixty days or less.

[9] Model Penal Code Section 3.02.

[10] Craig L. Carr, "Duress and Criminal Responsibility," *Law and Philosophy* 10 (1990): 161.

[11] Ibid.

[12] Ibid.

[13] Ibid.

[14] American Bar Association Standing Committee on Association Standards for Criminal Justice, *Proposed Criminal Justice Mental Health Standards* (Chicago American Bar Association, 1984).

[15] Ireland, *Dictionary of Criminal Justice.*

[16] Federal Defense Reform Act of 1984.

[17] See Chapter 6 for a discussion about Sir Robert Peel and his contributions to modern policing.

[18] Ireland, *Dictionary of Criminal Justice.*

[19] Durham v. U.S., 214 F.2d 862 (D.C. Cir. 1954).

[20] American Law Institute, *Model Penal Code: Official Draft and Explanatory Notes* (Philadelphia: American Law Institute, 1985).

[21] Sorrells v. United States, 287 U.S. 435 (1932).

$\mathcal{C}$HAPTER OVERVIEW

© Gary Blakeley, 2011. Used under license from Shutterstock, Inc.

Policing in America, like much of our criminal justice system, was originally based on the model that was developed in England. In this chapter we will take a brief look at the history of policing in England from its medieval beginnings to the formation of the London Metropolitan Police in 1829 and how it has evolved to the present day. There are over 17,000 law enforcement agencies operating in the United States today at every level of government including: federal, state, county, and city, as well as specialized police agencies that operate at various levels.

The basic functions of police work will be identified and discussed and the importance of patrol will be emphasized. Much of police work is reactive in nature, in that the police are called to a situation that has already taken place and then they must react to it. Community policing, together with problem solving, are proactive approaches utilized by police departments and are among the most effective methods of crime prevention.

The final sections of this chapter will look at the issues and laws involved when a police officer is required to use force, including deadly force, in the line of duty. The appropriate U.S. Supreme Court cases will be discussed and analyzed.

CHAPTER LEARNING OBJECTIVES

After reading this chapter you will be able to:

1. Understand how policing in America grew out of the English model.
2. Describe the philosophy of the London Metropolitan Police.
3. Explain the different levels of policing in the United States.
4. List and explain the different functions of police.
5. Understand the importance of police patrol.
6. Explain the concept of community policing and how it is an effective method of crime prevention.
7. Understand the SARA model of police problem solving.
8. Understand the concept of police discretion.
9. Identify when police are authorized to use force and when force is considered to be unreasonable or excessive.

─────────────── KEYWORDS ───────────────

Tything	Shire-reeve
Watchmen	Sir Robert Peel
Metropolitan Police Act	Bobbies
Federal Law Enforcement	FBI
DEA	ATF
U.S. Marshals Service	State Law Enforcement
Sheriff	City (Municipal) Police
Specialized Police Agencies	Enforcing the Laws
Providing Services	Criminal Investigation
Preventing Crime	Patrol
Kansas City Experiment	Community Policing
Problem Solving	SARA
Tennessee v. Garner	Deadly Force

EARLY ENGLISH HISTORY

Tything

The tything system which was used in early England made all citizens responsible for law and order in each community.

Prior to 1066,[1] the structure for securing order in early England was the "**tything**" system. This was a system where the people were responsible for law and order. Under the tything system, the people within counties were divided into divisions of ten and these divisions were called "tythings." Each of these tythings was represented by a tything-man. These groups of ten were then made a part of a larger group comprised of ten tythings which were organized under a "hundred-man." Each of the hundred-men was responsible to the **Shire-reeve** who was the Sheriff of the County.

During the 1600s and 1700s, the tything-man became the parish constable and the Shire-reeve became the Justice of the Peace to whom the constable reported to. The constable was elected or appointed within the parish for one year of unpaid duty as an unarmed watchman. The towns within each parish eventually set up a system of paid citizens, called **watchmen**, who patrolled the streets at night and guarded the gates of the town.

England saw a rapid rise in the populations of towns and cities as people moved into them because of tremendous social and economic changes that were taking place within the country. The watch system was unable to control the influx of people and subsequent rise in criminal activity, and began to fail in the late 1700s and became completely ineffective by the early 1800s.

London was a city of several million people by the 1800s and social unrest led to several riots in the streets. The watchmen could not control the growing unrest and the military was called in to quell the disruptions and maintain order in the city. The military used heavy-handed tactics to handle the riots, including shooting and beating many of the citizens of London. These tactics angered the citizens even more and the problems compounded themselves.

Shire-reeve

The Shire-reeve was the Sheriff of the County in early England.

Watchmen

The watchmen were citizens who were paid to patrol the streets and guard the gates of the town in 1600 and 1700 England.

*L*ONDON METROPOLITAN POLICE

Sir Robert Peel was the Home Secretary of England and was very concerned about the rising crime and unrest that was taking place in London. In 1829, he finally persuaded the British Parliament to pass the **Metropolitan Police Act** which established the London Metropolitan Police. The new police department was referred to as the "new police" or the "met," and the officers were nicknamed "**bobbies**" after Sir Robert "Bobbie" Peel. The London Metropolitan Police Department was not started on a small scale. During the first six months of operation 3,247 men were recruited and trained; however, 1,644 (51 percent) of the original recruits were dismissed.[2]

Sir Robert Peel

Georgios Kollidas/Shutterstock.com

Sir Robert Peel

Sir Robert Peel (1788–1850) was responsible for getting the Metropolitan Police Act passed in 1829 in England, which established the London Metropolitan Police.

Metropolitan Police Act

This act was passed in 1829 in England and established the London Metropolitan Police.

Bobbies

Named after Sir Robert "Bobbie" Peel, this is the nickname given to the police officers of the London Metropolitan Police.

PHILOSOPHY

The new police were founded on several basic operating philosophies that were established by Sir Robert Peel:

1. To reduce tension and conflict between law enforcement officers and the public.
2. To use nonviolent means in keeping the peace.
3. To relieve the military from controlling urban violence.
4. To be judged on the absence of crime rather than through high-visibility police action.[3]

Two of these operating philosophies are the backbone of the London Metropolitan Police even today, and separate the 'bobbies' from many of the other police departments around the world. The police officers (constables) of the 'met' do not carry firearms on routine patrol or when answering calls for service. The constables rely on their extensive training which stresses community involvement and effective communication skills.

The personal qualities that a person must possess in order to become a constable with the 'met' are:

1. Respect for diversity
2. Teamworking
3. Community and customer service
4. Effective communication
5. Problem solving
6. Personal responsibility
7. Resilience[4]

"To be judged on the absence of crime rather than through high-visibility police action" is the basic philosophy for crime prevention in London. Constables are expected to work with the communities they are assigned to and are not judged by the number of arrests they make; rather, they are judged by the reduction of crime in their area. The constables are encouraged to be proactive in their approach to crime rather than relying on a reactive methodology (see later in this chapter).

HISTORY OF POLICING IN AMERICA

Policing in America, just like our laws, was originally modeled after the British system. The American Colonies had constables and watchmen that were mostly unpaid citizens charged with maintaining order within their respective jurisdictions. As our cities grew, policing became more formalized.

POLICE TODAY

There are three distinct levels of law enforcement in the United States that correspond with our separate levels of government: federal, state, and local. Each level operates independently of each other and is further divided into specialties. While each department is autonomous, there is a tremendous amount of cooperation between them that has been increasing steadily since September 11, 2001. The tragedy of 9/11 was a wake-up call to law enforcement throughout the country since it clearly pointed out the need for improved communication and cooperation between all levels of policing in the United States. It has been speculated that the attack on the United States on 9/11 could have been prevented if all of the individual bits of information that different law enforcement agencies possessed had been shared and compiled at one location.

FEDERAL

Federal law enforcement is comprised of a diverse assortment of agencies. Almost every agency within the federal government has an enforcement division that enforces the policies and laws of that particular agency. These agencies include:

1. Department of the Treasury (Internal Revenue Service)
2. Department of Agriculture
3. Department of the Interior
4. Department of Commerce
5. Department of State
6. U.S. Postal Service
7. Department of Defense

Federal Law Enforcement
Federal law enforcement includes all law enforcement agencies within the federal government.

The Department of Justice oversees some of the more familiar federal law enforcement agencies including:

1. Federal Bureau of Investigation (FBI)
2. Drug Enforcement Agency (DEA)
3. Bureau of Alcohol, Tobacco, Firearms, and Explosives (ATF)
4. U.S. Marshals Service

FBI

FBI
Federal Bureau of Investigation

© Peter Kim, 2011. Used under license from Shutterstock, Inc.

The Federal Bureau of Investigation (**FBI**) is considered by many to be the primary law enforcement agency of the federal government. The FBI was established in 1908 by President Theodore Roosevelt who saw a need for a federal investigative force made up of well-disciplined experts to investigate and fight corruption.[5]

Today, the FBI is comprised of 36,074 employees of whom 13,911 are special agents.[6] The FBI currently has fifty-six field offices located in major cities throughout the United States as well as more than four hundred smaller offices (resident agencies) in cities and towns across the nation.[7] The FBI also has sixty international offices around the world.

The present-day priorities of the FBI are:

1. Protect the United States from terrorist attack.
2. Protect the United States against foreign intelligence operations and espionage.
3. Protect the United States against cyber-based attacks and high-technology crimes.
4. Combat public corruption at all levels.
5. Protect civil rights.
6. Combat transnational/national criminal organizations and enterprises.
7. Combat major white-collar crime.
8. Combat significant violent crime.
9. Support federal, state, local, and international partners.
10. Upgrade technology to successfully perform the FBI's mission.[8]

DRUG ENFORCEMENT ADMINISTRATION

DEA
Drug Enforcement
Administration

The Drug Enforcement Administration (**DEA**) was established in 1973 by President Richard Nixon in order to establish a single unified command to combat "an all-out global war on the drug menace."[9] Today the DEA has more than 5,200 Special Agents that are deployed throughout the United States and around the world. The mission of the DEA is to enforce the controlled substances laws and regulations of the United States and to reduce the availability of illicit controlled substances on the domestic and international markets.[10]

BUREAU OF ALCOHOL, TOBACCO, FIREARMS, AND EXPLOSIVES

The Bureau of Alcohol, Tobacco, Firearms, and Explosives (**ATF**) has a long history in the United States. In 1789 the first Congress of the United States imposed a tax on imported alcohol in order to help offset the debts that had accumulated from fighting the Revolutionary War. The Department of the Treasury was given the responsibility with enforcing this tax and the original agents assigned to this duty were the foundation of the modern ATF. Since that time the ATF has undergone many modifications and missions, as well as name changes, until it was officially given the title of Bureau of Alcohol, Tobacco, and Firearms in 1968. In 1972 the ATF was officially given the duties related to explosives,[11] but has retained the initials ATF. On January 24, 2003 the Bureau of Alcohol, Tobacco, Firearms, and Explosives was transferred to the U.S. Department of Justice.

ATF
Alcohol, Tobacco, Firearms, and Explosives

U.S. MARSHALS SERVICE

The **U.S. Marshals Service** is the oldest federal law enforcement agency in the United States. On September 24, 1789, President George Washington appointed the first thirteen U.S. Marshals following the passage of the first Judiciary Act.[12] Today, there are ninety-four U.S. Marshals (one for each federal district court) and almost four thousand deputy U.S. Marshals and criminal investigators.

U.S. Marshals Service
The U.S. Marshals Service is the oldest federal law enforcement agency.

The U.S. Marshals Service has a variety of responsibilities. Marshals provide security in all federal courts and transport all federal prisoners. They serve federal court documents and warrants and apprehend fugitives from justice. They are also responsible for maintaining the Witness Security Program that provides for the security, health, and safety of government witnesses, and their immediate dependents, whose lives are in danger as a result of their testimony against drug traffickers, terrorists, organized crime members, and other major criminals.[13]

STATE LAW ENFORCEMENT

Every state has a variety of **state law enforcement** agencies. Just like the federal government, states have enforcement arms for many of their state agencies. These include everything from brand inspectors to revenue agents. Many states also have stand-alone investigative agencies such as Nevada's Department of Public Safety Investigations Division and Georgia's Bureau of Investigation. These types of agencies typically assist local agencies with complex criminal investigations, provide training, maintain crime labs, and investigate higher level drug crimes.

State Law Enforcement
State law enforcement consists of all of the law enforcement agencies operating at the state level within individual states.

The most visible of the state law enforcement agencies are the highway patrol or the state police agencies. Every state, with the exception of Hawaii, has one of these two types of agencies. States that utilize the highway patrol system typically assign them the responsibility to enforce traffic laws and conduct accident investigation on state roads and federal (interstate) highways. These agencies usually also maintain weigh stations and enforce commercial trucking laws. While the officers (or troopers) who are assigned to state highway patrol agencies generally

© Darryl Vest, 2011. Used under license from Shutterstock, Inc.

have state-wide police authority, their primary role is not answering calls for service outside of traffic related incidents.

State police agencies customarily do the same functions as the highway patrol but have additional duties of more local law enforcement. State police are also routinely assigned patrol responsibilities in rural areas of the state and answer calls for service and conduct criminal investigations. While these are the general procedures for highway patrols and state police, there are many exceptions and modifications that individual states have implemented to meet their specific needs.

COUNTY LAW ENFORCEMENT

Sheriff

Most commonly the sheriff is considered to be the chief law enforcement officer in a county.

Most county law enforcement is conducted by sheriff's departments. In 2013, there were 3,012 sheriff's offices employing 352,000 full-time sworn and civilian personnel in the United States.[14] **Sheriffs** are often considered to be the chief law enforcement official in the county and most are elected by the populace within their jurisdiction.[15] Sheriff departments perform a variety of functions depending on the jurisdiction that they serve. Most are responsible for maintaining the county jail facilities, providing court security, and serving civil papers and criminal warrants. In some jurisdictions they are also responsible for routine patrol as they are the law enforcement agency for the county.

CITY LAW ENFORCEMENT

City (Municipal) Police

City police are the largest and most visible segment of law enforcement in the United States.

City (municipal) police comprise the largest and most visible segment of law enforcement in the United States, with over 12,500 local police departments employing over 477,000 sworn officers.[16] These departments range in size from one sworn officer to almost 35,000 in New York. About half of all local police departments in the United States employ fewer than ten sworn officers.[17]

© SVLuma, 2011. Used under license from Shutterstock, Inc.

Local police are the mainstay of policing in this country. These are the officers who routinely answer calls for service, are the first on the scene of most major crimes, and investigate everything from shoplifting to murder.

SPECIALIZED POLICE AGENCIES

In addition to the three basic levels of law enforcement (federal, state, and local), there are a host of **specialized police agencies** that have limited jurisdiction over specific areas of concern. These specialized agencies include:

1. School District Police
2. Campus Police
3. Park Police
4. Constables
5. Transit Police
6. City and County Marshals
7. Bailiffs
8. Game Wardens

Specialized Police Agencies
Specialized police departments have limited jurisdiction over specific areas of concern.

*T*HE FUNCTION OF POLICE

There has been considerable debate over the last several decades concerning what the exact functions of police should be and how they should carry out their duties. One purpose of the police that society has seemingly agreed upon is that they are mandated to control crime and make our country a safer place to live. The police attempt to accomplish this not so easy task by:

1. Enforcing the law
2. Providing services
3. Criminal investigation
4. Preventing crime

ENFORCING THE LAWS

Police officers are sworn to enforce all of the laws within their jurisdiction. This is the part of the job that most citizens, as well as many police officers, see as the primary job of law enforcement. Enforcing the laws equates to arresting "bad guys" in the eyes of many. The reality is that police spend less than half of their time actually enforcing the laws.

It is almost impossible to truly enforce all laws. There are many laws that are on the books that police do not have the time, the resources, or the inclination to enforce.

Every state and the federal government have laws that prohibit the sale and distribution of obscenity (pornography), yet very few jurisdictions actively pursue these laws if the pornography does not involve children. There are many other laws in every jurisdiction that are either obscure, not popular, or antiquated; and consequently police departments routinely ignore them. Police discretion, which will be discussed later in this chapter, also has an impact on the enforcement of some minor offenses.

PROVIDING SERVICES

The phrase "To Serve and Protect" is inscribed on police cars throughout the United States. A large portion of a police officer's time is spent assisting citizens and answering non-emergency calls for service. Many times people call the police (as well as fire departments) when they have a non-emergency problem and do not know where else to turn. Police can be called to respond to an almost endless variety of non-criminal situations, including: missing children, missing elderly persons, loud neighbors, barking dogs, loose animals, natural disasters, non-criminal injuries, and conducting welfare checks.

© Alexandru-Radu Borzea, 2011. Used under license from Shutterstock, Inc.

CRIMINAL INVESTIGATION

Criminal investigation is one of the primary ways that police identify and apprehend criminals. A criminal investigation can be a very complex and time consuming occurrence or it can be accomplished in a matter of seconds. Police respond to crimes in progress and to crimes that may have occurred hours, days, weeks, and even years earlier. If the crime is in progress when the police arrive, the officer may actually see the event and immediately arrest the suspect. Depending on the type and seriousness of the crime, trained criminal investigators (or detectives) may still conduct an investigation in order to gather the evidence necessary to bring the suspect to trial and obtain a conviction. When the police arrive on the scene of a crime that has taken place at an earlier time, a criminal investigation is necessary in order to collect evidence, develop leads, and attempt to solve the crime.

PREVENTING CRIME

Crime prevention is one of the most difficult and controversial tasks that we assign to police departments in the United States. Crime prevention involves being proactive and stopping crime before it takes place. The two tactics that police have traditionally utilized to prevent crime in a community are patrol and community policing (see the following sections). While these tactics do have an impact on the reduction of crime, they are arguably very limited in their overall effectiveness.

True crime prevention is a joint effort between law enforcement and the citizens within the individual communities. The police cannot effectively prevent crime by themselves. Whenever crime rates rise, communities demand that the police do more to control it. When crime rates decline, police leaders are quick to take credit for the decrease. The reality is that police have only a minimal effect on the swings (both up and down) that the crime rates go through in the short term. Obviously crime would be astronomical if there were no police, but overall they maintain a balance when they do not have community involvement.

PATROL

Patrol is the considered to be the backbone of police work at the local and state levels of law enforcement. The largest single expense item in police department budgets is putting uniform officers on the street to patrol and answer calls for service. Patrol puts the visible face on police. Citizens see police riding in their cars or walking a beat and this visibility is one of the ways that police deter crime. Police, depending on the location, accomplish their patrol duties in a variety of ways:

Patrol

Patrol is considered to be the backbone of police work at the local and state levels of law enforcement. Patrol is also the most expensive item in police department budgets.

1. Automobiles (the most common)
2. Foot patrol
3. Horse patrol
4. Bicycle patrol
5. Aircraft and helicopters
6. Boat patrol
7. Motorcycles

© SVLuma, 2011. Used under license from Shutterstock, Inc.

© Tom Plesnik, 2011. Used under license from Shutterstock, Inc.

© daseaford, 2011. Used under license from Shutterstock, Inc.

© Ivan Cholakov Gostock-dot-net, 2011. Used under license from Shutterstock, Inc.

© Oculo, 2011. Used under license from Shutterstock, Inc.

Most police departments divide their jurisdictions into smaller beats or sectors and assign one or more officers to patrol each of these smaller areas. Patrolling smaller geographic areas positions officers to be able to quickly respond to calls for service. It also reduces the area that an individual officer has to patrol which allows for more proactive patrol and more visibility to the community. Proactive patrol allows the officers to spend time in higher crime areas within their assigned area to locate crimes in progress, and to prevent or deter crimes from taking place.

THE KANSAS CITY PREVENTIVE PATROL EXPERIMENT

Kansas City Experiment

Conducted during 1972 and 1973, the Kansas City experiment attempted to show that crime could be curtailed and citizens would feel safer if there was more police visibility. The experiment failed to prove either hypothesis.

The **Kansas City experiment** was conducted in 1972/1973 and attempted to confirm two widely accepted theories concerning the effectiveness of police patrol[18]:

1. That visible police presence prevents crime by deterring potential offenders.
2. That the public's fear of crime is diminished by police presence.

Patrol was thought to both prevent crime and reassure the public and alleviate their fears concerning crime. The experiment used three controlled levels of routine preventive patrol in the experimental areas. The first area, termed "reactive," received no preventive patrol. Officers entered the area only in response to citizen calls for assistance, which in effect substantially reduced police visibility in that area. The second area was called "proactive." In this area, police visibility was increased two to three times its usual level. The third area was the "control" area. In this area, the normal level of patrol was maintained.[19]

Analysis of the data gathered revealed that the three areas experienced no significant differences in the level of crime, citizens' attitudes toward police services, citizens' fear of crime, police response time, or citizens' satisfaction with police response time. Even with the discouraging results from this experiment, patrol has always been, and will continue to be, the backbone of police work and is an effective strategy as long as there is cooperation amongst the community.

ℭOMMUNITY POLICING

Community Policing

Community policing is a strategy that involves a working relationship between police and the community to deter and prevent crime.

The United States Department of Justice defines **community policing** by stating that it "... is a philosophy that promotes organizational strategies, which support the systematic use of partnerships and problem-solving techniques, to proactively address the immediate conditions that give rise to public safety issues such as crime, social disorder, and fear of crime."[20]

Community policing, also called community-oriented policing, is a strategy that involves a working relationship between the police and the community. It is a policing style that emphasizes the idea that the public should play a more active role in crime control and prevention. Community policing is a collaborative partnership between the community, the local government, and the police. This approach involves proactive problem solving and community involvement to address the causes of crime, the fear of crime, and community quality of life issues. The four major elements of community policing are[21]:

© carolyn brule, 2011. Used under license from Shutterstock, Inc.

1. Organize community-based crime prevention.
2. Direct and reorient patrol activities to emphasize non-emergency service to the community.
3. Increase police accountability to the local communities.
4. Decentralize the command structure of police departments to allow for more lower-level decision making.

This strategy is one of the most proactive ways that a police department can operate and it is a proven way to increase public support and cooperation. The more positive interaction there is between the police and the public, and in neighborhoods in particular, the more people begin to trust the police and become a part of the crime solution.

PROBLEM SOLVING

A major part of community oriented policing is that of problem solving. Problem solving is the process of engaging in a proactive and systematic examination in order to identify problems and evaluate effective ways of dealing with them. Instead of responding to crime after it occurs (reactive policing), community policing encourages agencies to proactively develop solutions to the immediate underlying conditions that are contributing to and causing public safety problems. Police agencies have to develop new and innovative ways to approach community problems that affect public safety.[22]

SARA MODEL

SARA (Scanning, Analysis, Response, and Assessment) is a problem-solving model that is used by many police agencies throughout the country.[23]

SARA
Scanning, Analysis, Response, and Assessment

- **Scanning**: Identifying and prioritizing problems. Problems can be a type of behavior, a place, a person(s), a special event or time, or any combination of these. The police, with input from the community, should identify and prioritize these concerns.
- **Analysis**: Researching what is known about the problem. Analysis is the heart of the problem-solving process. It is here that an understanding of the problem is developed.

- ■ **Response**: Developing solutions to bring about lasting reductions in the number and extent of the problems. This is where the police and the community work together to find and implement solutions to the problem.
- ■ **Assessment**: Evaluating the success of the responses. This requires follow-up by the police to determine if the response had the desired effect and was successful.

PROBLEM ANALYSIS TRIANGLE

To understand a problem, many problem solvers have found it useful to visualize links between the victim, offender, and location (the crime triangle) and those aspects that could have an impact on them; for example, capable guardians for victims, handlers for offenders, and managers for locations.[24]

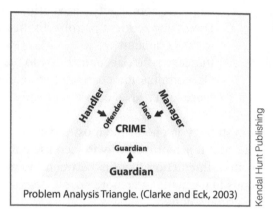

Problem Analysis Triangle. (Clarke and Eck, 2003)

Kendal Hunt Publishing

POLICE USE OF FORCE

Police officers are authorized to use that amount of force necessary to overcome resistance and to accomplish an arrest. An essential element in law enforcement is the potential for suspect resistance and police use of, or threatened use of, force. In 2008, police officers in the United States had 40.0 million face-to-face contacts with citizens, with the majority of the contacts initiated by traffic stops (44.1 percent).[25] While 90 percent of those persons reported that the police acted in a professional manner, an estimated 574,000 persons (1.4% of all contacts) of the 40 million reported that they experienced force or the threat of force by the police. Additionally, the majority of persons involved in police use of force incidents in 2008 felt that the police acted improperly and 13.7 percent of those stated that they filed a complaint against the police.[26]

The type of force used by police ranged from shouting or cursing at the suspect to pointing a gun at them[27]:

One of the most visible and controversial issues confronting police today is that of excessive force. Excessive force is defined by the International Association of Chiefs of Police as "the application of an amount and/or frequency of force greater than that required to compel compliance from a willing or unwilling subject."[28] Whenever we see or hear about an actual or alleged incident involving excessive force by police, the image of law enforcement as a whole is tarnished. Even though police contacts with the public are perceived as professional 90 percent of the time, it only takes a few well-publicized cases to negatively impact the public perception.

TYPES OF FORCE USED OR THREATENED BY POLICE IN 2008	
TYPE OF FORCE USED	PERCENT OF CONTACTS WITH POLICE IN WHICH FORCE WAS USED OR THREATENED OR THREATENED BY POLICE
Total	100%
Police actually used force	
Pushed or grabbed	53.5
Kicked or hit	12.6
Sprayed chemical/pepper spray	4.9
Electroshock weapon (stun Gun)	4.1
Pointed gun	25.6
Threatened force	76.6
Shouted at resident	75.5
Cursed at resident	39.1
Actual Number in Thousands	574

Data Source: U.S. Department of Justice Contacts Between Police and the Public, 2008
Note: Percentages to not equal 100% because many respondents reported that police used more than one type of force

$\mathscr{D}$EADLY FORCE

Deadly force is that force that could be reasonably expected to cause death or serious bodily harm. There are no definitive statistics on the number of times that police officers fire their weapons at suspects (or use other means of deadly force); however, we do know that the police were justified in killing 406 suspects in 2009.[29]

The United States Supreme Court in the 1985 case of *Tennessee v. Garner* set forth the procedures that law enforcement must follow when using deadly force.[30] Prior to this case, many police departments followed what was called the "fleeing felon doctrine." This doctrine allowed police officers to shoot suspects who were fleeing from police if the police had probable cause to believe that they had just committed a felony. In the case that led up to this Supreme Court decision, two Memphis, Tennessee police officers were dispatched to a prowler call. When they arrived, they saw the suspect fleeing the scene of a home burglary. The officers chased the suspect to a chain link fence where they saw that he was unarmed and they ordered him to halt. The suspect then began to climb over the fence at which time one of the officers fired one round striking the suspect in the

Deadly Force

Deadly force is that force that could be reasonably expected to cause death or serious bodily harm.

Tennessee v. Garner

This is the 1985 U.S. Supreme Court landmark case that set forth the procedures that law enforcement must follow when using deadly force.

head. The suspect, who turned out to be a fifteen-year-old juvenile, died a short time later in the hospital.

The Supreme Court ruled that it was unreasonable to shoot an unarmed felon just because he failed to stop and was attempting to flee the police. Deadly force can be used in the defense of life of the officer or a third party, and officers may shoot a fleeing felon only if that felon poses an imminent danger of serious bodily harm or death to the officers or a third party.

In the 1989 U.S. Supreme Court case of *Graham v. Conner,* the court looked further into the application of force, including deadly force, when used by police officers. In this case, the court established a new standard of "reasonableness" that is to be applied to every use-of-force decision that an officer makes. The court stated:

"Determining whether the force used to effect a particular seizure is "reasonable" under the Fourth Amendment requires a careful balancing of "the nature and quality of the intrusion on the individual's Fourth Amendment interests". . ."

"Because "[t]he test of reasonableness under the Fourth Amendment is not capable of precise definition or mechanical application,". . . its proper application requires careful attention to the facts and circumstances of each particular case, including the severity of the crime at issue, whether the suspect poses an immediate threat to the safety of the officers or others, and whether he is actively resisting arrest or attempting to evade arrest by flight. . . (the question is "whether the totality of the circumstances justifie[s] a particular sort of . . . seizure")."

"The "reasonableness" of a particular use of force must be judged from the perspective of a reasonable officer on the scene, rather than with the 20/20 vision of hindsight. . .As in other Fourth Amendment contexts, however, the "reasonable" inquiry in an excessive force case is an objective one: the question is whether the officers' actions are "objectively reasonable" in light of the facts and circumstances confronting them, without regard to their underlying intent or motivation."

In summary, the U.S. Supreme Court stated that, when looking at whether or not an officer used excessive or unreasonable force in any given situation, the courts (and individual departments) must look at each of the following:

1. The severity of the crime
2. Whether the suspect poses an immediate threat to the safety of the officer or others
3. Whether the suspect is resisting arrest or attempting to evade arrest by flight

They must then take into consideration the totality of the circumstances from the perspective of what a "reasonable" officer would have done, at the time of the incident, given the same set of facts and circumstances.

REVIEW QUESTIONS:

1. _____ persuaded the British Parliament to pass the London Metropolitan Police Act in 1829.

2. The three distinct levels of law enforcement in the United States today are the _____, _____, and _____.

3. The Federal Bureau of Investigation was established in 1908 by President _____.

4. Every state has a state highway patrol or a state police agency except _____.

5. The largest segment of law enforcement in the United States is at the _____ level.

6. The chapter discusses _____ different functions of the police in the United States.

7. The most controversial task (or function) that is assigned to police in the United States is that of

    _____ _____.

8. _____ is the backbone of police work.

9. A strategy of policing that involves a working relationship between the police and the community is

    called _____ _____.

10. _____ is a problem solving model that is used by many police agencies throughout the United States.

11. The application of an amount and/or frequency of force greater than that required to compel compliance from a willing or unwilling subject is considered to be _____ _____.

CRITICAL THINKING QUESTIONS:

1. Discuss how the operating philosophy of the London Metropolitan Police differs from that of most police agencies in the United States.

2. The "bobbies" in London do not carry firearms when answering routine calls for service and while on patrol. Do you think that police in the United States could operate without their firearms? Explain your opinion in detail.

3. Identify and explain the function of at least three federal law enforcement agencies that were NOT mentioned in this chapter.

4. Explain, in your own words, why crime prevention is one of the most difficult and controversial tasks that is assigned to our police departments.

5. Discuss the significance of the Kansas City Preventive Patrol Experiment and explain why patrol is still one of the most important functions of police work today.

6. Describe how the SARA Model of problem solving works and explain why it is important today.

7. Explain why community policing is one of the most effective methods of crime prevention in our society.

8. When a police officer is accused of using excessive force it tarnishes the reputation of all police. Explain what excessive force is and what police departments can do to reduce the number of instances of it.

—————————— NOTES ——————————

CHAPTER 6

[1] 1066 is when William the Conqueror invaded the island now called Britain.

[2] Gary Mason, *The Official History of the Metropolitan Police: 175 Years of Policing London,* (Carlton, 2004).

[3] Peter K. Manning, *Police Work—The Social Organization of Policing,* 2nd Edition (Prospects Heights, Illinois: Waveland Press, Inc., 1997).

[4] Metropolitan Police New Constable requirements accessed November, 2010 at http://www.met.police.uk/careers/newconstable/who_we_are_looking_for.html.

[5] A Brief History of the FBI, accessed November, 2010 at http://www.fbi.gov/about-us/history/brief-history.

[6] As of April 4, 2011 according to The Federal Bureau of Investigation quick facts, accessed June, 2011 at http://www.fbi.gov/about-us/quick-facts.

[7] Ibid.

[8] Ibid.

[9] U.S. Drug Enforcement Administration home web-page, accessed January, 2011 at http://www.justice.gov/dea/history.htm.

[10] DEA Mission Statement, accessed November, 2010 at http://www.justice.gov/dea/agency/mission.htm.

[11] George Thomas Kurian, *A Historical Guide to the U.S. Government* (New York: Oxford University Press, 1998).

[12] U.S. Marshals Service home web-page, accessed December, 2010 at http://www.usmarshals.gov/history/timeline.html.

[13] Ibid. Accessed December, 2010 at http://www.usmarshals.gov/witsec/index.html.

[14] U.S. department of Justice, Office of Justice Programs, Bureau of Justice Statistics, *Sheriff's Office Personnel, 1993-2013,* June, 2016

[15] The two exceptions to elections for sheriff are Hawaii and Rhode Island, where the sheriffs are appointed.

[16] Bureau of justice Statistics, *Local Police Departments, 2013: Personnel, Policies, and Practices,* May, 2015.

[17] Ibid.

[18] George L. Kelling, Tony Pate, Duane Dieckman, and Charles E. Brown, *The Kansas City Preventive Patrol Experiment—A Summary Report,* (Washington, DC: Police Foundation 1974).

[19] Ibid.

[20] COPS—Community Oriented Policing Services, *Community Policing Defined,* United States Department of Justice, 2009.

[21] Connie Estrada Ireland and George E. Rush, *The Dictionary of Criminal Justice With Summaries of Supreme Court Cases Affecting Criminal Justice,* 7th Edition, (New York: McGraw-Hill Companies, Inc., 2011).

[22] COPS, *Community Policing Defined,* 12.

[23] Ibid.

[24] Ibid.

[25] Matthew R. Durose, Christine Eith, *Contacts Between Police and the Public, 2008,* U.S. Department of Justice, Office of Justice Programs, Bureau of Justice Statistics, October, 2011.

[26] Ibid.

[27] Ibid.

[28] International Association of Chiefs of Police, *Police Use of Force in America, 2001* (Alexandria, Va: IACP, 2001).

[29] Federal Bureau of Investigation, *Crime in the United States,* accessed March, 2011 at http://www2.fbi.gov/ucr/cius2009/offenses/expanded_information/data/shrtable_14.html.

[30] Tennessee v. Garner, et al., 471 U.S. 1.

[31] Graham v. Conner, 490 U.S. 386

[32] Ibid

CHAPTER OVERVIEW

Police procedures are the accumulation of United States Supreme Court decisions that have dealt with the way that police must conduct themselves while performing their duties. This chapter will examine many of the important procedures that every law enforcement officer must have a working knowledge of in order to comply with the law and with the constitutional requirements as interpreted by the courts. The chapter will also examine many of the landmark U.S. Supreme Court cases that have had tremendous impact on the way police must now conduct themselves in a lawful manner.

The laws of arrest and the laws of search and seizure are derived from the Fourth Amendment and will be examined in detail. The concept of probable cause must be understood by all police officers and students of criminal justice because it is a requirement of all arrests and searches that are conducted in this country. The courts have also allowed police to detain suspects without arresting them in certain limited situations. These detentions require a level of evidence known as reasonable suspicion which is less stringent than that of probable cause.

There are many exceptions to the requirement that a search warrant must be obtained by the police prior to conducting any type of search in the United States. This chapter will discuss and explain some of the more common exceptions that have been allowed by the courts and are encountered by police on a regular basis. A discussion of when the police may conduct a lawful interrogation of a suspect and the implications of the infamous Miranda decision will conclude the chapter.

CHAPTER LEARNING OBJECTIVES

After reading this chapter you will be able to:

1. Explain the requirements necessary for the police to conduct a lawful arrest.
2. Understand the legal concept of probable cause.
3. Understand the legal concept of reasonable suspicion.
4. Distinguish between a lawful arrest and a lawful detention.
5. Explain what the exclusionary rule is and when it is applied.
6. Identify and explain the exceptions to the exclusionary rule.
7. List and explain at least five of the exceptions to the search warrant requirement.
8. Understand the requirements of the *Miranda* decision and know when the rights granted by that decision must be given to a suspect.

KEYWORDS

Arrest	Warrant
Probable Cause	Stop & Frisk
Terry v. Ohio	Reasonable Suspicion
Pat Down Search	Search
Search with a Warrant	Exclusionary Rule
Mapp v. Ohio	Good Faith Exception
Inevitable Discovery Exception	Poison Tree Doctrine
Search Warrant Exceptions	Search incident to a Lawful Arrest
Plain View Doctrine	Consent Searches
Exigent Circumstances	Carroll Doctrine
Miranda v. Arizona	

U.S. SUPREME COURT HANDS-OFF POLICY PRIOR TO THE 1960S

Prior to the 1960s, the United States Supreme Court decided very few cases that dealt with police procedures on the state level. Although there were exceptions, the Supreme Court limited itself to cases that dealt primarily to federal law enforcement in the area of police procedures. Beginning in the 1960s, the Warren Court[1] began deciding a host of cases that directly impacted police procedures at the state level. In particular, the Court has made numerous interpretations of the Fourth, Fifth, and Sixth Amendments to the U.S. Constitution that have directly affected the way that police must conduct themselves procedurally.

*A*RREST

An **arrest** is the legal detention of a person to answer for criminal charges. An arrest must be based on probable cause, and depending on the circumstances may be made with or without a **warrant**. An arrest is the 'seizure' of a person; therefore an arrest, just like the laws and procedures dealing with searches, is based upon the Fourth Amendment to the U.S. Constitution.

Arrest

An arrest is the legal detention of a person to answer for criminal charges. An arrest must be based on probable cause.

Warrant

A warrant is a court order issued by a judge that authorizes a police officer to make an arrest or conduct a search.

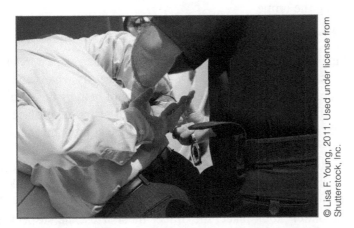

© Lisa F. Young, 2011. Used under license from Shutterstock, Inc.

There are two ways to make a lawful arrest, with a warrant and without a warrant. An arrest with a warrant is accomplished when an investigation has been conducted and probable cause has been developed which is then presented to a judge who reviews the probable cause and then issues the warrant. Any police officer can then serve the warrant and arrest the suspect. There are times when a judge will issue a warrant from the bench during a court session. These warrants are called bench warrants and can be issued for a variety of reasons, but are normally issued when a defendant does not appear in court for a scheduled hearing or trial.

The majority of arrests that are made by police officers are made without a warrant. A police officer may arrest a suspect without a warrant when any of the following has taken place[2]:

1. The person to be arrested has committed a felony or misdemeanor in the officer's presence.
2. The person to be arrested has committed a felony not in the officer's presence.
3. A felony has been committed and the officer has probable cause to believe that the person to be arrested has committed it.
4. The officer has reasonable grounds to believe that a felony has been or is being committed and has probable cause to believe that the person to be arrested has committed it or is committing it.

In summary, a police officer can usually make an arrest without a warrant for felonies that have or have not taken place in their presence, provided that they have probable cause. Most jurisdictions in the United States do not allow a police office to arrest a person for a misdemeanor crime unless that crime has taken place in the officer's presence. There are several ways that a crime can take place in an officer's 'presence':

1. Seeing the crime
2. Smelling the crime
3. Hearing the crime

Obviously if the officer sees the crime, he can make an arrest. There are times that an officer can 'smell' a crime. The most common way is when an officer smells drugs that are being smoked even though they are not being smoked directly in his presence. An officer may also hear a misdemeanor crime take place. The officer may hear a fight taking place but when he arrives the combatants are just standing next to each other.

Some jurisdictions have enacted laws that mandate police officers to make an arrest for domestic battery, a misdemeanor, even if the crime took place up to twenty-four hours prior to the arrival of the police officer. If there is physical evidence that the battery took place, the officer must arrest the suspect under these laws.

PROBABLE CAUSE

Probable Cause

A simplified working definition (not a legal definition) of probable cause for an arrest is: *It is more likely than not that the person being arrested committed the crime that they are being arrested for.*

The Fourth Amendment to the U.S. Constitution states that "no warrants shall issue, but upon probable cause." The U.S. Supreme Court has equated **probable cause** to the concept of reasonableness.[3] The Court has further stated that the facts and circumstances that lead to an arrest or a seizure must be sufficient to persuade a reasonable person that an illegal act has been or is being committed. Probable cause is an issue of law and therefore the final determiner of whether probable cause exists is a judge, not the police officer.

STOP AND FRISK

We have seen that the police may stop and arrest a suspect when they have probable cause to believe that the suspect has committed a crime. There are times when the police need to stop individuals in order to question them about possible criminal activity even though they do not have probable cause to arrest them. Prior to 1968, police officers were very limited in their ability to do this. While a police officer could always ask a suspicious person questions, they did not have the power or authority to actually detain them while investigating criminal activity.

TERRY V. OHIO

In 1968 the United States Supreme Court ruled on the case of **Terry v. Ohio**.[4] This landmark case established a new level of evidence that allows police officers to detain suspicious individuals, for a limited amount of time, while investigating criminal activity. This new level of evidence is reasonable suspicion. Reasonable suspicion also allows the police to pat-down a person while being lawfully detained.

The following is the summary of the facts as reflected in the Supreme Court decision that took place leading up to the decision in the *Terry* case. The court looked at all of the facts in this case in order to come up with their decision. The Court concluded that police officers are in a distinctive position to be able to draw "rational inferences" based upon "specific and articulable facts" because of their training and experience. In 1989, in the case of *United States v. Sokolow,*[5] the

Terry v. Ohio

The landmark U.S. Supreme Court case that established the level of evidence of reasonable suspicion.

Court clarified and refined these criteria to include the "totality of the circumstances" when considering if reasonable suspicion is present in any particular case.

—————————————————— TERRY V. OHIO ——————————————————

Officer McFadden testified that, while he was patrolling in plain clothes in downtown Cleveland at approximately 2:30 in the afternoon of October 31, 1963, his attention was attracted by two men, Chilton and Terry, standing on the corner of Huron Road and Euclid Avenue. He had never seen the two men before, and he was unable to say precisely what first drew his eye to them. However, he testified that he had been a policeman for 39 years and a detective for 35, and that he had been assigned to patrol this vicinity of downtown Cleveland for shoplifters and pickpockets for 30 years. He explained that he had developed routine habits of observation over the years, and that he would "stand and watch people or walk and watch people at many intervals of the day." He added: "Now, in this case, when I looked over, they didn't look right to me at the time."

His interest aroused, Officer McFadden took up a post of observation in the entrance to a store 300 to 400 feet away from the two men. "I get more purpose to watch them when I seen their movements," he testified. He saw one of the men leave the other one and walk southwest on Huron Road, past some stores. The man paused for a moment and looked in a store window, then walked on a short distance, turned around and walked back toward the corner, pausing once again to look in the same store window. He rejoined his companion at the corner, and the two conferred briefly. Then the second man went through the same series of motions, strolling down Huron Road, looking in the same window, walking on a short distance, turning back, peering in the store window again, and returning to confer with the first man at the corner. The two men repeated this ritual alternately between five and six times apiece—in all, roughly a dozen trips. At one point, while the two were standing together on the corner, a third man approached them and engaged them briefly in conversation. This man then left the two others and walked west on Euclid Avenue. Chilton and Terry resumed their measured pacing, peering, and conferring. After this had gone on for 10 to 12 minutes, the two men walked off together, heading west on Euclid Avenue, following the path taken earlier by the third man.

By this time, Officer McFadden had become thoroughly suspicious. He testified that, after observing their elaborately casual and oft-repeated reconnaissance of the store window on Huron Road, he suspected the two men of "casing a job, a stick-up," and that he considered it his duty as a police officer to investigate further. He added that he feared "they may have a gun." Thus, Officer McFadden followed Chilton and Terry and saw them stop in front of Zucker's store to talk to the same man who had conferred with them earlier on the street corner. Deciding that the situation was ripe for direct action, Officer McFadden approached the three men, identified [p7] himself as a police officer and asked for their names. At this point, his knowledge was confined to what he had observed. He was not acquainted with any of the three men by name or by sight, and he had received no information concerning them from any other source. When the men "mumbled something" in response to his inquiries, Officer McFadden grabbed petitioner Terry, spun him around so that they were facing the other two, with Terry between McFadden and the others, and patted down the outside of his clothing. In the left breast pocket of Terry's overcoat, Officer McFadden felt a pistol. He reached inside the overcoat pocket, but was unable to remove the gun. At this point, keeping Terry between himself and the others, the officer ordered all three men to enter Zucker's store. As they went in, he removed Terry's overcoat completely, removed a .38 caliber revolver from the pocket and ordered all three men to face the wall with their hands raised. Officer McFadden proceeded to pat down the outer clothing of Chilton and the third man, Katz. He discovered another revolver in the outer pocket of Chilton's overcoat, but no weapons were found on Katz. The officer testified that he only patted the men down to see whether they had weapons, and that he did not put his hands beneath the outer garments of either Terry or Chilton until he felt their guns. So far as appears from the record, he never placed his hands beneath Katz' outer garments. Officer McFadden seized Chilton's gun, asked the proprietor of the store to call a police wagon, and took all three men to the station, where Chilton and Terry were formally charged with carrying concealed weapons.[6]

REASONABLE SUSPICION

Reasonable suspicion can be defined as the level of evidence that a police officer needs in order to justify the detention of an individual who is suspected of engaging in criminal activity. The officer must be able to articulate that the suspicion was reasonable and may do so based upon their training and experience. The criminal activity being investigated may be past, present, or future activity. A mere hunch is not sufficient; they must be able to articulable their suspicion.

The amount of time that a person may be detained under a reasonable suspicion stop has not been ruled on by the courts; however, the person may not be detained for an "unreasonable" amount of time. There must be an active investigation to determine if the detained person has in fact been involved in criminal activity. Some jurisdictions have limited investigative detentions to a maximum of sixty minutes.

The Supreme Court, in the 2004 case of *Hiibel v. Sixth Judicial District Court of Nevada, Humbult County, et al.,*[7] ruled that police officers can require persons who are detained under a *Terry* stop to identify themselves to the officer.

Reasonable Suspicion

Reasonable suspicion can be defined as the level of evidence that a police officer needs in order to justify the detention of an individual who is suspected of engaging in criminal activity.

© B Christopher/Shutterstock.com

Pat-down Search

A pat-down search is a cursory search of the outer clothing for the purpose of determining if the suspect has a weapon.

PAT-DOWN SEARCH

The ruling under the *Terry* stop allows officers, in some circumstances, to 'pat-down' persons who are being detained. A **pat-down search** is a cursory search of the outer clothing for the purpose of determining if the suspect has a weapon. There are certain conditions that must be met in order for the police to be able to conduct a pat-down; it is not automatically allowed just because there is reasonable suspicion to detain the suspect. In order to justify a pat-down the officer must be able to articulate that there was reason to believe that the suspect may have a weapon. The search may than be conducted for the safety of the officer or other citizens. The search cannot be a "fishing expedition" to look for other illegal substances; it must be for weapons only.[8] If illegal substances are found during a lawful pat-down, that evidence may be used against the suspect.

$\mathscr{S}$EARCH

One of the fundamental freedoms that Americans enjoy is the right to privacy. The Fourth Amendment to the U.S. Constitution states: "The right of the people to be secure in their persons, houses, paper, and effects, against unreasonable searches and seizures, shall not be violated . . ." In order for the police to intrude on the privacy of a person, they must have a lawful reason and, with very limited exceptions, they must have probable cause.

$\mathscr{S}$EARCH WITH A WARRANT

The Fourth Amendment specifically states that ". . . no warrant shall issue, but upon probable cause, supported by oath or affirmation, and particularly describing the place to searched, and the persons or things to be seized." This protection insures that a neutral party, a judge or magistrate, reviews the police officers probable cause before a search warrant is issued and the actual search is conducted. Even though it was written over two hundred years ago, the procedures set forth in the Fourth Amendment for obtaining a warrant are still the process used today.

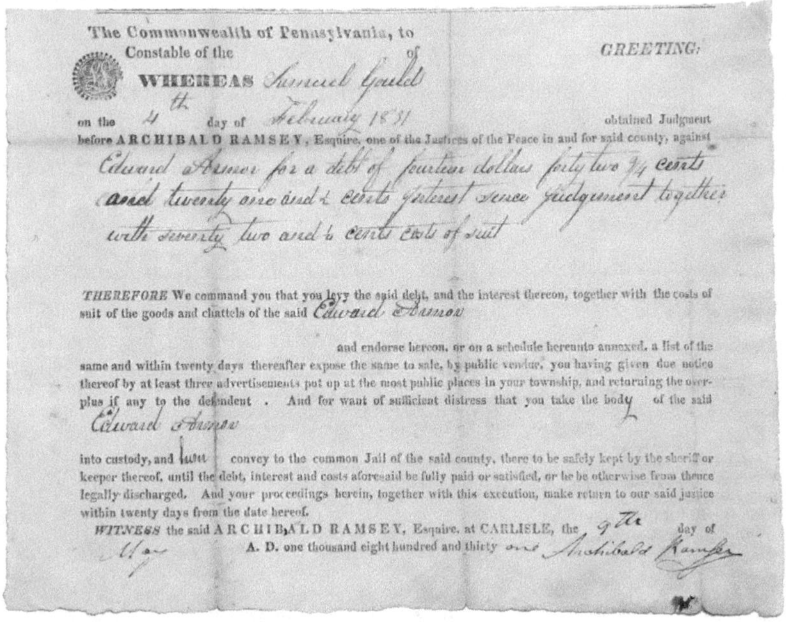

© Kenneth V. Pilon, 2011. Used under license from Shutterstock, Inc.

EXCLUSIONARY RULE

The **exclusionary rule** states that any evidence that is illegally seized by the police will be inadmissible in a criminal trial. The exclusionary rule was first introduced by the U.S. Supreme Court in the 1914 case of *Weeks v. U.S.*[9] This case established the exclusionary rule for federal agents and the federal court system. State and local police were still allowed to enter illegally seized evidence into court, and were able to do so until 1961, except in those states that wrote their own exclusionary rule statutes. During the interim period of time, federal officers often exploited a loophole in the wording of the *Weeks* case that said "evidence illegally seized by federal officers is inadmissible." The federal officers would often simply ask state or local officers to make illegal seizures on their behalf and then use the evidence in federal court.[10] This practice was referred to as the "silver platter" doctrine because it appeared that state and local police were handing over illegally seized evidence to the federal officers on a "silver platter."

The Supreme Court applied the exclusionary rule to the states in 1961 in the case of *Mapp v. Ohio*.[11]

Exclusionary Rule

The exclusionary rule states that any evidence that is illegally seized by the police will be inadmissible in a criminal trial.

Mapp v. Ohio

This is the 1961 landmark U.S. Supreme Court case that applied the exclusionary rule to the states.

—————————————————— MAPP V. OHIO ——————————————————

On May 23, 1957, three Cleveland police officers arrived at appellant's residence in that city pursuant to information that a person [was] hiding out in the home, who was wanted for questioning in connection with a recent bombing, and that there was a large amount of policy paraphernalia being hidden in the home.

Miss Mapp and her daughter by a former marriage lived on the top floor of the two-family dwelling. Upon their arrival at that house, the officers knocked on the door and demanded entrance, but appellant, after telephoning her attorney, refused to admit them without a search warrant. They advised their headquarters of the situation and undertook a surveillance of the house.

The officers again sought entrance some three hours later when four or more additional officers arrived on the scene. When Miss Mapp did not come to the door immediately, at least one of the several doors to the house was forcibly opened and the policemen gained admittance. Meanwhile Miss Mapp's attorney arrived, but the officers, having secured their own entry, and continuing in their defiance of the law, would permit him neither to see Miss Mapp nor to enter the house. It appears that Miss Mapp was halfway down the stairs from the upper floor to the front door when the officers, in this highhanded manner, broke into the hall. She demanded to see the search warrant. A paper, claimed to be a warrant, was held up by one of the officers. She grabbed the "warrant" and placed it in her bosom. A struggle ensued in which the officers recovered the piece of paper and as a result of which they handcuffed appellant because she had been "belligerent" in resisting their official rescue of the "warrant" from her person. Running roughshod over appellant, a policeman "grabbed" her, "twisted [her] hand," and she "yelled [and] pleaded with him" because "it was hurting." Appellant, in handcuffs, was then forcibly taken upstairs to her bedroom where the officers searched a dresser, a chest of drawers, a closet and some suitcases. They also looked into a photo album and through personal papers belonging to the appellant. The search spread to the rest of the second floor including the child's bedroom, the living room, the kitchen and a dinette. The basement of the building and a trunk found therein were also searched. The obscene materials for possession of which she was ultimately convicted were discovered in the course of that widespread search.[12]

At the trial, the police were unable to produce a search warrant and the Court ruled that the exclusionary rule now applied to all police officers throughout the country.

FRUIT OF THE POISONOUS TREE DOCTRINE

The fruit of the poisonous tree doctrine was established in the 1920 Supreme Court case of *Silverthorne Lumber Co. v. U.S.*[13] The Court ruled that if evidence that is seized is inadmissible in court, any other evidence that was obtained as a result of the illegally seized evidence would also be inadmissible. The Court ruled that if the tree is poisoned (the original illegally seized evidence), then the fruit (evidence seized that is based on the original) would also be poisoned.

© kosam, 2011. Used under license from Shutterstock, Inc.

EXCEPTIONS TO THE EXCLUSIONARY RULE

The U.S. Supreme Court has established several exceptions to the exclusionary rule. Two of the most significant exceptions are the good faith exception and the inevitable discovery exception.

GOOD FAITH EXCEPTION

The Supreme Court has ruled that there are times that even when evidence is seized pursuant to a defective search warrant it can still be admitted into court. The 1984 case of *United States v. Leon* established what is now known as the **good faith exception** to the exclusionary rule.[14] In this case, an officer from the Burbank, California police department applied for a search warrant that was reviewed by several Deputy District Attorneys and signed by a state-court judge. Large quantities of drugs and other evidence were seized. The case was appealed and the appellant court found that the probable cause in the affidavit was insufficient and the evidence was ruled inadmissible under the exclusionary rule. The Supreme Court disagreed and said that even though the affidavit was defective, the officer acted in good faith when he executed the search warrant, and therefore the evidence was admissible. The Court did point out that if the officer had known that the warrant was defective prior to executing it, any evidence seized would be excluded.

Good Faith Exception

In the 1984 U.S. Supreme Court case of *United States v. Leon* the court allowed for the admission of evidence that would normally not be admissible under the exclusionary rule, if the officers acted in good faith.

© Shawn Hempel, 2011. Used under license from Shutterstock, Inc.

INEVITABLE DISCOVERY EXCEPTION

Inevitable Discovery Exception

In the 1984 case of *Nix v. Leon*, the court established an exception to the exclusionary rule stating that if illegally seized evidence would have been found legally in the normal course of an investigation (it would have been inevitably discovered), it can be admitted into court.

In the Supreme Court case of *Nix v. Williams,* that was decided the same year as the *Leon* case in 1984, the Court established another exception to the exclusionary rule that is known as the **inevitable discovery exception**.[15] In this case police officers from Davenport, Iowa, were driving an arrested suspect back to Des Moines. The suspect had been arrested for the murder of a ten-year-old girl, but the body had not been found yet. On the way back to Des Moines, the officers engaged the suspect in a conversation saying that he should tell the officers where the body of the girl was, because if he didn't, the body may never be found and would not be able to have a Christian burial. The suspect then led the officers to where the body was. In court, the defense argued that the suspect had been given his rights and therefore the evidence of the body should not be allowed into court as evidence based on the exclusionary rule. On appeal, the Supreme Court ruled that the body would have been discovered independently since there were large search parties looking for it. The Court ruled that the body was admissible because it would inevitably have been discovered.

ℰXCEPTIONS TO THE SEARCH WARRANT REQUIREMENTS

The Fourth Amendment specifically states that before they may conduct a search, they are required to obtain a search warrant. Over the years, the U.S. Supreme Court has established several exceptions to the warrant rule. These exceptions allow officers to conduct searches without a prior determination of probable cause by a judge and conduct the search without a warrant. Some of the more common exceptions are:

1. Search incident to a lawful arrest
2. Plain view
3. Consent
4. Exigent circumstances
5. Vehicle searches

Search Incident to a Lawful Arrest

When the police make a lawful arrest, they are allowed to conduct a complete search of the person arrested as well as the area within the immediate control of the arrestee.

SEARCH INCIDENT TO A LAWFUL ARREST

When the police make a lawful arrest, they are allowed to conduct a complete search of the person arrested as well as the area within the immediate control of the arrestee. This type of search is called a '**search incident to a lawful arrest**.' The Supreme Court in the case of *United States v. Robinson* (1973) stated that there are two reasons that the police may conduct this type of search[16]:

1. Officer safety—officers may search for and confiscate any weapons that the suspect has.
2. Prevent the destruction of evidence.

The Supreme Court further refined the area that may be searched without a warrant when a suspect is arrested in a home. In the case of *Chimel v. California* (1969) the Court held that a search incident to an arrest in a home is limited to "the area into which an arrestee might reach in order to grab a weapon or other evidentiary items."[17] This established "area of immediate control" has been referred to as the arms reach doctrine.

PLAIN VIEW

The "**plain view doctrine**" was established in the 1968 Supreme Court case of *Harris v. United States.*[18] The "plain view doctrine" states that if a police officer is lawfully at a location and he sees contraband within his view, he may seize it without a warrant. Contraband is anything that is illegal on its face; that is, the officer does not have to move it or inspect it to determine that it is illegal. Contraband includes such things as illegal drugs, drug paraphernalia, and certain illegal weapons. If the officer has to move the item to read a serial number to determine if it is stolen, it is probably not contraband.

 If an officer is invited into a home to take a police report and sees illegal drugs on the kitchen counter, the officer may legally seize the drugs and charge the owner. The officer was legally in the home and in a position where he could see the contraband.

Plain View Doctrine
The "plain view doctrine" states that if a police officer is lawfully at a location and he sees contraband within his view, he may seize it without a warrant.

CONSENT SEARCHES

A person may waive their Fourth Amendment rights and voluntarily allow the police to search their property (or themselves) without a warrant by giving their **consent** to do so. The person who is giving consent must have "standing" to do so. Standing means that the person who gives the permission has the legal right to do so. The owner of a house may give consent for the police to search the home, but a guest of the homeowner may not give consent because they do not have standing to do so. The guest has no legal right to allow the search because they have no ownership.

 A roommate who lives in one bedroom of a two bedroom apartment and pays half of the rent, could give the police consent to search only the common areas of the apartment as well as their own room, but could not give permission to search the roommate's room. A landlord could not give consent to search a tenants apartment and a hotel cannot give consent to search a paying customers room.

 In order to give consent, it must be given voluntarily and knowingly. The police cannot coerce or threaten a person in order to obtain consent to search. Once consent is given, it may be withdrawn at any time. The person can also put limitations on the search. The person could tell the police that they have permission to

Consent
A person may waive their Fourth Amendment rights and voluntarily allow the police to search their property (or themselves) without a warrant by giving their consent to do so.

search particular rooms of a house but not others. They could also put a time limit on the search by telling the police that they only have a specified amount of time to conduct the search and then they must leave.

EXIGENT CIRCUMSTANCES

Exigent (emergency) Circumstances

Exigent (emergency) circumstances necessitate that police officers enter a home or other building, or extend the parameters of a search, without obtaining a warrant.

There are times when **exigent (emergency) circumstances** necessitate that police officers enter a home or other building, or extend the parameters of a search, without obtaining a warrant. If a police officer sees a fire in a home they may enter to look for or warn the occupants. If an officer on patrol hears gunshots or screams coming from a home they could enter to investigate. If the police are chasing a suspect who is known to be armed and poses an immediate threat, and that suspect enters a home, they could follow him without first obtaining a warrant.

The Supreme Court has also said that if police are executing an arrest warrant in a home, they may search the premises for other people who may be hiding and could potentially cause a danger to the officers.[19]

© Wade H. Massie, 2011. Used under license from Shutterstock, Inc

Carroll Doctrine

The Supreme Court as early as 1925 in the case of *Carroll v. U.S.* recognized that vehicles are highly mobile and police officers often do not have time to obtain search warrants.

VEHICLE SEARCHES

Motor vehicles are a major exception to the warrant requirement of the Fourth Amendment. The Supreme Court as early as 1925 in the case of *Carroll v. U.S.* recognized that vehicles are highly mobile and police officers often do not have time to obtain search warrants.[20] The *Carroll* case established what is known as the "**Carroll doctrine**" or the "mobility doctrine." The "Carroll doctrine" states that because vehicles are mobile, police cannot routinely obtain search warrants for them and therefore, if the officer has probable cause that a crime has been committed, they may search without a warrant.

© Lisa F. Young, 2011. Used under license from Shutterstock, Inc.

If the police stop a vehicle and arrest the driver, they may conduct a search of the entire front and rear compartments as well as any unlocked containers within that area of the vehicle. This extended area of search was made permissible in the 1981 Supreme Court case of *New York v. Belton*.[21] The *Belton* case expanded *Chimel* limits of a search when vehicles are involved. Areas officers may search under the *Belton* ruling include: under the front seat, under the dashboard, the entire back seat (including being able to move items to look under them), over the visors, and any unlocked interior compartments.

In 2009, the Supreme Court of the United States further clarified and restricted the *Belton* ruling in the case of *Arizona v. Gant*.[22] The court ruled that the police may search the passenger compartment of a vehicle incident to a recent occupant's arrest only if it is reasonable to believe that the arrestee might access the vehicle at the time of the search or that the vehicle contains evidence of the offense that the occupant is being arrested for. If the arrestee is in handcuffs or otherwise restrained so that they cannot access the vehicle, the police are restricted in their warrantless search.

A police officer may search an entire vehicle, including locked compartments and the trunk, if the officer has probable cause. The Court in the case of the *United States v. Ross* (1982) ruled that "Police officers who have legitimately stopped an automobile and who have probable cause to believe that contraband is concealed somewhere within it may conduct a warrantless search of the vehicle that is as thorough as a magistrate could authorize by warrant."[23]

*I*NTERROGATION

Miranda v. Arizona
This 1966 United States Supreme Court case established the rights that must be given to a suspect who is in custody and being questioned by the police.

Without a doubt, the most famous U.S. Supreme Court case dealing with police procedures would have to be the 1966 case of **Miranda v. Arizona**.[24] This case established the rights that must be given to a suspect who is in custody and being questioned by the police. The basis for this decision comes from the Fifth Amendment protection that we all have against self-incrimination. This right dictates that no one can be forced to testify, or give any statements to authorities, that could implicate them in any criminal act.

Prior to the 1936 Supreme Court case of *Brown v. Mississippi,* police would routinely coerce, and at times even physically abuse suspects, in order to obtain confessions.[25] In 1964, the U.S. Supreme Court again addressed how confessions could be obtained from suspects in the case of *Escobedo v. Illinois*.[26] In this case the Court recognized for the first time

© Bettmann/Contributor/Getty Images

that suspects need to be advised that they are entitled to have an attorney present whenever they are a suspect and are being questioned by the police. The ruling in *Escobedo* left some questions unanswered concerning exactly what rights needed to be given to suspects prior to questioning, other than the right to an attorney, and also left several other issues unanswered. The Court clarified their decision in the *Escobedo* case when they decided the *Miranda* case two years later in 1966.

_____ MIRANDA V. ARIZONA _____

To summarize, we hold that, when an individual is taken into custody or otherwise deprived of his freedom by the authorities in any significant way and is subjected to questioning, the privilege against self-incrimination is jeopardized. Procedural safeguards must be employed to protect the privilege, and unless other fully effective means are adopted to notify the person of his right of silence and to assure that the exercise of the right will be scrupulously honored, the following measures are required. ***He must be warned prior to any questioning that he has the right to remain silent, that anything he says can be used against him in a court of law, that he has the right to the presence of an attorney, and that, if he cannot afford an attorney one will be appointed for him prior to any questioning if he so desires.*** *Opportunity to exercise these rights must be afforded to him throughout the interrogation. After such warnings have been given, and such opportunity afforded him, the individual may knowingly and intelligently waive these rights and agree to answer questions or make a statement. But unless and until such warnings and waiver are demonstrated by the prosecution at trial, no evidence obtained as a result of interrogation can be used against him.*[27]

WHEN IS MIRANDA REQUIRED?

The Miranda Rights are required to be given to a suspect prior to any questioning when the suspect is going to be questioned in a custodial setting. A custodial setting would be anytime the suspect is under arrest or is otherwise being deprived of the freedom to leave.

WHEN IS MIRANDA NOT REQUIRED?

There are many situations that involve contact with the police that do NOT require the issuing of the Miranda Rights. Miranda is not required when:

1. The suspect makes a statement to the police before they ask a question.
2. The suspect gives a confession to a third party who is not the police. In these cases the third party may testify to what they were told.
3. The suspect is booked into a jail and is asked routine "booking questions" that include asking the suspect their name, address, date of birth, etc.

4. The suspect is stopped for a routine traffic violation.
5. The suspect is temporarily detained during a *Terry* stop.
6. The suspect is in the custody of the police but is not being asked any questions that would be "testimonial" in nature.
7. The suspect is intoxicated or does not understand English.

It is important to note that failing to give Miranda Rights to an arrested subject DOES NOT negate or make an arrest illegal. Miranda has nothing to do with the actual arrest; it only has to do with the questioning of a suspect in a custodial setting.

REVIEW QUESTIONS:

1. Prior to the 1960s, the United States Supreme Court maintained a _____ policy when it came to interfering with the procedures used by state and local police.

2. All arrests and search and seizures are based on the _____ Amendment to the U.S. Constitution.

3. All arrests must be based upon _____ _____.

4. In the 1968 case of _____, the U.S. Supreme Court ruled that a police officer may, under certain conditions, lawfully detain a suspect without arresting them.

5. _____ _____ is the level of evidence that a police officer needs in order to conduct a "stop and frisk."

6. The exclusionary rule was originally established in the U.S. Supreme Court case of _____.

7. _____ was the 1961 Supreme Court case that made the exclusionary rule applicable to all police officers in the United States.

8. The good faith exception and the inevitable discovery exception are both exceptions to the

   _____ _____.

9. _____ _____ _____ _____ _____ _____ allows an officer to conduct a complete search of an arrested person as well the area within their immediate control.

10. The _____ _____ doctrine states that if a police officer is lawfully at a location and he sees contraband within his view, he may seize it without a warrant.

11. In the 1925 Supreme Court case of _____, the Court first recognized that vehicles are highly mobile and police do not usually have time to obtain a search warrant.

12. It wasn't until _____ in the case of *Brown v. Mississippi* that the Supreme Court recognized that police could not coerce or physically abuse suspects in order to obtain a confession.

13. The Miranda Rights are required to be given to a suspect prior to any questioning, when the suspect

    is going to be questioned in a _____ setting.

CRITICAL THINKING QUESTIONS:

1. Explain the circumstances under which a police officer may make a lawful misdemeanor arrest without a warrant.

2. Discuss the differences between probable cause and reasonable suspicion and what each of these levels of evidence allow a police officer to do.

3. How does the fruit of the poisonous tree doctrine expand the exclusionary rule?

4. Select and explain two of the exceptions to the search warrant requirements that are discussed in this chapter.

5. Discuss at least three of the circumstances when a police officer does not have to advise an arrested suspect of his Miranda Rights.

NOTES

CHAPTER 7

[1] U.S. Supreme Courts are named for the Chief Justice who presides over the Court. Earl Warren served as Chief Justice of the United States Supreme Court from 1953 until 1969.

[2] Connie Estrada Ireland and George E. Rush, *The Dictionary of Criminal Justice With Summaries of Supreme Court Cases Affecting Criminal Justice,* 7th Edition, (New York: McGraw Hill Companies, Inc., 2011).

[3] Brinegar v. United States, 338 U.S. 160 (1949).

[4] Terry v. Ohio, 392 U.S. 1 (1968).

[5] United States v. Sokolow, 490 U.S. 1 (1989).

[6] Ibid.

[7] Hiibel v. Sixth Judicial Court of Nevada, Humbult County, et al., 542 U.S. 177 (2004).

[8] Minnesota v. Dickerson, 508 U.S. 366 (1993).

[9] Weeks v. U.S. 232 U.S. 383 (1914).

[10] Ireland, *Dictionary of Criminal Justice,* pg 420.

[11] Mapp v. Ohio, 367 U.S 643 (1961).

[12] Ibid.

[13] Siverthorne Lumber Co. v. U.S., 251 U.S. 385 (1920).

[14] United States v. Leon, 468 U.S. 897 (1984).

[15] Nix v. Williams, 467 U.S. 431 (1984).

[16] Robinson v. United States, 414 U.S. 234 (1973).

[17] Chimel v. California, 395 U.S. 752 (1969).

[18] Harris v. United States, 390 U.S. 234 (1968).

[19] Maryland v. Buie, 494 U.S. 325 (1990).

[20] Carroll v. U.S., 267 U.S. 132 (1925).

[21] New York v. Belton, 453 U.S. 454 (1981).

[22] Arizona v. Gant, 556 U.S. 332 (2009).

[23] United States v. Ross, 456 U.S. 798 (1982).

[24] Miranda v. Arizona, 384 U.S. 436 (1966).

[25] Brown v. Mississippi, 297 U.S. 278 (1936).

[26] Escobedo v. Illinois, 378 U.S. 478 (1964).

[27] Miranda v. Arizona, 384 U.S. 436 (1966).

CHAPTER OVERVIEW

There are two distinct court systems in the United States, the federal system and the courts of the individual states. Within this dual system, are also two primary divisions which consist of our civil courts and our criminal courts. This chapter focuses on the criminal court systems and the distinctions between them. In order to appreciate the court system in this country, you must first understand the concept of jurisdiction and be familiar with the various types of jurisdiction that individual courts may have.

The federal courts are comprised of a three tiered system with the district courts acting as the trial court, the U.S. Circuit Courts of Appeal are the intermediary appellate courts, and the U.S. Supreme Court is the highest court in the United States. The state court systems are diverse in their structure and consist of either two or three tiered systems, depending on the individual state.

CHAPTER LEARNING OBJECTIVES

After reading this chapter you will be able to:

1. Describe the difference between civil courts and criminal courts.
2. Understand the concept of jurisdiction as it applies to the courts.
3. Distinguish between the different types of judicial jurisdiction.
4. Explain the basic structure of the federal court system.
5. Compare the differences between the federal court system and that of the various states.
6. Describe how the United States Supreme Court selects the cases that it decides to hear.

--------- KEYWORDS ---------

Dual Court System	Preponderance of the Evidence
United States Supreme Court	Jurisdiction
Original Jurisdiction	Limited Jurisdiction
General Jurisdiction	Appellate Jurisdiction
Federal Court System	Federal District Courts
Federal Circuit Courts of Appeal	U.S. Supreme Court
John G. Roberts, Jr.	Rule of Four
Writ of certiorari	State Courts
Trial Courts	Appellate Courts

DEVELOPMENT OF THE AMERICAN COURT SYSTEM

Dual Court System

The United States of America has a dual court system which is comprised of the federal court system and the courts of the individual states.

The United States of America has a **dual court system** which is comprised of the federal court system and the courts of the individual states. Courts are established by statute or constitution and have the authority to make decisions on cases, controversies in law, and disputed matters of fact that are brought before it.[1]

Courts have been a part of America since settlers began coming here in the 1600s. By the time the United States became a country in 1776, each of the colonies had established their own court system. Today, all fifty states have their own court systems that operate independently and are established by the constitution and the statutes of the individual states. The federal court system was established by Article III, Section 1 of the United States Constitution which specifically set up the U.S. Supreme Court and gave congress the authority to set up and establish lower courts when it deemed necessary.

CIVIL AND CRIMINAL COURTS

The court system in the United States is divided into two primary divisions which are the civil system and the criminal system. Civil courts handle legal disputes between private parties, whether they are a person or a company or corporation. When a person brings a civil lawsuit, they are usually seeking a monetary award to reimburse actual damages inflicted (compensatory damages) or a monetary award to punish the one who was at fault for damages (punitive damages).

© Tomislav Forgo, 2011. Used under license from Shutterstock, Inc.

A person may also seek an injunction against the opposing party. An injunction is a court order that commands a person to a specific act, or to refrain from doing an act that would injure another by violating their personal or property rights. There are two ways to bring a case into civil court, which are a tort action or a breach of contract. A tort is a civil wrong that amounts to a breach of duty to an individual that results in damages to them.

In civil cases, the party that brings the suit is called the plaintiff and the party that is defending the action against them is the defendant. The level of evidence used to determine the outcome of a civil case is called the **preponderance of the evidence**. A preponderance of the evidence is much less stringent than the level of proof needed in a criminal case, which is proof beyond a reasonable doubt. In a civil case, the winner is determined by which party has the most impressive or convincing evidence.

Preponderance of the Evidence

This is the level of evidence used to determine the outcome of a civil case. The winner of a civil case is determined by which party has the most impressive or convincing evidence.

Criminal cases are brought forward by the government who is charging an individual with a criminal offense. The government is represented by a prosecutor who may be a District Attorney, an Attorney General, a Solicitor, a city or county attorney, or other government prosecutor depending on the jurisdiction of the case. The person who is charged with the crime is called the defendant, and as previously mentioned, in order to find a defendant guilty of a crime the government must prove its case beyond a reasonable doubt. This level of evidence is the highest standard of evidence that we have in this country.

© zimmytws, 2011. Used under license from Shutterstock, Inc.

JURISDICTION

Jurisdiction is the territory, subject matter, or persons over which a court has legal authority to hear and decide a certain type of case. State courts have jurisdiction over crimes committed within their geographic area. This is also often referred to as venue, which is the geographic area over which a court has territorial jurisdiction to decide cases. On the state level, a crime must be tried in the county in which it was committed. Federal courts have jurisdiction over federal laws.[2]

ORIGINAL JURISDICTION

Original jurisdiction is the authority of a court to hear and decide a lawsuit or criminal case that arises within a specific geographic area or territory.

LIMITED JURISDICTION

Courts of limited jurisdiction have original jurisdiction only over specific subject matter that is given to it by law. These are usually specialty courts and courts that hear and decide misdemeanor and ordinance type cases. Civil cases heard in these courts are usually limited to small claims. Municipal courts, justice courts, magistrate courts, traffic courts, and probate courts are all examples of courts of limited jurisdiction. Municipal courts, for example, are courts of limited jurisdiction because their original jurisdiction is restricted to city ordinances and violations of city laws. Traffic courts are limited to hearing traffic issues, probate courts hear issues that only deal with probate, and so on.

GENERAL JURISDICTION

Courts of general jurisdiction have original jurisdiction over all subject matter that is not specifically assigned to a court of limited jurisdiction. These are typically the trial courts for felonies and the courts that hear and decide civil lawsuits. Courts

THE DIFFERENCES BETWEEN FEDERAL AND STATE COURTS	
STRUCTURE	
THE FEDERAL COURT SYSTEM	THE STATE COURT SYSTEM
■ Article III of the Constitution invests the judicial power of the United States in the federal court system. Article III, Section 1 specifically creates the U.S. Supreme Court and gives Congress the authority to create the lower federal courts.	■ The Constitution and laws of each state establish the state courts. A court of last resort, often known as a supreme court, is usually the highest court in a state. Some states also have an intermediate court of appeals. Below these appeals courts are the state trial courts. Some are referred to as circuit or district courts.

Continued

■ Congress has used this power to establish the 13 U.S. courts of appeals, the 94 U.S. district courts, the U.S. Court of Claims, and the U.S. Court of International Trade. U.S. bankruptcy courts handle bankruptcy cases. Magistrate judges handle some district court matters.	■ States also usually have courts that handle specific legal matters; e.g., probate court (wills and estates), juvenile court, family court, etc.
■ Parties dissatisfied with a decision of a U.S. district court, the U.S. Court of Claims, and/or the U.S. Court of International Trade may appeal to a U.S. court of appeals.	■ Parties dissatisfied with the decision of the trial court may take their cases to the intermediate court of appeals.
■ A party may ask the U.S. Supreme Court to review a decision of the U.S. Court of Appeals, but the Supreme Court usually is under no obligation to do so. The U.S. Supreme Court is the final arbiter of federal constitutional questions.	■ Parties have the option to ask the highest state court to hear the case.
	■ Only certain state court cases are eligible for review by the U.S. Supreme Court.

of general jurisdiction will often also hear appeals from courts of limited jurisdiction. District courts, superior courts, and circuit courts are examples of courts with general jurisdiction.[3]

APPELLATE JURISDICTION

Courts with appellate jurisdictions can hear appeals from lower courts and review the judgments of those courts. Appeals are not trials, they are a review of the court transcripts, evidence, and legal briefs of the attorneys from both sides.

THE DIFFERENCES BETWEEN FEDERAL AND STATE COURTS—CONTINUED	
SELECTION OF JUDGES	
THE FEDERAL COURT SYSTEM	THE STATE COURT SYSTEM
(Article III, Section 1 of the Constitution) Federal judges are nominated by the President and confirmed by the Senate. They hold office during good behavior, typically, for life. Through congressional impeachment proceedings, federal judges may be removed from office for misbehavior.	**State court judges are selected in a variety of ways, including:** ■ election, ■ appointment for a given number of years, ■ appointment for life, and ■ combinations of these methods; e.g., appointment followed by election.

Continued

TYPES OF CASES HEARD	
THE FEDERAL COURT SYSTEM	THE STATE COURT SYSTEM
■ Cases that deal with the constitutionality of a law, ■ Cases involving the laws and treaties of the U.S., ■ Cases involving ambassadors and public ministers, ■ Disputes between two or more states, ■ Admiralty law, ■ Bankruptcy, and ■ Habeas corpus issues.	■ Most criminal cases ■ Probate (involving wills and estates) ■ Most contract cases ■ Tort cases (personal injuries) ■ Family law (marriages, divorces, adoptions, etc.) State courts are the final deciders of state laws and constitutions. Their interpretations of federal law or the U.S. Constitution may be appealed to the U.S. Supreme Court. The Supreme Court may choose to hear or not to hear such cases.

Source: Administrative Office of the U.S. Courts, at: http://www.uscourts.gov/FederalCourts/UnderstandingtheFederal Courts/Jurisdiction/DifferencebetweenFederalAndStateCourts.aspx.

FEDERAL COURT SYSTEM

Federal Court System

The federal court system is a three tiered system that was originally set up by Article III of the U.S. Constitution.

The **federal court system**, as we have seen, was originally set up by the U.S. Constitution. The federal court system is a three tiered system, which means that it has intermediate appellate courts between the trial courts and the Supreme Court. Federal courts hear cases involving:

1. The constitutionality of law
2. Laws and treaties of the United States
3. Ambassadors and public ministers
4. Disputes between two or more states
5. Admiralty law
6. Bankruptcy cases

The three tiers of the federal court system are:

1. District Courts
2. Federal Circuit Courts of Appeals
3. United States Supreme Court

DISTRICT COURTS

Federal District Courts

Federal district courts are the trial courts of the federal government.

Federal district courts are the trial courts of the federal government. The district courts have jurisdiction over almost every category of federal cases, including both criminal and civil cases. There are currently ninety-four federal judicial districts,

THE UNITED STATES FEDERAL COURTS
SUPREME COURT
—United States Supreme Court
APPELLATE COURTS
—U.S. Court of Appeals ■ 12 Regional Circuit Courts of Appeals ■ 1 U.S. Court of Appeals for the Federal Circuit
TRIAL COURTS
—U.S. District Courts ■ 94 judicial districts ■ U.S. Bankruptcy Court —U.S. Court of International Trade —U.S. Court of Federal Claims
FEDERAL COURTS AND OTHER ENTITIES OUTSIDE THE JUDICIAL BRANCH
—Military Courts (trial and appellate) —Court of Veterans Appeals —U.S. Tax Court —Federal administrative agencies and boards

Source: http://www.uscourts.gov/FederalCourts/UnderstandingtheFederalCourts/FederalCourtsStructure.aspx

which includes at least one district for every state, plus one district in each of the following: the District of Columbia, Puerto Rico, the Virgin Islands, Guam, and the Northern Mariana Islands. The federal district courts also include the U.S. Bankruptcy Courts. The U.S. Court of International Trade and the U.S. Court of Federal Claims are separate from the district courts, but are considered on the same judicial level.

There were 92,789 criminal cases brought into U.S. District Courts in 2012, of which 90.7 percent were for felonies.[4] Most of these defendants (93.4 percent) were convicted and 80.7 percent of those were sentenced to a term of incarceration in federal prison. The average prison sentence in 2012 was 56.6 months, with the longest sentences given to those who were convicted of violent crimes (122.9 months), felony weapons charges (79.6 months), and felony drug charges (75.5 months) It is interesting to note that there were a total of 26,806 people convicted of drug offenses in the Federal District Courts in 2012. Of these, only 82 people were convicted of federal possession and other lesser drug offenses. The remainder, 26,724 cases, were for drug trafficking.[5]

FEDERAL CIRCUIT COURTS OF APPEALS

The **Federal Circuit Courts of Appeals** consists of the ninety-four United States judicial districts which are organized into twelve regional circuits, each of which has a United States court of appeals. There is also one U.S. Court of Appeals for

Federal Circuit Courts of Appeals

The Federal Circuit Courts of Appeals consists of the ninety-four United States judicial districts which are organized into twelve regional circuits (plus the Federal Circuit), each of which has a United States court of appeals.

the Federal Circuit that is located in Washington D.C. and has nationwide appellate jurisdiction to hear appeals in specialized cases such as those involving patent laws. These appellate courts hear appeals from the district courts within their circuit, as well as appeals of decisions from federal administrative agencies.

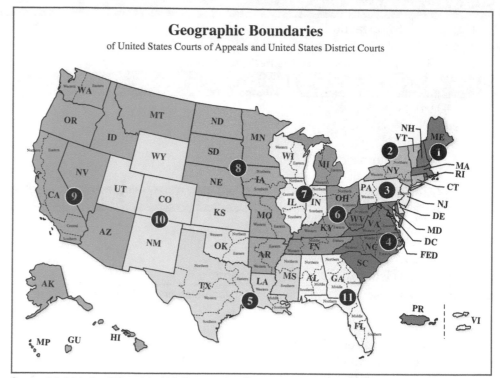

Geographic Boundaries
of United States Courts of Appeals and United States District Courts

Source: Administrative Office of the U.S. Courts at: http://www.uscourts.gov/uscourts/images/CircuitMap.pdf

THE UNITED STATES SUPREME COURT

United States Supreme Court

The United States Supreme Court is the highest court in the federal Judiciary and in the United States.

John G. Roberts Jr.

The current Chief Justice of the United states Supreme Court.

The **United States Supreme Court** is the highest court in the federal Judiciary and in the United States. The Supreme Court consists of the Chief Justice of the United States and eight associate justices. Supreme Court justices are appointed by the president and confirmed by the U.S. Senate, and once confirmed they serve for life. The current Chief Justice of the U.S. Supreme Court is **John G. Roberts, Jr.**

While the Supreme Court has original trial jurisdiction in some very specific and limited circumstances, the primary purpose of the Court is judicial review of lower court decisions. It is here that the Court determines if lower court decisions, as well as laws and statutes, comply with the intent of the United States Constitution. The Court is the final interpreter of the U.S. Constitution.

John G. Roberts, Jr.

There are between 6,000 and 7,000 requests for cases to be heard by the Supreme Court. These cases are reviewed and the Court selects about 80 of these cases that it will hear and rule on. The Court has complete control over what cases it will accept for review. In order for a case to be accepted for review, at least four of the Justices must agree to hear the case. This is called the "**rule of four**." Once the case is accepted for review, the Court issues a *writ of certiorari*, which is a court order that is issued to the lower court telling them to send up the record of the proceedings of the case.

Rule of Four

In order for a case to be accepted for review, at least four of the Justices must agree to hear the case.

Writ of Certiorari

A *writ of certiorari* is a court order that is issued by an appeals court to a lower court telling them to send up the record of the proceedings of the case.

STATE COURT SYSTEM

Each of the fifty states has its own court system. Some of these systems are similar to the structure of the federal system, in that they have a three tier system that utilizes an intermediate appellate court. Other states, those with less population, use a two tier system and eliminate the intermediate appellate court. In these states, appeals from the trial court go directly to the highest court in the state.

In 2015, over 86.2 million cases were filed in the state court systems within the United States. The majority of these cases (54 percent) were traffic cases. The remaining cases included civil cases, domestic relations, criminal, and juvenile cases.[6]

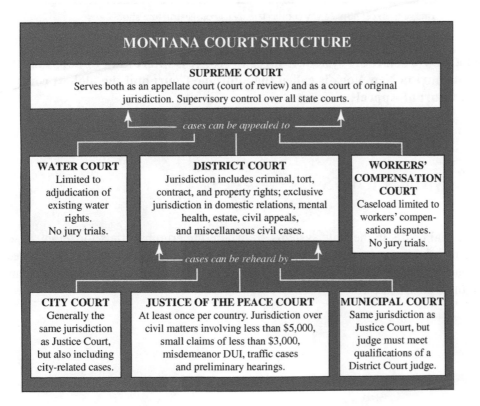

MONTANA COURT STRUCTURE

SUPREME COURT
Serves both as an appellate court (court of review) and as a court of original jurisdiction. Supervisory control over all state courts.

cases can be appealed to

WATER COURT
Limited to adjudication of existing water rights.
No jury trials.

DISTRICT COURT
Jurisdiction includes criminal, tort, contract, and property rights; exclusive jurisdiction in domestic relations, mental health, estate, civil appeals, and miscellaneous civil cases.

WORKERS' COMPENSATION COURT
Caseload limited to workers' compensation disputes.
No jury trials.

cases can be reheard by

CITY COURT
Generally the same jurisdiction as Justice Court, but also including city-related cases.

JUSTICE OF THE PEACE COURT
At least once per country. Jurisdiction over civil matters involving less than $5,000, small claims of less than $3,000, misdemeanor DUI, traffic cases and preliminary hearings.

MUNICIPAL COURT
Same jurisdiction as Justice Court, but judge must meet qualifications of a District Court judge.

The court system of Montana is a two tier system.

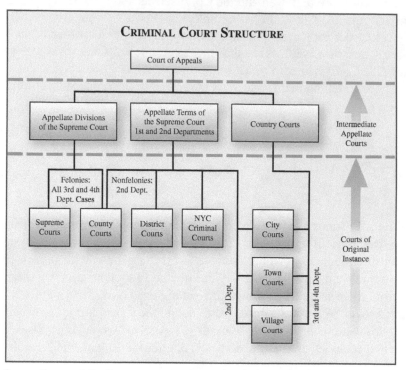

The New York court system is three tiered. It is interesting to note that the trial court in New York is called the Supreme Court and the highest court is the Court of Appeals.

𝒯RIAL COURTS

The trial courts in the state systems are where the criminal trials for felony cases are heard. These courts are the busiest in the entire United States. In 2015, an estimated 18.1 million criminal cases were heard by the various state court systems in the United States.[7]

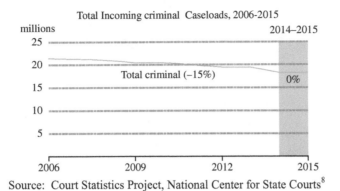

Total Incoming criminal Caseloads, 2006-2015

Source: Court Statistics Project, National Center for State Courts[8]

APPELLATE COURTS

The appellate courts in the state systems have appellate jurisdiction and review cases from the trial courts that are sent up on appeal. The state appellate courts review cases and base their rulings on the constitution of their respective states. In states with a three tier system, the initial appeal goes to the intermediate appeals court. Rulings that are appealed from these courts would then go to the state court of last resort, which is the equivalent of the Supreme Court at the state level. In states that have a two tier system, appeals from the trial courts of general jurisdiction would be sent directly to the court of last resort in the state.

REVIEW QUESTIONS:

1. The two primary divisions of the court system in the United States are the _____ and the

    _____ courts.

2. A _____ is a civil wrong.

3. _____ is the territory, subject matter, or persons over which a court has legal authority to hear and decide a certain type of case.

4. Article _____, Section _____ of the U.S. Constitution specifically creates the United States Supreme Court.

5. The federal court system is a _____ tier system.

6. The trial court in the federal court system is the _____ court.

7. There are _____ Regional Circuit Courts of Appeal in the federal court system.

8. _____ _____ is the current Chief Justice of the United States Supreme Court.

9. Once a case is accepted for review by the U.S. Supreme Court, the Court issues a _____

    _____ _____.

10. In states that have a two tiered court system, appeals from the trial court go directly to the court of

    _____ _____ within that state.

CRITICAL THINKING QUESTIONS:

1. Define, in your own words, the level of evidence referred to as the preponderance of the evidence.

2. Select and explain any two of the different types of jurisdiction that are discussed in this chapter.

3. Describe some of the key differences between the federal court system and the state court systems.

4. Explain the different ways that judges are selected in the state court systems.

5. Describe how a case is selected and heard by the U.S. Supreme Court.

——————————————————— NOTES ———————————————————

CHAPTER 8

[1] Connie Estrada Ireland and George E. Rush, *The Dictionary of Criminal Justice With Summaries of Supreme Court Cases Affecting Criminal Justice,* 7th Edition (New York: McGraw-Hill Companies, Inc., 2011).

[2] Ibid.

[3] Ibid.

[4] *Federal justice Statistics, 2012—Statistical Tables,* Bureau of Justice Statistics, U.S. Department of Justice, January 2015, accessed March, 2017 athttps://www.bjs.gov/content/pub/pdf/fjs12st.pdf.

[5] Ibid

[6] R. Schauffler, R. LaFountain, S. Strickland, K. Holt, & K. Genthon Examining the Work of State Courts: An Overview of 2015 State Court Caseloads (National Center for State Courts 2016)

[7] Ibid

[8] Ibid

PRETRIAL ACTIVITIES, THE CRIMINAL TRIAL, AND SENTENCING

CHAPTER OVERVIEW

© Andrea Donti, 2011. Used under license from Shutterstock, Inc.

A person enters the criminal justice system when they are arrested and charged with a criminal act. Once the person becomes a part of the system, they become a defendant and their Sixth Amendment rights are immediately (and automatically) put into effect. This chapter will explain all of these rights and how they are applied from the pretrial phases through the actual criminal trial. The stages of a criminal trial will be examined and explained in this chapter, from jury selection until the verdict is rendered by a judge or a jury.

Once a person has been found guilty of a felony in a federal or state court in the United States, a presentence investigation is typically requested by the court prior to the actual sentencing of the defendant. This report is a detailed background history of the defendant that is used to assist the judge in determining the proper sentence that should be imposed. This report is typically written by the probation department and also contains a recommended sentence that is based on results of the report.

Sentencing in the United States has undergone some major reform since the 1970's. Prior to this time the goal of sentencing was the rehabilitation of the offender. This philosophy of sentencing soon gave way to an emphasis on the punishment of the offender. This change came about because of increased crime rates and a new "get tough on crime" attitude that spread throughout the country. With this new reform movement came several new sentencing models that are now in use, in one form or another, in both the federal judicial system and those of the individual states.

The most severe sentence that can be imposed is that of the death penalty. This chapter will discuss the history of the death penalty in the United States as well as the legal issues that have been raised since the death penalty has been implemented. Methods of execution and the status of the death penalty today will also be discussed.

*C*HAPTER LEARNING OBJECTIVES

After reading this chapter you will be able to:

1. Understand the bail system and the alternative pretrial release procedures that may be used in different criminal cases.
2. Identify and explain the various pretrial activities that are used in the American court system.
3. Compare the grand jury system with the preliminary hearing and explain how they are both used to determine whether an arrest was lawful.
4. Explain what a plea bargain is and why it has become an important aspect of our judicial system.
5. List the rights that are afforded under the Sixth Amendment to the U.S. Constitution.
6. Identify the various stages of a criminal trial.
7. List the various section contained in a presentence report.
8. Explain how sentencing in the United States has changed since this 1970's.
9. Identify and various sentencing models that are currently in use in the United States.
10. Compare the indeterminate sentencing model with that of the structured sentencing model.
11. Understand the difference between aggravating and mitigating circumstances as they relate to sentencing.
12. Explain how the U.S. Supreme Court has dealt with the administration of the death penalty in the United States since 1967.
13. List the various methods that are legally used to execute prisoners in the United States today.

--------------------------- KEYWORDS ---------------------------

Booking	Bail
ROR	First Appearance
Preliminary Hearing	Grand Jury
Information	Arraignment
Plea Bargaining	Speedy Trial
Right to Counsel	Jury Selection
Venire	*Voir Dire*
Challenge for Cause	*Peremptory Challenge*
Opening Statements	Burden of Proof
Motion for Directed Verdict	Closing Arguments
Jury Instructions	Deliberation
Hung Jury	*Allen* Charge
Verdict PSI	Three Strike" Law

Truth in Sentencing
Structured Sentencing
Mandatory Sentences
Sentence Reform Act of 1984
Aggravating Circumstances
Concurrent Sentence
Furman v. Georgia

Indeterminate Sentencing
Determinate Sentencing
Presumptive Sentencing
Mitigating Circumstances
Consecutive Sentence
Georgia v. Gregg

Entering the Criminal Justice System

© corepics, 2011. Used under license from Shutterstock, Inc.

A person enters the criminal justice system when they are arrested and charged with a criminal act (a crime). When the police make an arrest, they will charge the suspect with a crime based upon the probable cause that they determined was present at the time of the arrest. The crime that the suspect is initially charged with is often changed by the prosecutor during the pretrial process (see plea bargaining).

BOOKING

After a person is arrested, they are taken to a jail facility where they are booked. The booking process consists of:

© Alita Bobrov, 2011. Used under license from Shutterstock, Inc.

1. Filing of the arrest report.
2. Taking fingerprints of the suspect.
3. Photographing the suspect ("mug" shot).
4. Obtaining the personal information of the suspect (name, address, birthdate, and other identifiers).

Once the person is booked, they are housed in the jail until such time that they can make bail or are brought to court for their first appearance (see following section).

BAIL AND PRETRIAL RELEASE

One of the basic presumptions of the criminal justice system in America is that of the presumption of innocence. All persons arrested of a crime are presumed to be innocent until proven guilty by a court. It is this presumption that allows for the provision of bail. **Bail**, while not a guaranteed right, is provided for in the Eighth Amendment of the United States Constitution. The Eight Amendment states that "excessive bail shall not be required."

Bail is a way for an accused individual to be released from custody prior to trial. Bail is the posting of money, property, or other collateral by the arrested person, as

Bail

Bail is a way for an accused individual to be released from custody prior to trial by posting money or some other form of collateral.

a way of guaranteeing they will appear in court to answer the charges against them. This is one of the foremost reasons for the allowing of bail in our system. This reason, release to guarantee appearance, has to be weighed against protecting society from the possible commission of more crimes by the suspect if they are released back into the community. Since bail is not a guarantee, certain charges are considered serious enough that no bail is allowed. Persons charged with capital offenses (those that could result in a sentence of death) and other serious offenses are routinely denied bail. The "excessive bail" provision also does not mean that a person cannot be given a bail totaling millions of dollars. This type of bail is routinely given in high level drug trafficking cases and in cases involving large amounts of embezzled or stolen property.

In many jurisdictions around the country, there are standard bail amounts that are posted in the booking facilities that will allow those accused to post a set amount of bail for certain crimes. These standard bails are usually agreed upon in advance by the judges within that jurisdiction. This type of procedure allows many of those accused of crimes to be released within a short amount of time without having to wait for an appearance before a judge or magistrate.

In addition to the posting of bail, there are other ways that an accused person can be released from jail prior to going to trial. Many factors are taken into consideration when making release decisions:

1. Prior criminal history of the accused.
2. The seriousness of the crime for which the person is currently charged.
3. Flight risk.
4. Job stability, family relationships, and other indicators that tie the accused to the community.

ROR

Release on recognizance (ROR) allows a person to be released from jail prior to trial on their promise to refrain from criminal activity and to return to court at the date and time specified without having to post collateral.

Many jurisdictions offer a variety of alternatives to releasing a person on bail. One of the most common of these is releasing on recognizance (ROR). **ROR** is allowing the accused to be released on their promise to refrain from criminal activity and to return to court at the date and time specified. The ROR release only requires the signature of the defendant. This type of release is often used for lesser crimes (certain misdemeanors) and is a way to alleviate overcrowding in the jails.

Another common alternative to bail is to be released on a program of house arrest. House arrest can be monitoring either electronically through the use of a bracelet and monitoring device, or with a curfew accompanied by a requirement of reporting daily to the jail or other facility for status checks.

$\mathcal{E}$NTERING THE COURT SYSTEM— PRETRIAL ACTIVITIES

FIRST APPEARANCE

If an arrested person is unable to make bail, they must be brought before a judge or magistrate "without unnecessary delay."[1] Depending on the jurisdiction, the accused person must be brought to court within forty-eight or seventy-two hours of their arrest. This time includes weekends and holidays. While jurisdictions can vary the time lapse required for a **first appearance**, the U.S. Supreme Court requires courts to determine whether or not the arrest was valid and was based upon probable cause within forty-eight hours of arrest.[2] Courts throughout the country have set up a variety of procedures to insure that this requirement is met, particularly on holiday weekends when courts are not actually in session.

When the arrested person is brought before the court for their first appearance, they are given formal notice of the charges against them. They are also read their Sixth Amendment rights, and if they request an attorney (and they qualify) one will be appointed for them at this time. This is also the time when bail can be set or other pretrial release sanctions can be discussed and imposed.

First Appearance

If an arrested person is unable to make bail, they must be brought before a judge or magistrate "without unnecessary delay" for their first appearance in court.

PRELIMINARY HEARING

About half of all states utilize the **preliminary hearing** and the other half (and the federal government) use a grand jury system (see the following). The preliminary or probable cause hearing is a formal court preceding that is used to determine if there is probable cause to justify the arrest and to send the case over to the grand jury (in some jurisdictions) or to the trial court.

The preliminary hearing is held in a courtroom and has many similarities to a trial. The prosecution presents witnesses who are sworn, and may present other evidence. The defendant is present with his/her attorney and may or may not present any evidence at this time. The prosecution does not have to present their entire case, they only have to present enough evidence and/or testimony to convince the judge or magistrate that the arrest was legal and the charges are based upon probable cause.

Preliminary Hearing

The preliminary or probable cause hearing is a formal court preceding that is used to determine if there is probable cause to justify the arrest and to send the case over to the grand jury (in some jurisdictions) or to the trial court.

THE GRAND JURY

The purpose of the **grand jury** is the same as that of the preliminary hearing; to determine if there was probable cause to justify the arrest and, if so, to send the case to the trial court. Grand juries usually consist of twenty-three citizens who have been subpoenaed to serve on the jury for a specified period of time. In most jurisdictions the grand jury meets in secret and the defendant is not notified of the hearing. The prosecutor calls witnesses into the grand jury room one at a time and swears them in. The prosecutor then asks the witness questions, after which time the jurors themselves may question the witness if they want. There is no cross examination since the defense is not even present. Similar to the preliminary hearing, the prosecutor does not have to present the entire case against the defendant, only enough to establish probable cause.

Grand Jury

The grand Jury serves the same purpose as the preliminary hearing except that this is not a trial type setting. Instead the evidence is heard by a jury of twenty-three (usually) citizens.

When the prosecutor finishes presenting the evidence, the grand jury meets alone and deliberates. If the jury determines that there is probable cause, they will issue an indictment, or a "true bill." The case is then sent to the trial court. If the grand jury does not find probable cause, they will issue a "no bill" and the case is over.

INFORMATION

Information

The information is a formal accusation submitted to the court by a prosecutor and alleges that a specific person(s) has committed a specific offense(s).

Once a defendant has been bound over to the trial court, either by a determination by the judge in the preliminary hearing or by indictment of the grand jury, the prosecutor files an **information**. The information is a formal accusation submitted to the court by a prosecutor and alleges that a specific person(s) has committed a specific offense(s).[3]

ARRAIGNMENT

Arraignment

The arraignment is the first time the defendant is brought before the court that has the jurisdiction to actually conduct the trial.

The **arraignment** is the first time the defendant is brought before the court that has the jurisdiction to actually conduct the trial. The arraignment is a formal hearing where the defendant stands before the judge and is:

1. Informed or the charges for which they will be tried.
2. Read their Sixth Amendment rights.
3. Enter a plea.

When asked to enter a plea, the defendant has several options. The defendant may enter a plea of not guilty in which case the judge will then set a trial date. If the defendant enters a plea of guilty, a date will then be set for sentencing. Sentencing usually occurs thirty to sixty days after the plea in order to allow enough time to have a pre-sentence report submitted to the court (see Chapter 10). The defendant may also enter

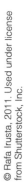

a plea of *nolo contendere* (no contest). *Nolo contendere* has the same effect as a guilty plea; however, it is usually used in cases where there may be civil proceedings filed against the defendant at a later date because it is not an admission of guilt in civil court.[4] If the defendant refuses to enter a plea, they "stand mute" and the judge will enter a plea of not guilty for the defendant and set a trial date.

© Cupertino, 2011.
Used under license from
Shutterstock, Inc.

*P*LEA BARGAINING

Plea bargaining is the negotiation between the prosecutor and the defendant (usually the defendants attorney) which results in the defendant entering a plea of guilty in exchange for a reduction of charges, or the prosecutors promise to recommend a more lenient sentence than the defendant would ordinarily receive.[5] The U.S. Supreme Court allowed the use of plea bargaining in the 1970 case of *Brady v. United States.*[6]

In 2006, state courts in the United States sentenced 1,232,290 persons for felony convictions and plea bargaining was used in 94 percent of these cases.[7] Plea bargaining receives a lot of criticism because it seems like the courts just give offenders a "slap on the wrist." The reality is, without plea bargaining, our entire criminal justice system would probably collapse. Our court system could not possibly handle 1.2 million actual trials every year. There just are not enough courthouses, judges, or staff to allow for that. An often overlooked fact is that 69 percent of those felons who do plead guilty under plea bargain agreements are actually sentenced to a period of confinement (41 percent to state prison and 28 percent to local jails).[8]

Plea Bargaining

Plea bargaining is the negotiation between the prosecutor and the defendant (usually the defendants attorney) which results in the defendant entering a plea of guilty in exchange for a reduction of charges or sentence.

*L*EGAL ISSUES

There are two very important legal issues, both of which are contained in the Sixth Amendment, that impact the court system in the United States: the right to a speedy trial and the right to an attorney.

SPEEDY TRIAL

The Sixth Amendment of the United States Constitution states: "In all criminal prosecution, the accused shall enjoy the right to a speedy and public trial." The U.S. Supreme Court has recognized that there is in fact a right to a **speedy trial**

Speedy Trial

While the Sixth Amendment of the United States Constitution states that the accused in any criminal prosecution is entitled to a speedy and public trial, the Court has left it up to the states to define the time constraints.

for all citizens accused of crimes,[9] however, they have never actually defined the time frame in which a trial must be commenced in order to comply with this provision. In the 1967 case of *Barker v. Wingo*[10] the Court stated that only in the case of delays that are unwarranted and prejudicial can the defendant claim a violation of their Sixth Amendment rights. The provision providing for a speedy trial was applied to the states in 1973 in the case of *Strunk v. U.S.*[11]

Many states have enacted their own statutes that define the time frames that courts must follow in order to comply with the provisions of a speedy trial within their respective jurisdictions. The United States Congress passed the federal Speedy Trial Act in 1974 (which was amended in 1979), which defines the time frames that federal courts must follow in order to comply with the speedy trial provisions. The federal Speedy Trial Act states that there can no more than[12]:

1. Thirty days between arrest and indictment.
2. Ten days between indictment and arraignment.
3. Sixty days between arraignment and trial.

RIGHT TO COUNSEL

Like most of the rights afforded by the U.S. Constitution, the Sixth Amendment guarantee "... to have assistance of counsel for his defense" has undergone a transition over the years by the U.S. Supreme Court:

- 1932—states must appoint counsel for indigent in capital cases.[13]
- 1938—indigent defendants are entitled to appointed counsel in federal criminal cases.[14]
- 1963—indigent defendants are entitled to appointed counsel in state felony cases.[15]
- 1972—states must provide counsel to indigents in any case where they may receive a sentence of imprisonment.[16]
- 2002—counsel must be provided to the indigent even for minor offenses if there is even a slight chance of the defendant getting a sentence of incarceration.[17]

© Andrey Burmakin, 2011. Used under license from Shutterstock, Inc.

The question of who qualifies for government funded counsel has been left up to the individual states and local jurisdictions. Generally the defendant who asks for appointed counsel will be required to fill out a financial questionnaire that will be reviewed by the court to determine if the person qualifies.

There are several ways that the state and local courts comply with the appointment of counsel for the poor. The most common is the use of public defenders. Public defenders are full-time, government-paid attorneys who are assigned indigent cases from the court during the pretrial stages of the court process. The public defender system has come under a considerable amount of criticism over the years because of their high caseloads and the fact that they are a part of the government run court system. Proponents, on the other hand, point out that public defenders know the local court system better than other, outside attorneys and handle only criminal defense cases.

Another system that some courts use to provide indigent counsel is that of court-appointed counsel. In these jurisdictions, the court assigns local attorneys cases as they come up and the attorneys are paid a fee for defending the accused. Critics of this system are quick to point out that the fees paid the attorneys are generally very low and consequently they are very reluctant to take a case to trial.

The third method used to provide indigent counsel is the use of contract attorneys. Local attorneys and law firms bid for contracts from the local government in order to provide defense services for the court.

*T*HE CRIMINAL TRIAL

A trial is the examination in a court of the issues of fact and law in a case for the purpose of reaching a judgment.[18] There are two basic types of trials: bench and jury trials. A bench trial (or a nonjury trial) is a trial where there is no jury, just a judge. The judge is responsible for hearing the facts of the case and issuing rulings on matters of law. A jury trial is one in which a jury is empanelled and they are to determine the issues of fact in a case and render a verdict. The judge is still responsible for deciding and ruling on all issues of law.

JURY SELECTION

The first order of business in a jury trial is the **selection of the jury**. The jurors, or the jury pool, are selected randomly from the citizens of the community where the trial is going to be held. Depending on the jurisdiction, prospective jurors are

Selection of the Jury
The first order of business in a jury trial is the selection of the jury.

© Ginae McDonald, 2011. Used under license from Shutterstock, Inc.

usually selected from the voter registration lists or the driver license rolls. Once
the jurors have been summoned, they form the *venire*. The **venire** is the group of
prospective jurors summoned by the court to report at a specified date and time.

Once the *venire* has been summoned, the next step is to question the prospective jurors to determine their qualifications to serve on the jury. This questioning
is called the **voir dire**. The defense attorney, the prosecutor, and the judge get to
ask questions of the prospective jurors during the *voir dire* in order to determine if
they have any relationship to any of the parties involved in the trial (the defendant,
attorneys, judge, or any of the anticipated witnesses), or have any preconceived
prejudices or bias.

Both the prosecution and the defense may challenge the jurors during the *voir
dire*. Challenging a juror is a way of removing that juror from the *venire*. There are
two types of challenges that are used; challenge for cause and peremptory challenge. A **challenge for cause** is a challenge where the attorney (either prosecution
or defense) must state a reason why they feel that juror should not serve on the jury.
Challenges for cause are usually used when the prospective juror shows any type
of prejudice or bias towards the case, indicates that they have a relationship with
any of the members of the trial, or state that they have already formed an opinion
on the case. There is no limit to the number of challenges for cause by either side.

Peremptory challenges are also made by both the prosecution and the defense. The attorneys do not have to state a reason for wanting a juror removed
from the jury pool when using peremptory challenges. Unlike the challenges for
cause, there are limits to the number of peremptory challenges that are allowed.
The number of these challenges is usually set by statute.

OPENING STATEMENTS

Once the jury has been selected, the trial begins. The first part of the trial is the
opening statements. The opening statements are made by both the prosecution
and the defense; however, neither side is required to make one. These statements
are a brief outline of the case that they will present. The attorneys can talk about
what evidence they intend to present and what they anticipate witnesses will say
during the trial. Opening statements are not evidence, and jurors are not to consider
these statements when they deliberate over the case at the conclusion of the trial.
The attorneys are required to limit their opening statements to comments about
what they believe will be presented during the trial.[19]

THE PROSECUTION'S CASE

Since the **burden of proof** is always on the prosecution to prove their case beyond
a reasonable doubt, they always present their case first. The prosecution will call
their witnesses to the stand and question them. When the prosecutor questions the
witness it is called direct examination. During direct examination, the prosecutor
may not ask the witness any leading questions. A leading question is one where the
answer is implied in the question itself. "You saw the defendant leave the scene of

the crime in a red car didn't you?" This would be an example of a leading question because the prosecutor is implying that the car was red.

When the prosecutor has concluded the questioning of the witness, the defense gets a chance to question that same witness. The Sixth Amendment of the United States Constitution states: "In all criminal prosecutions, the accused shall enjoy the right ... to be confronted with witnesses against him." This questioning is call cross-examination of the witness. Attorneys are allowed more leeway in the way they question witnesses during cross-examination.

This procedure of direct examination and cross-examination continues until all of the prosecutors witnesses have testified.

The prosecution will also present any physical evidence, documentary evidence, and any other type of evidence they may have during this phase of the trial. When all of the prosecutor's evidence has been submitted, the prosecution will rest its case.

MOTION FOR DIRECTED VERDICT

After the prosecution rests, the defense will many times make a motion for a directed verdict. When this motion is made, the defense is telling the judge that the prosecution failed to meet its burden of proof and did not prove all of the elements of the crime beyond a reasonable doubt. This motion is rarely granted, but if it is the judge will find the defendant not guilty and the trial is over.

THE DEFENDANT'S CASE

Once the prosecution rests, it is the defense's turn to present its case to the jury. The procedure is the same as that used to present the prosecution's case, except that the roles are reversed. The defense attorney will call up any witnesses that they have and the defense will question them first under direct examination. When the defense is finished questioning their witness the prosecutor gets to cross-examine them.

The purpose of the defense during their cross-examination of prosecution witnesses and the direct examination of their own witnesses is to raise reasonable doubt in the mind of the jurors. They attempt to do this in a variety of ways, and if they are successful they can win the case for their client, the defendant.

One of the most critical decisions that the defense must make is whether or not to have the defendant take the stand and testify in their own behalf. One of the biggest reasons for not putting the defendant on the stand is the fact that they will be subject to cross-examination by the prosecution. It is important to note that the prosecution is not allowed to comment to a jury on the defendant's refusal to take the stand on their own behalf.[20]

CLOSING ARGUMENTS

Closing Arguments

Closing arguments are a summary of all of the evidence that has been presented during the trial. Closing arguments are not evidence and are given by both the prosecutor and the defense attorney.

When both sides have presented all of their respective evidence and have rested their case, the attorneys are given one more opportunity to talk to the jury in the form of **closing arguments**. Closing arguments are a summary of all of the evidence that has been presented during the trial. The prosecutor will attempt to persuade the jury that they have met their burden of proof, have proven each and every element of the crime charged, and that the defendant is guilty. The defense will attempt to convince the jury that the prosecution did not prove their case beyond a reasonable doubt and that they, the jury, should find the defendant not guilty of the crime charged.

JURY INSTRUCTIONS

The last phase of the trial before the jury deliberates is the charge to the jury, or the jury instructions. During this phase the judge gives the jurors the applicable rules of law that pertain to the case. If the defendant did not take the stand, the judge will explain to the jury that they are not to draw any inferences, positive or negative, from the decision not to testify. The judge will also explain about the possible verdicts that the juror can render, and will tell the jurors the proper procedures to use from selecting a foreman to writing the verdict.

DELIBERATION

Hung Jury

If the jury cannot come to a unanimous verdict then they are a hung jury.

Once the jury has been given their instructions, the will be taken to the jury room and begin their deliberations. The deliberation, which is where the jury discusses the evidence of the case, is done in complete secrecy. Criminal cases in most jurisdictions require that the jury reach a unanimous verdict. If the jury is unable to reach a unanimous decision, it is a hung jury. If the jury cannot come to a verdict and are a **hung jury**, the case will go back to the prosecutor and a decision will have to be made as to whether to retry the case and start all over again at a later date.

Allen Charge

An *Allen* charge allows the judge to tell the jurors who are in the minority in a hung jury to reconsider their decision and see if they can change their mind and vote with the majority.

In some jurisdictions, if the jury tells the judge that they are "hung," the judge can send them back for further deliberation. If there are only a few jurors who are not in the majority, some states allow the judge to give what is called an **Allen charge**.[21] An *Allen* charge allows the judge to tell the jurors who are in the minority to reconsider their decision and see if they can change their mind and vote with the majority.

VERDICT

The jury can render one of three verdicts:

1. Guilty
2. Not guilty
3. Hung jury

If the jury finds the defendant guilty, the judge will set a sentencing date. If the jury finds the defendant not guilty, the judge will release the defendant from custody (if not on bail).

*P*RESENTENCE INVESTIGATION (PSI)

When a defendant is found guilty of a felony by a judge or jury in a trial, or pleads guilty before a judge, a date is set for a sentencing hearing. This hearing is routinely set thirty to sixty days in the future so that there is time to obtain a presentence investigation (**PSI**). The presentence investigation is a detailed background investigation that is conducted on the defendant to assist the judge in determining what sentence should be imposed.

In most jurisdictions, the presentence investigation is written by the probation department. The report looks into the defendant's background and includes:

PSI

The presentence investigation (PSI) is a detailed background investigation that is conducted on the defendant to assist the judge in determining what sentence should be imposed.

1. Family history, including where the defendant lives, who they live with, marriages, divorces, number of children, etc.
2. Educational history
3. Employment history
4. Military history
5. Criminal history
6. A summary of the offense for which they are going be sentenced on
7. A summary of an interview with the defendant
8. A written statement of the defendant if they want one included
9. A written statement from the victim of the crime
10. A recommendation for sentence

© Maaike Boot, 2011. Used under license from Shutterstock, Inc.

The recommendation for sentence is one of the most important sections of the presentence investigation. The probation department takes all of the information that they have gathered about the defendant and develops a recommended sentence based on several variables, including sentencing guidelines, risks and needs of the defendant, and other factors. The recommendation could be for prison or jail time, probation, or a combination of both. The recommendation will also include any special conditions that should be imposed, such as counseling, community service, fines, electronic monitoring, curfews, etc. The judge is the final determiner of the sentence; however, the PSI has a tremendous influence on what sentence will be imposed.

SENTENCING REFORM IN THE UNITED STATES

Starting around 1900, almost all of the states in the United States used an indeterminate criminal sentencing system. The primary goal of the system was to rehabilitate the offenders so they could re-enter society as productive and lawful citizens. The roles of the participants in the criminal justice system—the judges, correctional agencies, and parole officials—were clearly defined. This system provided for a relatively stable incarceration rate for almost seventy years.[22]

"Three-Strike" Laws
Some states have enacted mandatory sentencing laws called "three strikes" that mandate long term incarceration for offenders upon conviction of their third felony.

"Truth in Sentencing" Laws
States that have enacted truth in sentencing laws have done so in order to reduce the possibility of early release from incarceration.

Sentencing reform in the United States began in earnest in the late 1970s. The emphasis on rehabilitation began to give way to an emphasis on punishment as the primary goal of imprisonment. States and the federal government initiated a very serious "get tough on crime" policy. New policies and laws designed to identify hard-core criminals and insure longer sentences of imprisonment for them were being adopted throughout the country. **"Three-strike" laws** which required mandatory sentencing and **"truth in sentencing" laws** all gained popularity, and were significant contributing factors to the dramatic increase in prison populations in the United States. Additionally, there has been a substantial increase in the construction of prisons since the 1980s. It is also important to note that crime rates in the United States began to decrease significantly during this same period of time.[23]

SENTENCING MODELS

Since the sentencing reform movement in the 1970s and 1980s, there are now several sentencing models that are used in different parts of the United States:

1. Indeterminate sentencing
2. Structured sentencing
   A. Determinant sentencing
   B. Mandatory sentencing
   C. Presumptive sentencing

INDETERMINATE SENTENCING

Indeterminate sentencing is a sentence that provides for a range of time and includes a minimum time that the person must serve before becoming eligible for parole consideration, and a maximum amount of time that indicates the completion or discharge date. Indeterminate sentencing gives the sentencing judge considerable discretion in being able to adjust the sentence. Prior to the 1970s, virtually every state was using some form of indeterminate sentencing. States that have continued to utilize indeterminate sentencing also maintain parole boards. Once a person is sentenced to prison under an indeterminate sentence, they become eligible for parole after serving the minimum part of the sentence. The parole board then has the discretion to decide whether or not to release the inmate on parole.

© Andrey Burmakin/Shutterstock.com Inc.

Indeterminate Sentencing
This is a sentence that that provides for a range of time and includes a minimum time that the person must serve before becoming eligible for parole consideration, and a maximum amount of time that indicates the completion or discharge date.

STRUCTURED SENTENCING

There are many opponents to the indeterminate model of sentencing. These opponents say that indeterminate sentencing allows for too much judicial discretion, which in turn allows for too much sentencing disparity. Offenders who commit the same crime, even within the same jurisdiction, often receive completely different sentences. The system became very offender specific, rather than offense specific, when it came to sentencing. This disparity in sentences was blamed on limitless judicial and parole board power and the fact that they made their decisions without having to show documentation as to why. Additionally, rising crime rates, the public's fear of crime, and the social problems of the 1960s (civil rights, Vietnam War protests, the widespread openness of the drug culture, etc.) became concerns of elected officials that led to a sentencing revolution in the United States in the 1970s.[24]

A variety of new sentencing models were implemented throughout the country. These new methods of sentencing were designed to reduce judicial discretion and were part of a "get tough on crime" approach to dealing with criminals. These new models fall under a general category of **structured sentencing**, and included determinate sentencing, mandatory sentencing, and presumptive sentencing.

Structured Sentencing
Structured sentences were designed to reduce judicial discretion when it comes to sentencing. Determinate sentencing, mandatory sentencing, and presumptive sentencing all fall under the heading of structured sentencing.

DETERMINATE SENTENCING

Determinate sentencing is a fixed term of incarceration. When offenders are sentenced in a determinate sentencing state, they are given their anticipated release date from prison on the day they are sentenced. Each state has established their own statutes that dictate how much "good time" a prisoner can earn while serving time in prison and that is calculated into the anticipated release date. Determinate sentencing is an

Determinate Sentencing
Determinate sentencing is a fixed term of incarceration.

attempt to reduce sentencing disparity by making the sentences offense specific and not offender specific. Under this model, all persons convicted of the same criminal offense (burglary, robbery, etc.) would, theoretically at least, receive the same sentence.

Determinate sentencing states have, for the most part, done away with parole boards because they are no longer necessary due to the fact that there is very little (or no) discretion concerning the release date of the prisoner. States that have retained parole boards have greatly reduced their discretionary decision making authority.

MANDATORY SENTENCING

Mandatory Sentences

Mandatory sentences require that a certain penalty will be set and carried out in all cases upon conviction for a specified offense (e.g., all persons convicted of burglary would get the same sentence).

Mandatory sentences are an attempt to severely reduce sentencing discretion by setting all punishments for specific crimes statutorily. It is a statutory requirement that a certain penalty will be set and carried out in all cases upon conviction for a specified offense.[25] All states have at least some form of mandatory sentencing for some crimes. Many states have enacted laws that mandate a specific penalty for a third conviction of DUI or domestic battery that the courts are required to impose upon conviction.

© matis, 2011. Used under license from Shutterstock, Inc

Arguably the most extreme form of mandatory sentencing would be the "three strikes" laws that have been adopted in one form or another by at least twenty-five states.[26] "Three strikes" laws are a type of mandatory minimum sentencing structure in which judges have little or no discretion and must impose lengthy terms of incarceration on defendants who have two serious or violent felony convictions on their record prior to being convicted of a third.[27] California has had the most visible form of "three strikes" laws in that it states that any felony could be charged and counted as the third strike. California saw a rise in their prison population of third strike offenders from 254 in 1994 to 7,234 in 2003.[28]

PRESUMPTIVE SENTENCING

Presumptive Sentencing

Presumptive sentencing is a model that combines the use of indiscriminate sentencing with that of determinate sentencing.

Sentencing Reform Act of 1984

The goal of the Sentencing Reform Act of 1984 was to eliminate sentencing disparity through the use of guidelines that were based on both offense and offender characteristics.

Presumptive sentencing is a model that combines the use of indeterminate sentencing with that of determinate sentencing. This model allows for more judicial discretion than the other forms of structured sentencing, but not as much as the indeterminate model allows for. The discretion is limited by sentencing guidelines that are set up by state sentencing commissions. The federal government passed the Sentencing Reform Act of 1984 that was a form of presumptive sentencing and became a model for the sentencing reform of several states. The Sentencing Reform Act of 1984 was established as a part of the Comprehensive Crime Control Act and set up the U.S. Sentencing Commission. The purpose of the Commission is to review and adjust the sentencing guidelines annually.

The goal of the **Sentencing Reform Act of 1984** was to eliminate sentencing disparity through the use of guidelines that were based on both offense and offender characteristics. The federal government, when they adopted this form of sentencing, eliminated the Federal Parole Commission, which in turn eliminated the need for federal parole officers. Federal prisoners must serve 85 percent of their sentence prior to being released from prison. When the prisoner has served the mandatory amount of time, they are "conditionally released" and are supervised by federal probation officers.

Under presumptive sentencing, the judge must take aggravating and mitigating circumstances (see later in this chapter) into consideration before sentencing the offender. Once these factors have been considered and applied, the judge must use the Federal Sentencing Guideline Manual to determine the actual sentence that will be imposed.[29]

*I*SSUES IN SENTENCING

Even with all of the sentencing reforms over the past three decades, several factors are often taken into consideration prior to the actual sentencing of a convicted person.

AGGRAVATING AND MITIGATING CIRCUMSTANCES

Aggravating circumstances are factors that relate to the commission of a specific crime that cause its severity to be greater than that of a typical instance of the same type of offense. Aggravating circumstances may justify a harsher sentence for the defendant. **Mitigating circumstances** are those that favor the defendant and tend to reduce some of the blame for the crime. These circumstances may justify a reduced sentence for the defendant.

TYPICAL AGGRAVATING CIRCUMSTANCES

1. Use of a weapon during the commission of the crime

© jules2000, 2011.
Used under license from Shutterstock, Inc.

Aggravating Circumstances

Aggravating circumstances are factors that relate to the commission of a specific crime that cause its severity to be greater than that of a typical instance of the same type of offense.

Mitigating Circumstances

Mitigating circumstances are those that favor the defendant and tend to reduce some of the blame for the crime.

2. Prior convictions for the same type of offense
3. Causing serious bodily harm

4. Committing a crime for hire

5. Crime was committed to avoid or prevent lawful arrest
6. The victim was elderly
7. The victim was a child

8. The crime was gang related
9. The victim of the crime was selected because of race, ethnicity, sexual orientation, religion, or because of the mental or physical disability of the victim

TYPICAL MITIGATING CIRCUMSTANCES

1. The crime was committed while the defendant was under extreme mental or emotional disturbance

© robodread, 2011.
Used under license from Shutterstock, Inc.

2. The victim was a participant in the defendant's criminal conduct
3. The defendant had no prior criminal history
4. The defendant acted under duress or under the domination of another person
5. The young age of the defendant

© Sascha Burkard, 2011.
Used under license from Shutterstock, Inc.

CONCURRENT AND CONSECUTIVE SENTENCES

In cases where a defendant is found or pleads guilty to more than one crime or more than one count of a single crime, the judge, in most cases, has the option of sentencing the defendant to concurrent or consecutive time. If the judge gives the defendant a **concurrent sentence**, that means the defendant will serve each of the separate sentences at the same time. **Consecutive sentencing** means that the defendant will serve the first sentence and only then will the second sentence start.

If the defendant is sentenced on two counts of burglary and given a five year sentence on each count, under a concurrent sentence, both five year sentences will be served at the same time. The defendant will complete the sentence at the end of five years (less good time). If that same defendant is given a consecutive sentence, the first five year sentence must be completed (less good time) before the second sentence begins.

Concurrent Sentence

Concurrent sentencing that means the defendant will serve each of the separate sentences at the same time.

Consecutive Sentencing

Consecutive sentencing means that the defendant will serve the first sentence and only then will the second sentence start.

© Junial Enterprises, 2011. Used under license from Shutterstock, Inc.

VICTIM CONSIDERATIONS

Prior to the 1970s, sentencing decisions gave little or no consideration to the needs or concerns of the victims of crime. Since that time, the needs of the victim have become a major concern of the courts. Every state has written laws dealing with the legal rights of victims. In addition to the statutory rights of victims, thirty-two states have adopted state victims' rights constitutional amendments that have been made a part of their state constitutions. The federal government has proposed, on several occasions, a constitutional amendment dealing with victim's rights.

The victims' bills of rights that have been incorporated into the various state constitutions and/or state laws generally include the following rights[30]:

1. To be notified of proceedings and the status of the defendant
2. To be present at certain criminal justice proceedings
3. To make a statement at sentencing or other times
4. To receive restitution from a convicted offender
5. To be consulted before a case is dismissed or a plea bargain is entered
6. To a speedy trial
7. To keep the victim's contact information confidential

DEATH PENALTY

© Boris15, 2011. Used under license from Shutterstock, Inc.

The death penalty is, obviously, the most severe sentence that our judicial system can impose. The death penalty is reserved for only the most heinous of crimes. Prior to America becoming a country, in the 1600s a person could be put to death for such crimes as murder, adultery, sodomy, witchcraft, and blasphemy. The 1700s saw people put to death for robbery, forgery, and illegally cutting down a tree.[31] Today, the death penalty is reserved for first degree murder in the thirty-five states that still utilize the death penalty. The federal government also has a death penalty that is reserved for thirty-two separate offenses, most of which deal with the murder of various federal officials, treason, and terrorist related activities.[32]

THE LEGALITY OF THE DEATH PENALTY

Over the years, there have been many Supreme Court challenges to the death penalty, with the majority of them raising the Eighth Amendment guarantee against "cruel and unusual punishment." In 1967, the Supreme Court reviewed the way the death penalty was administered in the United States and found several serious concerns in the process. As a result, the Court put a moratorium on executions that remained in effect until 1977, when it was lifted and executions were again allowed. In 1972, the court ruled in the case of *Furman v. Georgia*, that the death penalty was often used arbitrarily and seemed to be disproportionally used based on race and not on the seriousness of the crime.[33] The Court did not say that the death penalty was constitutionally invalid, just that the procedures used had to be restructured to provide a fair and equitable way of deciding who qualified for execution.

The State of Georgia developed new laws and procedures in an attempt to satisfy the conditions for applying fairness and equity in the death penalty requirements. Another Georgia case, *Georgia v. Gregg*, reached the U.S. Supreme Court in 1976. The Court stated that the new procedures as used in this case met the standards of fairness and equity, and reinstated the death penalty in the United States.[34]

The new procedures for applying the death penalty incorporated the use of a bifurcated, or two-stage, process for deciding if a defendant qualified for the death penalty. The bifurcated system is used in capital cases and requires that the jury first listen to the evidence, as in a regular trial, and then deliberates to determine the guilt or innocence of the defendant. If the defendant is found guilty, a second hearing is held using the same jury. This second hearing is used to determine whether to sentence the defendant to death or to give a life sentence. The evidence that is presented in this second hearing deals with the aggravating and the mitigating circumstances of the case. If the jury decides that there are statutory aggravated circumstances, and they outweigh the mitigating circumstances, they can decide to impose the death penalty.

Since 1977, the U.S. Supreme Court has made several rulings that have restricted the types of crimes that are eligible for the death penalty and the categories of offenders who can receive a sentence of death. In 1977 the Court ruled that the death penalty cannot be used in cases of rape if the woman did not die during the commission of the crime.[35] The Court banned the execution of "mentally retarded" persons in 2002[36] and banned the execution of persons who were under the age of eighteen (at the time the offense was committed) in 2005.[37] In 2008, the Court invalidated a Louisiana law that allowed for the execution of child rapists.[38] In this case the Court argued that the execution for a crime where the victim is still alive is not proportional.

Furman v. Georgia
A 1972 U.S. Supreme Court case that suspended all executions in the United States because the death penalty was often used arbitrarily and disproportionally used based on the race of the defendant.

Georgia v. Gregg
A 1976 U.S. Supreme Court case that reinstated the death penalty in all states that use a bifurcated (two-stage) process for deciding if a defendant qualified for the death penalty.

METHODS OF EXECUTION

While many forms of execution have been employed throughout history, the only methods that are currently sanctioned are:

1. Lethal injection

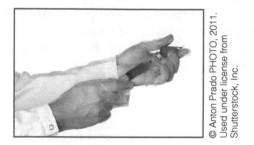

2. Electrocution

3. Gas chamber
4. Hanging

5. Firing squad

Lethal injection is the most commonly used method of execution and has been adopted as the primary device in all states that employ the death penalty, as well as the federal government.

THE DEATH PENALTY TODAY

At year-end 2013, there were 2,979 inmates under a sentence of death in thirty-five states and the federal government. Of these inmates, 55.8 percent of these were white and 41.9 percent were black; and 98.1 percent were male and only 1.9 percent were female. In 2014 there were a total of 35 executions in the United States and all were carried out by lethal injection.

SUMMARY FINDINGS

STATUS OF THE DEATH PENALTY, DECEMBER 31, 2013				
EXECUTIONS DURING 2013		NUMBER OF PRISONERS UNDER SENTENCE OF DEATH, 12/31/2013		JURISDICTIONS WITHOUT DEATH PENALTY, 12/31/2013
Texas	16	California	735	Alaska
Florida	7	Florida	398	District of Columbia
Oklahoma	6	Texas	273	Hawaii
Ohio	3	Pennsylvania	190	Illinois
Missouri	2	Alabama	190	Iowa
Arizona	2	North Carolina	151	Maine
Alabama	1	Ohio	136	Maryland
Georgia	1	Arizona	122	Massachusetts
Virginia	1	Louisiana	84	Michigan
		Georgia	82	Minnesota
		Nevada	81	New Jersey
		Tennessee	75	North Dakota
		Federal Bureau of Prisons	56	Rhode Island
		Mississippi	50	Vermont
		Oklahoma	48	West Virginia
		21 otherjurisdictions*	308	Wisconsin
Total	39	**Total**	2,979	

*New Mexico repealed the death penalty for offenses committed on or after July 1, 2009; Connecticut repealed the death penalty for offenses committed on or after April 25, 2012; and Maryland repealed the death penalty effective October 1, 2013. As of December 31, 2013, 2 men in New Mexico, 10 men in Connecticut, and 5 men in Maryland were a under previously imposed sentence of death.

Source: Bureau of Justice Statistics, National Prisoner Statistics Program (NPS-8), 2013.

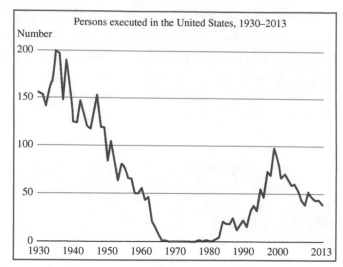

Source: Bureau of Justice Statistics, National Prisoners Statistics Program (NPS-8), 2013

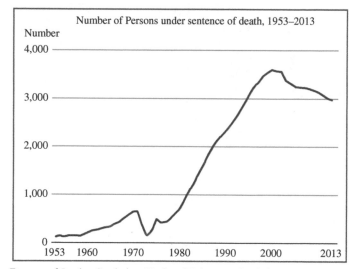

Source: Bureau of Justice Statistics, National Prisoners Statistics Program (NPS-8), 2013

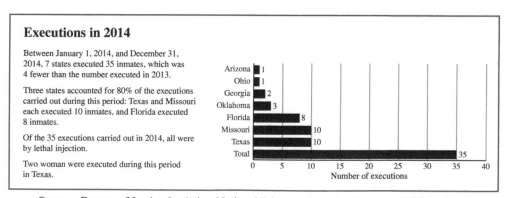

Source: Bureau of Justice Statistics, National Prisoners Statistics Program (NPS-8), 2013

REVIEW QUESTIONS:

1. The posting of money, property, or other collateral, by an arrested person to guarantee that they will appear in court to answer the charges against them is called _____.

2. The _____ is the first time the defendant is brought before the court that has the jurisdiction to actually conduct the trial.

3. The _____ Amendment guarantees the right to a speedy trial as well as the right to counsel.

4. The _____ is the group of prospective jurors summoned by the court to report at a specified date and time.

5. The burden of proof in a criminal trial is always on the _____.

6. The questioning of prospective jurors to determine their qualifications to serve on the jury is called the _____ _____.

7. The report that is filed with the court prior to sentencing by the probation department is called the _____ _____.

8. _____ sentencing is a fixed term of incarceration.

9. _____ circumstances are factors that relate to the commission of a specific crime that causes its severity to be greater than that of a typical instance of the same type of offense.

10. If a judge sentences two or more counts to run one after another, it is called a _____ sentence.

11. The _____ Amendment establishes the guarantee against "cruel and unusual punishment".

12. In 1972 the U. S. Supreme Court ruled in the case of _____ that the death penalty was often used in an arbitrary manner and was disproportionally used on race and not on the seriousness of the crime.

13. The most common method of legal execution in the United States in _____ _____.

CRITICAL THINKING QUESTIONS:

1. Discuss the concept of plea bargaining in the United States. Why is it used? Why is a necessary component of the judicial system?

2. Explain the bail system that is used in this country. Why is it allowed? How does it work? What are some of the alternative ways that arrested persons can be released from jail prior to trial.

3. Explain why the burden of proof is always on the prosecution in criminal trials in the United States.

4. Discuss in detail the importance of the presentence report. What does it contain? Who writes it?

5. Compare and contrast indeterminate sentencing with that of determinate sentencing.

6. Explain the difference between a concurrent sentence and a consecutive sentence.

7. Decide whether or not the death penalty should be abolished. Support your answer with good reasoning.

—————————————— NOTES ——————————————

CHAPTER 9

[1] McNabb v. U.S., 318 U.S. 332 (1943).

[2] County of Riverside v. McLaughlin, 500 U.S. 44 (1991).

[3] Connie Estrada Ireland and George E. Rush, *The Dictionary of Criminal Justice With Summaries of Supreme Court Cases Affecting Criminal Justice,* 7th Edition (New York: McGraw-Hill Companies, Inc., 2011).

[4] Ibid.

[5] Ibid.

[6] Brady v. United States, 397 U.S. 742 (1970).

[7] Sean Rosenmerkel, Matthew Durose, and Donald Farole, Jr., *Felony Sentences in State Courts, 2006—Statistical Tables* (U.S. Department of Justice, Office of Justice Programs, Bureau of Justice Statistics, December, 2009; revised 11/22/2010).

[8] Ibid.

[9] Klopfer v. North Carolina, 386 U.S. 213 (1967).

[10] Barker v. Wingo, 407 U.S. 514 (1972).

[11] Strunk v. U.S., 412 U.S. 434 (1973).

[12] 18 U.S.C. Section 1361.

[13] Powell v. Alabama, 287 U.S. 45 (1932).

[14] Johnson v. Zerbst, 304 U.S. 458 (1938).

[15] Gideon v. Wainwright, 372 U.S. 335 (1963).

[16] Argersinger v. Hamlin, 407 U.S. 25 (1972).

[17] Alabama v. Sheldon, 535 U.S. 654 (2002).

[18] Ireland, *Dictionary of Criminal Justice.*

[19] United States v. Dinitz, 424 U.S. 600 (1976).

[20] Griffin v. California, 380 U.S. 609 (1965).

[21] Allen v. United States, 164 U.S. 492 (1896).

[22] National Council on Crime and Delinquency, *Criminal Justice Sentencing Policy Statement,* November 2005.

[23] Ibid.

[24] Ibid.

[25] Connie Estrada Ireland and George E. Rush, *The Dictionary of Criminal Justice With Summaries of Supreme Court Cases Affecting Criminal Justice,* 7th Edition (New York: McGraw-Hill Companies, Inc., 2011).

[26] NCCD, *Criminal Justice Sentencing Policy Statement.*

[27] Ireland, *Dictionary of Criminal Justice.*

[28] NCCD, *Criminal Justice Sentencing Policy Statement.*

[29] United States Sentencing Commission, *2010 Federal Sentencing Guidelines Manual & Supplement,* accessed June, 2011 at http://www.ussc.gov/Guidelines/2010_guidelines/ToC_PDF.cfm.

[30] National Center for Victims of Crime website, accessed June, 2011 at http://www.ncvc.org/ncvc/main.aspx?dbName=DocumentViewer&DocumentID=32697.

[31] Larry H. Gaines and Roger Leroy Miller, *Criminal Justice in Action—5th Edition* (Belmont, CA: Thomas Wadsworth, 2009).

[32] Tracy L. Snell, *Capital Punishment, 2013—Statistical Tables* (U.S. Department of Justice, Office of Justice Programs, Bureau of Justice Statistics, December 2010).

[33] Furman v. Georgia, 408 U.S. 238 (1972).

[34] Gregg v. Georgia, 428 U.S. 153 (1976).

[35] Coker v. Georgia, 433 U.S. 584 (1977).

[36] Adkins v. Virginia, 536 U.S. 304 (2002).

[37] Roger v. Simmons, 553 U.S. 35 (2005).

[38] Kennedy v. Louisiana, 129 S. Ct. 1 (2008).

CORRECTIONS: JAILS AND PRISONS

CHAPTER OVERVIEW

The history of corrections in America began in the 1600s when the first settlers
arrived on the continent. With the growth
of the population came the need for more
organization and structure in our prisons
and jails. The growth also brought about
different philosophies on how to handle
the punishment of offenders that were be-

© Freddy Eliasson, 2011. Used under
license from Shutterstock, Inc.

© Kenneth Dedeu,
2011. Used under
license from
Shutterstock, Inc.

ing incarcerated. The prison system evolved from the Great Law of the Quakers, to the Walnut
Street Jail system, to the Pennsylvania system, to the Auburn system, to the correctional systems in use today.

It is important for the student of criminal justice to understand the difference between
jails and prisons, since they serve different functions within our correctional system. The
difference between the two is discussed in detail in this chapter. The current philosophies of
punishment are also detailed.

The United States has the largest prison population in the world, and as such there are
many problems and issues facing the correctional system today. Overcrowding is one of those
problems that face almost every prison in America. Health issues, gangs, and our aging prison
population are just some of the other issues facing our correctional systems throughout the
country.

CHAPTER LEARNING OBJECTIVES

After reading this chapter you will be able to:

1. Describe the correctional systems in use in America from the 1600s to the present day.
2. Understand the difference between jails and prisons.
3. Recognize the different levels of security that are used in our correctional system today.
4. Describe the different philosophies of punishment that have been utilized in the United States.
5. Identify the various problems and issues facing the correctional system today.
6. Explain the unique problems associated with the incarceration of women in our prisons.

KEYWORDS

William Penn

Walnut Street Jail

Pennsylvania System

Federal Bureau of Prisons

Prison

Classification

"Supermax" Prison

Deterrence

Retribution

Just Deserts

Great Law of the Quakers

Penitentiary

Auburn System

Jail

Private Prisons

Levels of Security

Incapacitation

Restorative Justice

Lex Talionis

Rehabilitation

BRIEF HISTORY OF CORRECTIONS IN THE UNITED STATES

In the 1600s colonists from England began to settle in the American colonies and as the population increased, so did the need for courts and punishment for offenders. Early prisons and jails in America were small and used primarily as holding facilities for suspects who were awaiting trial or execution. Convicted persons were not routinely given lengthy sentences of incarceration in the early days of American colonization. Corporal punishment was a much more common sentence and was used for many petty crimes. More serious crimes were usually dealt with by execution, or more commonly, by banishment from the community. In the early settlement days, banishment was usually a death sentence, since the person had to fend for themselves in the harsh and untamed environment.

As more and more settlers came to America, crime began to increase, compelling the citizenry to begin looking at more humanitarian and long-term ways to deal with offenders. One of the original correctional philosophies in the American colonies was put forth by **William Penn** (1644–1718) who was the founder of Pennsylvania and the leader of the Quakers. The **Great Law of the Quakers** dictated a much more humane way to deal with those convicted of crimes than the system that was in place at the time. The Great Law was the body of laws in Pennsylvania that saw hard labor as a more effective punishment than corporal punishment and death for crimes, and also demanded compensation to the victims. This system of corrections was in place from 1682 until 1718.[1] Upon the repeal of the Great Law, Pennsylvania reverted back to a harsher criminal code similar to that still being employed by the other colonies.

William Penn

William Penn

William Penn (1644–1718) was the founder of Pennsylvania and the leader of the Quakers.

Great Law of the Quakers

The Great Law was the body of laws in Pennsylvania that saw hard labor as a more effective punishment than corporal punishment and death for crimes, and also demanded compensation to the victims.

Walnut Street Jail

The Walnut Street Jail was the first true penitentiary in the United States and was opened in Pennsylvania in the United States in 1790.

Penitentiary

The Quakers developed the concept of a "penitentiary," a place where prisoners could reflect on their crime in silence and repent over their wrong-doing.

WALNUT STREET JAIL

The **Walnut Street Jail** was the first true **penitentiary** in the United States and was opened in Pennsylvania in the United States in 1790. The Quakers developed the concept of a "penitentiary," a place where prisoners could reflect on their crime in silence and repent over their wrong-doing.[2] The penitentiary was originally a Philadelphia city jail that was built in 1773

to alleviate the overcrowding of the existing city jail. Following the American Revolution, a group of Quakers formed the Philadelphia Society for Alleviating the Miseries of Public Prisons whose goal was to encourage prison reform. The society's efforts finally paid off in 1790 when the Walnut Street Jail became the first penitentiary in the country.[3]

An addition was built in the courtyard of the Walnut Street Jail that was designed to hold individual prisoners in small cells. These cells were designed to prevent prisoners from communicating with each other and windows where built high in each cell so the prisoners could not look out of them. The only person prisoners had contact with was a prison guard for a brief period of time each day. The Quakers looked at this solitary confinement as a time for reflection and remorse, not a form of punishment.

PENNSYLVANIA SYSTEM

The Walnut Street Jail became a model for what became known as the **"Pennsylvania System"** of prison design and philosophy.[4] This philosophy was supported by such well-known patriots and reformers as Benjamin Franklin and Benjamin Rush. Other prisons built on the Pennsylvania System model included the Eastern State Penitentiary in eastern Philadelphia and the Trenton State Prison in New Jersey. While the Pennsylvania System drew great international interest, it was soon replaced by a different correctional model.

AUBURN SYSTEM

© vlad_star, 2011. Used under license from Shutterstock, Inc.

Ben Franklin

The Walnut Street model of providing for prisoners housed in single cells began to compete with a new prison system model that was based on a prison built in Auburn, New York. The new prison emphasized putting the prisoners to work at hard labor and reintroduced corporal punishment. As prison populations began to increase, the Walnut Jail type of prisons became very expensive to build since there had to be one cell for each prisoner and they had to remain separated from each other. The Auburn Prison was built with smaller cells that were used for sleeping only and they were built on tiers (cell blocks). The prisoners were forced to work during the day and were not isolated from each other; however, they were required to maintain silence at all times.[5]

The **Auburn System** was the model for more than thirty state prisons that were built over the next several decades, including Sing Sing prison built in New York in 1826. Many of these prisons were very large structures with the common theme of inside cellblocks that did not touch the outside walls of the prison. Many European countries adopted the Auburn system and continued building prisons following the design of cellblocks for the next 150 years.[6]

CORRECTIONAL SYSTEM IN THE UNITED STATES TODAY

The correctional system in the United States is the largest in the world and consists of jails, prisons, and community supervision (probation and parole which will be discussed in detail in Chapter 11). Over 6.7 million people were under some form of correctional supervision in the United States by the end of 2015.[7] This number reflects all persons in jails, in prisons, on probation, and on parole. One in every thirty-seven adults (2.7 percent) in the United States is in the correctional system.

The United States has less than 5 percent of the world's population, yet it has almost 22 percent of the world's prisoners (2.1 million criminals behind bars).[8] China, which has four times the population of the United States, is a distant second with 1.6 million people in prison. The Republic of San Marino, a small European country (twenty-four square miles) that is surrounded by Italy, has a population of about 30,000. This small Republic has the distinction of having the smallest prison population in the world with only two prisoners. the countries with the highest prison population rates (number of prisoners per 100,000 population) are the United States (698), Turkmenistan (583), and Cuba (510). Some of the lowest prison population rates include Nigeria (31), India (31), and Japan (48).[9]

Just like the police and court systems in the United States, the various states and the federal government both run correctional systems that are distinct and separate from each other. The federal correctional system is overseen by the **Federal Bureau of Prisons** and each of the fifty states run their prison systems under a variety of headings, both on the state level and locally.

Federal Bureau of Prisons
The federal correctional system is overseen by the Federal Bureau of Prisons.

DIFFERENCE BETWEEN JAILS AND PRISONS

While the terms are often used interchangeably, it is important for students of criminal justice to understand that there is a distinct difference between jails and prisons. The following explanations describe the general distinctions between jails and prisons in most states and the federal government. Six states (Connecticut, Rhode Island, Vermont, Alaska, Hawaii, and Delaware) utilize an integrated correctional system that combines jails and prisons.[10]

JAILS

Jails are local facilities that are usually run by municipalities and counties. There are about 728,200 prisoners being held in local jails in the United States.[11] Jails are short term facilities where those who have been convicted of crimes serve a sentence that is generally for a term of less than one year. This includes criminals convicted of misdemeanors (state and federal) and local crimes such as city or county ordinances. Jails also:

© trekandshoot, 2011. Used under license from Shutterstock, Inc.

Jails
Jails are short term facilities where those who have been convicted of crimes serve a sentence that is generally for a term of less than one year. Jails also hold a host of other persons who have not yet been convicted of a crime.

- receive individuals pending arraignment and hold those awaiting trial, conviction, or sentencing
- remit probation, parole, and bail-bond violators and absconders
- temporarily detain juveniles pending transfer to juvenile authorities
- hold mentally ill persons pending transfer to appropriate mental health facilities
- hold individuals for the military, for protective custody, for contempt, and for the courts as witnesses
- release inmates to the community upon completion of sentence

- transfer inmates to federal, state, or other authorities
- house inmates for federal, state, or other authorities because of crowding of their facilities
- sometimes operate community-based programs as alternatives to incarceration[12]

The local jail population in the United States as of 2015 was 728,200 which is an 8.7% decrease since 2007.[13]

PRISONS

Prisons are long term facilities that are run by the state or the federal government. Prisons generally house those who have been convicted of felonies and are serving sentences that are typically one year or longer in length. Unlike jails that can also house those awaiting trial and have not yet been convicted of a crime, those serving time in prison, with very little exception, have all plead guilty or have been found guilty by a court. As of 2015, the federal prison population was 195,700 and the state prisons held 1,526,800 prisoners. It is important to note that the overall prison population in the United States in 2015 (both state and federal) fell to the lowest level since 2004, with a current combined population of 2,173,800.[14]

Prisons

Prisons are long term facilities that are run by the state or the federal government. Prisons generally house those who have been convicted of felonies and are serving sentences that are typically one year or longer in length.

Private Prisons

Private prisons in the United States are run by private corporations under the supervision of government correctional agencies.

PRIVATE PRISONS

In addition to the correctional facilities that are run by federal, state, and local governments, there are also **private prisons** in the United States that are run by private corporations under the supervision of government correctional agencies. Privatizing correctional facilities is a way for governments, at all levels, to attempt to reduce the costs associated with the incarceration of prisoners. Private companies that operate prisons usually charge a per inmate rate that is less than the amount of money the government is able to maintain their own facilities for. There are many pros and cons associated with private correctional facilities, however many states and the federal government both utilize them. Approximately 8 percent of all federal and state prisoners are housed in private prisons.

PERSONS HELD IN CUSTODY IN STATE OR FEDERAL PRISONS OR IN LOCAL JAILS, 2000, 2010, AND 2014–4015						
	NUMBER				PERCENT OF ALL PRISONERS	PERCENT OF ALL PRISONERS
PERSONS IN CUSTODY	2000	2010	2014	2015		
Total	1,938,500	2,266,500	2,217,900	2,168,400	1.0%	-2.2%
Federal prisoners[a]	140,100	207,000	209,600	195,800	2.9%	-6.6%
Prisons	133,900	198,300	200,100	186,700	2.9	-6.7
Federal facilities	124,500	173,100	169,500	160,700	2.2	-5.2
Privately operated facilities	9,400	25,200	30,500	26,000	8.4	-14.8
Community corrections centers[b]	6,100	8,600	9,500	9,200	3.2	-3.2
State prisoners	1,177,200	1,310,800	1,264,800	1,244,400	0.5%	-1.6%
State facilities[c]	1,101,200	1,216,700	1,173,100	1,153,100	0.5	-1.7
Privately operated facilities	76,100	94,100	91,700	91,300	1.3	-0.4
Local jails	621,100	748,700	744,600	728,200	1.3%	-2.2%
Incarceration rate[d]	690	700	690	670	--	-2.9%
Adult incarceration rate[e]	920	910	900	870	-0.2%	-3.3%

Sources: Bureau of Justice Statistics. Annual Survey of Jails, and National Prisoner Statistics program, 2000, 2010, and 2014–24 2015; and U.S. Census bureau, postcensal estimated restident populations for January 1 of the following year, 2001, 2011, 2015, and 2016.

THE CLASSIFICATION PROCESS

One of the first orders of business when an inmate enters a prison facility is the classification process. **Classification** is an assessment of the prisoner's risks and needs. The risks that are assessed include the type of crime they were convicted of, the potential for violence, their escape risk, and their prior criminal history. An assessment of the prisoners needs is also conducted. The needs include such things as the health of the inmate, education level, job skill level, and prior and current drug and/or alcohol use.

Classification

Classification is an assessment of a new prisoner's risks and needs.

The risk assessment is then used to determine what level of confinement the prisoner will be assigned to (see following) and the types of programs they will be placed into. Programs include such things as education programs (literacy and GED), job training, and mental health, drug, and alcohol counseling.

© dundanim, 2011.
Used under license from
Shutterstock, Inc.

© cosma, 2011. Used under license from Shutterstock, Inc.

© Katrina Brown, 2011. Used under license from
Shutterstock, Inc.

LEVELS OF SECURITY

Levels of Security

Prisons are divided into different levels of security: minimum, medium, maximum, and "supermax." The type of prison is based on the types of security features that are included in the construction of the facility as well as the type of prisoner that is housed there.

Prisons are divided into different **levels of security**: minimum, medium, maximum, and "supermax." The type of prison is based on the types of security features that are included in the construction of the facility as well as the type of prisoner that is housed there. Minimum security prisons house those prisoners that pose the least amount of risk to themselves, other inmates, and the staff. Minimum level prisons have the least amount of security and many times are classified as prison camps. Here inmates live in dormitory housing and can spend their days outside of the prison facility on work details such as fighting forest and brush fires. Minimum security prisons often house those inmates who have proven themselves as low risk and are getting near the end of their sentence, or who will shortly be eligible for parole.

Medium security prisons are the most common and house the greatest number of prisoners at both the state and federal level. Medium security prisons have more security features than the minimum facilities and usually include several layers of fencing, high outer walls and correctional officers in fixed posts in towers. Prisoners are usually housed in small two man cells or in dormitory style living conditions; however, they are not routinely confined to them except during the evening hours. These prisoners spend much of their day assigned to work details, counseling sessions, education, and recreation.

Maximum security prisons are even more secure facilities, and house the more dangerous prisoners. Security in these prisons is elaborate and usually contains many levels. Prisoners are very restricted in their movement and do not get anywhere near the freedom that is allowed even in the medium security facilities. Almost every state correctional department has at least one maximum security prison.

"Supermax" Prisons

These facilities house the worst and most dangerous prisoners. These prisoners are usually sent to these facilities when they have killed other prisoners or have assaulted correctional officers.

Several states as well as the federal government maintain what is commonly called **"supermax" prisons**. These facilities house the worst and most dangerous prisoners. These prisoners are usually sent to these facilities when they have killed other prisoners or have assaulted correctional officers. Confinement in a "supermax" is restricted to twenty-three hours a day in a small single cell and any movement of the prisoner is escorted by one or two correctional officers.

THE PHILOSOPHIES OF PUNISHMENT

One of the most controversial issues concerning the correctional system in the United States is the question "Why do we put criminals in prison?" Our correctional system has gone through several different philosophies concerning why we incarcerate criminals over the past two hundred years:

1. Incapacitation
2. Deterrence
3. Restorative Justice
4. Retribution and Just Deserts
5. Rehabilitation

INCAPACITATION

Incapacitation has taken on different meanings over time. Early use of incapacitation was banishment. When a person was banished, they were sent into the wilderness on their own and were never allowed to return. This accomplished the ultimate goal of incapacitation which is to remove the problem from society. The person could no longer be a threat to the community. The modern implication of incapacitation is putting criminals in prison with the ultimate goal of removing them as a threat to society so that they cannot commit any additional crimes. One of the inherent problems with this philosophy is that in most cases it is only temporary. Unless the criminal is given a life sentence or the death penalty, they will eventually return to society. Incapacitation is often referred to as warehousing.

Incapacitation

The modern implication of incapacitation is putting criminals in prison with the ultimate goal of removing them as a threat to society so that they cannot commit any additional crimes.

© James Steidl, 2011. Used under license from Shutterstock, Inc.

DETERRENCE

Deterrence is a philosophy that says we should punish criminals in order to deter others from committing crimes. There are two general theories of deterrence: general and specific. General deterrence says that we should punish criminals so that others see the punishment and will not want to be subject to the same penalties. Specific deterrence is based on the theory that we should punish criminals so that we prevent that specific criminal from wanting to repeat their criminal ways.

In order for deterrence to be effective, punishments must be swift and certain and must be severe enough to make potential criminals think twice before committing a criminal act. In some countries, deterrence seems to work quite well. European and Scandinavian countries do not have the problem with DUI (drunk driving) that we do in the United States. The punishments for driving impaired are severe and certain enough to deter citizens from driving under the influence. There is also tremendous peer pressure on those who are impaired to keep them

Deterrence

Deterrence is a philosophy that says we should punish criminals in order to deter others from committing crimes.

© Andy Dean Photography, 2011. Used under license from Shutterstock, Inc.

from driving. In the United States, the punishments in most jurisdictions for DUI are relatively minor in comparison, and there is not the stigma attached to it in order to deter people from doing it. The stark reality is that about 1.5 million people are arrested each year in the United States for driving under the influence.[16]

RESTORATIVE JUSTICE

Restorative Justice

The concept of restorative justice focuses on the needs of the victim and society, as well as the offender.

The concept of **restorative justice** focuses on the needs of the victim and society, as well as the offender. This philosophy is in use, at least in part, in many jurisdictions around the country. "Making the victim whole" is the catch phrase of restorative justice. If a criminal steals the property of victim, restorative justice says that the offender must make restitution to the victim in order to reduce the harm caused by the act of stealing. Community service is another way that the offender can make society whole again, by giving time and work to the community as part of the restorative sentencing. Restorative justice is often used in conjunction with other philosophies of punishment.

RETRIBUTION AND JUST DESERTS

Retribution

A more modern philosophy based on the concept of *lex talionis* that states the actual punishment should match the crime as closely as possible so that the offender can feel the same pain as they caused the victim.

Retribution is a philosophy that goes back over two hundred years in the United States, and is based on the concept of *lex talionis* or "an eye for an eye." This early philosophy was based on the idea that the punishment should equal the crime. If a person stole his neighbors horse, the neighbor could take the offenders horse. If a person killed his neighbor's

© Dusan Jankovic, 2011. Used under license from Shutterstock, Inc.

Lex talionis

The concept of *lex talionis* or "an eye for an eye," was an early philosophy based on the idea that the punishment should equal the crime.

wife, the victim could kill the offender's wife, and so on. The idea is that the actual punishment should match the crime as closely as possible so that the offender can feel the same pain as they caused the victim.

Since the mid-1990s, there has been a movement back towards the concept of retribution; however, it is now referred to as "just deserts." **Just deserts** incorporates the idea that criminals are responsible for their own actions and their decisions, and that punishment is the natural consequence of those actions. The United States began "getting tough" on crime in the 1990s. Sentencing reforms, building of more prisons, and laws like the "three strikes and you're out," all contributed to this modern get tough with criminals model.

Just Deserts

Just deserts incorporates the idea that criminals are responsible for their own actions and their decisions, and that punishment is the natural consequence of those actions.

Many of the proponents of just deserts argue that this philosophy of punishment is one of the primary reasons that crime rates have declined in this country during the same period of time. Their argument seems to have validity when you consider that more criminals have been incarcerated for longer periods of time and have not been on the streets committing more crimes. While this philosophy is still popular, economics may bring this era to a rapid end. State governments have been experiencing very severe budget problems and many have been forced to reduce funding to corrections. This has resulted in the closing of prisons and the release of many prisoners long before the completion of their prescribed sentences.

REHABILITATION

Rehabilitation is the philosophy premised on the idea that criminals can be "cured" and made to change their criminal ways. Over the past several decades, billions of dollars have been spent expanding and developing prison and community programs aimed at rehabilitating criminals. Counseling programs, job skills training, education, and a host of other programs have been geared toward reforming criminals who become a part of our correctional system. The proponents of rehabilitation argue that people can be forced to change their ways and criminals can be shown that crime is a poor alternative to a productive and successful life. They argue that we should not throw away a segment of our society just because they have made some poor choices.

Opponents to rehabilitation point to the fact that many studies have shown that rehabilitative efforts have had little or no effect on the overall recidivism rates of prisoners being released from prison. They also point out the fact that society cannot 'force' a person to change, if a criminal decides to end their criminal activity they will do so whether or not they have been in any program. The opponents also argue that many times the best rehabilitative programs are quickly forgotten when the prisoner returns to the same environment that he/she lived in prior to getting caught and going to prison.

Rehabilitation
Rehabilitation is the philosophy premised on the idea that criminals can be "cured" and made to change their criminal ways.

PROBLEMS AND ISSUES FACING THE CORRECTIONAL SYSTEM

The modern correctional system has a host of problems and issues that have to be dealt with on a daily basis. This section will briefly identify some of the more prominent of these.

OVERCROWDING

Prison overcrowding has become an issue in almost every state. Overcrowding is the direct result of many of the same factors previously discussed in the section on retribution and just deserts. Economics over the past several years has curtailed the building of new prisons which, in turn, has contributed greatly to the overcrowding of the existing prisons.

In a 2011 case, the United States Supreme Court ruled the overcrowding of the California prisons constituted a violation of the Eighth Amendment requirement against cruel and unusual punishment.[17] The Court ruled that overcrowding deprives prisoners of basic substance including adequate medical care. The Court concluded that the State of California correctional facilities were holding 156,000 prisoners which were almost double the designed capacity of the prisons and has ordered the release of up to 37,000 prisoners. The Court further said that "overcrowding has overtaken the limited resources of prison staff; imposed demands well beyond the capacity of medical and mental health facilities; and created unsanitary and unsafe conditions that make progress in the provision of care difficult or impossible to achieve."

HEALTH ISSUES

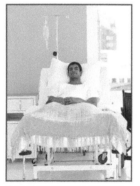

© wavebreakmedia ltd, 2011. Used under license from Shutterstock, Inc.

One of the most dangerous and expensive aspects of the correctional system is that of health issues. Correctional facilities are responsible for the health needs of the inmates. Providing health services to an ever growing jail and prison population takes a large bite out of the operational budgets of the agencies tasked with maintaining the facilities.

In addition to "routine" health problems that are encountered amongst any large group of people, from colds and flu to heart attacks, there are a number of diseases that are more prevalent in jails and prisons than in the general population. Such blood borne diseases as HIV, AIDS, hepatitis B and C, as well as the air borne disease of tuberculosis, can become epidemic in correctional facilities. These diseases are not only a concern of the inmates, but with the correctional staff as well. The staff is required to have close contact with the inmates on a daily basis. Searches of inmates and cells, altercations, and just routine supervision put the staff at risk on a daily basis.

PRISON GANGS

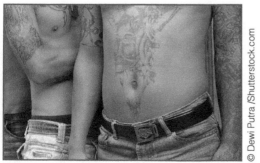

An ever growing problem in jails and prisons today is that of prison gangs. There are members of almost every gang represented within the confines of correctional institutions. There are also gangs that are unique to the prisons themselves, which are formed many times solely for the protection of inmates who have no other affiliations. Correctional staff has to be careful when assigning new inmates to housing units, taking care not to put a member of one gang in an area populated by rival gang members.

The prison gangs routinely control the sale and distribution of contraband within the prison walls. Drugs, alcohol, cigarettes, work assignments, and a host of other commodities are among the items that can be controlled by gangs. Gangs also establish their own "turf" on the recreation yards as well as the housing units, and encroachment of this territory can result in physical assaults and even murder.

SEX IN PRISON

Sex in prisons and jails has become such a problem that President George W. Bush signed the Prison Rape Elimination Act of 2003 (PREA) into law on September 4, 2003. The Act applies to all correctional facilities, including prisons and jails; juvenile, military, and Indian country facilities; and Immigration and Customs Enforcement (ICE) facilities. The act requires the Bureau of Justice Statistics to[18]:

- "carry out, for each calendar year, a comprehensive statistical review and analysis of the incidence and effects of prison rape"
- "include, but not be limited to the identification of the common characteristics of—(A) both victims and perpetrators of prison rape; and (B) prisons and prison systems with a high incidence of prison rape"
- Utilize "a random sample, or other scientifically appropriate sample, of not less than 10 percent of all Federal, State, and county prisons, and a representative sample of municipal prisons"
- "use surveys and other statistical studies of current and former inmates"
- provide "a listing of those institutions in the representative sample, separated into each category … and ranked according to the incidence of prison rape in each institution" and "a listing of any prisons in the representative sample that did not cooperate with the survey"

There were 7,444 reported allegations of sexual victimizations in jails and prisons in 2008.

NATIONAL ESTIMATES OF TOTAL ALLEGATIONS OF SEXUAL VICTIMIZATION, BY TYPE OF FACILITY, 2005–2008[19]								
	NUMBER OF ALLEGATIONS				RATE PER 1,000 INMATES			
FACILITY TYPE	2008*	2007	2006	2005	2008*	2007	2006	2005
Total	7,444	7,374	6,528**	6,241**	3.18	2.95	2.91**	2.83**
Prisons (a)	5,796	5,535**	4,958**	4,791**	3.82	3.62**	3.37**	3.33**
Public-federal (b)	368	309**	242**	268**	2.22	1.86**	1.50**	1.71**
Public-state	5,194	4,940**	4,516**	4,341**	4.20	3.98**	3.75**	3.68**
Jails (c)	1,633	1,823	1,533	1,406	2.04	1.89	2.02	1.86

*Comparison group.
**Difference with comparison group is significant at the 95 percent confidence level.
(a) Includes federal, state, and private prisons.
(b) Estimates for 2006 are not comparable to those in 2005 due to a change in reporting.
(c) Includes local and private jails.

© wavebreakmedia ltd, 2011. Used under license from Shutterstock, Inc.

AGING PRISON POPULATIONS

The aging of our prison populations is becoming one of the most critical issues that the correctional system is facing today. As the population of the United States gets older due to such factors as the aging of the "baby boomers," the populations of our prisons are getting older also. Inmates over the age of fifty-five have increased 534 percent between 1988 and 2012 for males and 680 percent for females during the same time period.[20,21] Elderly inmates mean that prisons will have to accommodate them with more expensive medical services. Prisons will have to begin construction of handicap facilities (wheelchair ramps, wider hallways and cell openings, convalescent facilities, etc.), provide nursing services, and increase hospital accommodations, to name but a few.

Budget constraints on prisons throughout the country are adding to the problem of caring for elderly inmates. The Eighth Amendment to the U.S. Constitution prohibits cruel and unusual punishment and deliberate indifference to the medical needs of inmates has been ruled to violate this right.[22] States are looking at alternatives for housing many of these elderly inmates. Early release, alternative sentencing, and community correctional centers are all being examined as ways to reduce this growing problem.

WOMEN IN PRISON

There are almost 105,000 women in state and federal prisons as of 2015 and this reflects a three percent increase since 2005.[23] This increase in female inmates poses several unique problems. Women are housed in separate prison facilities, and the increase in numbers equates to the need for additional prison facilities. Another major issue involving female inmates is that of pregnancy. There were more than 2,100 pregnant woman incarcerated in 2003 and more than 1,400 babies born in prison during the same time period.[24] Caring for pregnant inmates, and subsequently caring for newborns, adds to the medical expenses of the correctional facilities. Some prison systems are even allowing the babies to stay with the mother in prison for extended periods of time, which adds to the special needs that prisons must now provide.

REVIEW QUESTIONS:

1. The founder of Pennsylvania and the leader of the Quakers was _____ _____ .

2. The first true "penitentiary" in the United States was called the _____ _____ Jail.

3. Sing Sing prison in New York is an example of the _____ System that was a model for more than thirty state prisons throughout the eighteenth century.

4. _____ are local facilities that are usually run by municipalities and counties.

5. _____ are long term facilities that are run by the state or the federal government.

6. An assessment of a prisoner's risks and needs is referred to as _____ .

7. The most common security levels of prisons in the United States are the _____ security prisons.

8. The punishment philosophy of _____ _____ focuses on the needs of the victim, society, and the offender.

9. The concept of *lex talionis* or "an eye for an eye" is based on the early philosophy that punishment should equal the crime. Today we refer to this philosophy as _____ .

10. _____ is the philosophy that is premised on the idea that criminals can be "cured" and made to change their criminal ways.

CRITICAL THINKING QUESTIONS:

1. Discuss William Penn's contributions to the early correctional system used in America.

2. Explain how the punishment philosophy has changed in the United States as we progressed through the different systems from the 1600s to modern day.

3. Describe the differences between a jail and a prison.

4. Give an argument for or against the use of private prisons in the United States.

5. Discuss the different levels of security that are used in our prisons today. Include in your discussion the differences in the physical facilities of each level.

6. Select one of the philosophies of punishment and discuss why you believe it is the most compelling reason that we should put criminals in prison.

7. Describe, in some detail, at least three of the problems and issues that face our correctional system today.

NOTES

CHAPTER 10

[1] Henry E. Allen, Edward J. Latessa, and Bruce S. Ponder, *Corrections in America, an Introduction,* 12th Edition, (Upper Saddle River, NJ: Pearson Prentice Hall, 2010).

[2] Shirelle Phelps and Jeffrey Lehman, eds. *West's Encyclopedia of American Law,* 2nd ed. (Detroit: Gale, 2004).

[3] Ibid.

[4] Ibid.

[5] Allen, *Corrections in America.*

[6] Ibid.

[7] Danielle Kaeble and Lauren E. Glaze, *Correctional Populations in the United States, 2015* (U.S. Department of Justice, Office of Justice Programs, Bureau of Justice Statistics, December 2016).

[8] Andrew Cole, Helen Fair, Jessica Jacobson, and Roy Walmsley, *Imprisonment Worldwide: The Current Situation and an Alternative Future,* Policy Press, Bristol UK (2016)

[9] Ibid.

[10] *All Terms & Definitions,* U.S. Department of Justice, Office of Justice Programs, Bureau of Justice Statistics, accessed June, 2011 at http://bjs.ojp.usdoj.gov/index.cfm?ty=tda.

[11] Glaze, *Correctional Populations.*

[12] Todd D. Minton, *Jail Inmates at Midyear 2010--Statistical Tables* (U.S. Department of Justice, Office of Justice Programs, Bureau of Justice Statistics, April 2011).

[13] op cit Glaze.

[14] Ibid

[15] Ibid.

[16] Laura M. Marusack, *DWI Offenders Under Correctional Supervision* (U.S. Department of Justice, Office of Justice Programs, Bureau of Justice Statistics, June, 1999).

[17] Brown, Governor of California, et al. v. Plata et al., No. 09–1233, decided May 23, 2011.

[18] *Prison Rape Elimination Act (Sexual Violence in Correctional Facilities),* U.S. Department of Justice, Office of Justice Programs, Bureau of Justice Statistics, accessed June, 2011 at http://bjs.ojp.usdoj.gov/index.cfm?ty=tp&tid=20.

[19] *Prison Rape Elimination Act of 2003 (PREA), Sexual Victimization Reported by Adult Correctional Authorities, 2007–2008* (U.S. Department of Justice, Office of Justice Programs, Bureau of Justice Statistics, January, 2011).

[20] Allen, *Corrections in America,* pg 346.

[21] The actual increase for males has been from 13,955 in 1988 and is anticipated to be 74,531 in 2012; and 511 in 1988 and is anticipated to be 3,478 in 2012 for females.

[22] Allen, *Corrections in America.*

[23] E. Ann Carson and Elizabeth Anderson, *Prisoners in 2015* (U.S. Department of Justice, Office of Justice Programs, Bureau of Justice Statistics, December, 2016).

[24] Allen, *Corrections in America.*

CORRECTIONS: ALTERNATIVES TO INCARCERATION

Chapter 11

CHAPTER OVERVIEW

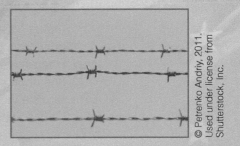

© Petrenko Andriy, 2011.
Used under license from
Shutterstock, Inc.

Probation is the most common form of punishment that is used in the United States today. Probation got its start in 1841 when John Augustus bailed out a "common drunkard" and helped reform his behavior before he had to return to court several weeks later. While there is no uniform structure of probation departments in the United States, there are some similarities among all of them. The probationer is required to follow conditions that are imposed by the sentencing court, and is supervised by a probation officer. Parole is a completely different system of supervision from probation, and the distinctions between the two are explained in this chapter.

The role of the probation and parole officers within our correctional system will be discussed as well as the detailed procedures that must be followed in order to revoke a person who violates any of the terms or conditions of their supervision. Several of the other alternatives to incarceration are also explained and detailed in this chapter.

CHAPTER LEARNING OBJECTIVES

After reading this chapter you will be able to:

1. Explain how John Augustus established the system that is now known as probation.
2. Understand the difference between probation and parole.
3. Describe the various organizational structures of probation in the United States today.
4. List at least six of the standard conditions of probation and parole.
5. List at least six of the special conditions that can be applied to a probationer or a parolee.
6. Understand the procedures that are required in order to revoke the probation or parole of an offender.
7. Explain the most common alternatives to incarceration that are used in the United States.

─────────────── KEYWORDS ───────────────

Judicial Reprieve
Probation Officer
Parole Boards
Special Conditions
Technical Violations
Preliminary Inquiry Hearing
Gagnon v. Scarpelli
Recidivism
Split Sentencing
Electronic Monitoring
Veterans Court

John Augustus Probation
Parole
Standard Conditions
Revocation Proceedings
New Charges
Morrissey v. Brewer
Revocation Hearing
Drug Court
Intensive Supervision
GPS monitoring

BRIEF HISTORY OF PROBATION IN THE UNITED STATES

Judicial Reprieve

The earliest form of probation was the English courts practice of judicial reprieve.

The earliest form of probation was the English courts practice of judicial reprieve. **Judicial reprieve** served as a temporary suspension of a sentence in order to allow the defendant to appeal their case in order to try to obtain a pardon from the King. Eventually the concept of judicial reprieve evolved into what we know today as a suspended sentence (see following sections). The practice of suspending sentences was adopted by the courts in Boston in 1830, and quickly spread to the other courts in the United States.[1]

John Augustus, the "Father of Probation," has been recognized as the first true probation officer. Augustus was the owner of a successful boot-making business in Boston and was a member of the Washington Total Abstinence Society. The Society members abstained from alcohol and believed that abusers of alcohol could be rehabilitated through understanding, kindness, and sustained moral persuasion, rather than through conviction and jail sentences. It was this membership that led Augustus to the Boston courts. In 1841, Augustus attended a police court to bail out a "common drunkard," who was to become the first probationer. The offender was ordered to appear in court three weeks later for sentencing. Augustus accompanied the man back to court, and to the surprise of the court the defendant was sober and his appearance and demeanor had changed dramatically.[2]

John Augustus began an eighteen-year career as a voluntary probation officer and was the first person to apply the term "probation" to the method he used to treat offenders. By 1858, Augustus had provided bail for 1,946 men and women. It has been reported that only ten of his probationers forfeited their bail and failed to return to court, or to complete their probation. Shortly after John Augustus's death, the State of Massachusetts passed the first probation law. Following the passage of these first statutes, probation gradually spread through the United States.[3]

John Augustus

John Augustus (1785–1859) is known as the "Father of Probation" based on his work with the Boston courts in the mid 1800s.

PROBATION TODAY

Probation is a form of sentencing where the offender is given a jail or prison sentence that is suspended, and is then placed on community supervision in lieu of actually serving time. The offender is then placed under the supervision of a **probation officer**. If the offender abides by the conditions set forth by the sentencing court, he/she will be discharged from probation and will never have to serve the underlying sentence of incarceration. If the offender violates any of the terms or conditions of their probation, they will be brought back before the sentencing judge for revocation proceedings. When a judge revokes an offender, they are subject to serving the original suspended sentence and to being sent to jail or prison. There were over 3.7 million offenders on probation in the United States by year-end 2015, making it the most common form of criminal sentencing.[4]

Probation

Probation is a form of sentencing where the offender is given a jail or prison sentence that is suspended, and is then placed on community supervision in lieu of actually serving time.

Probation Officer

Probation officers are responsible for the supervision of those offenders who have been placed on court ordered probation.

PROBATION DEPARTMENTS

There is no uniform standard for the way the probation departments are structured or operated in the United States. Probation departments can fall under a variety of organizational structures including:

1. Under state and/or county courts
2. Under state public safety

Number of persons supervised by U.S. adult correctional systems, by correctional status, 2000 and 2005–2015

Year	Total correctional population[a]	Community supervision			Incarcerated[b]		
		Total[a,c]	Probation	Parole	Total[a]	Local jail	Prison
2000	6,467,800	4,564,900	3,839,400	725,500	1,945,400	621,100	1,394,200
2005	7,055,600	4,946,600	4,162,300	784,400	2,200,400	747,500	1,525,900
2006	7,199,600	5,035,000	4,236,800	798,200	2,256,600	765,800	1,568,700
2007	7,339,600	5,119,000	4,293,000	826,100	2,296,400	780,200	1,596,800
2008	7,312,600	5,093,400	4,271,200	826,100	2,310,300	785,500	1,608,300
2009	7,239,100	5,019,900	4,199,800	824,600	2,297,700	767,400	1,615,500
2010	7,089,000	4,888,500	4,055,900	840,800	2,279,100	748,700	1,613,800
2011	6,994,500	4,818,300	3,973,800	855,500	2,252,500	735,600	1,599,000
2012	6,949,800	4,790,700	3,944,900	858,400	2,231,300	744,500	1,570,400
2013	6,899,700	4,749,800	3,912,900	849,500	2,222,500	731,200	1,577,000
2014	6,856,900	4,713,200	3,868,400	857,700	2,225,100	744,600	1,562,300
2015	6,741,400	4,650,900	3,789,800	870,500	2,173,800	728,200	1,526,800
Average annual percent change, 2007–2015	–1.1%	–1.2%	–1.6%	0.7%	–0.7%	–0.9%	–0.6%
Percent change, 2014–2015	–1.7%	–1.3%	–2.0%	1.5%	–2.3%	–2.2%	–2.3%

Note: Estimates were rounded to the nearest 100 and may be comparable to previously published BJS reports due to updated information or rounding. Counts include estimates for nonresponding jurisdictions. All probation, parole, and prison counts are for December 31; jail counts are for the last weekday in June. Detail may not sum to total due to rounding and adjustments made to account for offenders with multiple correctional statuses. See *Methodology*. See the *Key Statistics* page on the BJS website for correctional population statistics prior to 2000 or other years not included in this table.

[a]Total was adjusted to account for offenders with multiple correctional statuses. See *Methodology*.

[b]Includes offenders held in local jails or under jurisdiction of state or federal prisons.

[c]Includes some offenders held in a prison or jail but who remained under the jurisdiction of a probation or parole agency.

Source: Bureau of Justice Statistics, Annual Probation Survey, Annual Parole Survey, Annual Survey of Jails, Census of Jail Inmates, and National Prisoner Statistics Program, 2000 and 2005–2015.

3. Under municipal court systems
4. Under municipal and/or county juvenile courts
5. Under the U.S. District Courts (federal probation)

In some jurisdictions probation officers (or agents) are peace officers and carry firearms, while in other jurisdictions they are unarmed and have little or no peace officer authority. Federal probation officers are federal law enforcement officers and the individual officers have the option to carry firearms if they want.

STATE AND LOCAL

Adult probation departments are operated at either the state or the local level. About half of the states have agencies that supervise adult probationers and about half do not. In those states that do not have dedicated probation agencies, the responsibility for the supervision of offenders generally falls to the counties.

FEDERAL

The Office of Probation and Pretrial Services, Administrative Office of the United States Courts is the authority responsible for monitoring offenders charged with and convicted of federal crimes. In the federal system, the term Supervised Release

is used instead of parole. In 1987, the United States Federal Sentencing Guidelines discontinued parole for individuals convicted of federal crimes for offenses committed after November 1, 1987. Federal prisoners are required to serve 85 percent of their sentence under truth in sentencing legislation. The United States Parole Commission is the parole authority for individuals who committed federal offenses before November 1, 1987.

U.S. probation and pretrial services offices are located in ninety-three of the ninety-four U.S. District Courts[5] and each district is run by a chief probation officer who reports directly to the court for which they serve. Each Probation chief does their own hiring, manages their own budget, and decides how to run their own office. Each district is overseen nationally by the Criminal Law Committee of the Judicial Conference of the United States.[6]

JUVENILE

The juvenile system of probation is completely separate from the adult. Juvenile probation generally falls under the organizational structure of the juvenile courts at the county or municipal level. Just like adults, the most common form of sentence for juveniles is probation. Juvenile probation is often used as a way of diverting first time and status offenders from the harshness of the court system in an attempt to monitor them and prevent their progression into more serious problem behavior. Juvenile probation has been termed the "workhorse of the juvenile justice system" because 64% of juvenile delinquency cases in 2013 were given a term of probation (see chapter 12).[7]

© Sascha Burkard, 2011. Used under license from Shutterstock, Inc.

PAROLE

Parole refers to criminal offenders who are conditionally released from prison to serve the remaining portion of their sentence in the community under the supervision of a parole officer or agent. The primary difference between probation and parole is that probationers are released under supervision and have not served a sentence in jail or prison, and parolees have served at least a portion of their sentence incarcerated. In 2015, there were 870,500 offenders under parole supervision in the United States.[8]

© David Dea, 2011. Used under license from Shutterstock, Inc.

Parole

Parole refers to criminal offenders who are conditionally released from prison to serve the remaining portion of their sentence in the community under the supervision of a parole officer or agent.

PAROLE BOARDS

Parole Board

The parole board is a panel of individuals who decide whether an inmate should be released from prison on parole after serving a portion of their sentence.

The **parole board** is a panel of individuals who decide whether an inmate should be released from prison on parole after serving a portion of their sentence. The members of the parole board are appointed by the governor. In some states, the parole board is an independent agency, while in others it is part of the department of corrections. Many states, and the federal government, eliminated their parole boards when they adopted one of the various forms of structured sentencing models (see Chapter 9).

PAROLE DEPARTMENTS

Unlike probation departments that may be run by either the state or local government, parole departments are all state agencies and are tasked with monitoring those individuals who are released on parole. It is important to note, however, that some states (and the federal government) supervise the early release of prisoners by using their probation departments.

CONDITIONS OF SUPERVISION OF PROBATION AND PAROLE

While probation and parole are actually two separate organizations, the conditions that both probationers and parolees must follow are very similar. When they are initially placed on either probation or parole, there are two types of conditions that they must follow, the standard conditions and special conditions.

STANDARD CONDITIONS

Standard Conditions

Standard conditions of probation/parole are those which are included in all probation and parole agreements and must be followed by all offenders.

Standard conditions of probation/parole are those which are included in all probation and parole agreements and must be followed by all offenders. The conditions may vary from jurisdiction to jurisdiction, however, they typically include:

1. Submit to a search of their person, their residence, their vehicle, and any property under their control, at any time, by any probation or parole officer or law enforcement officer

2. A requirement that the offender maintain contact with, and report to the probation or parole authority at designated times

3. Prohibition of illegal substance use
4. Drug testing

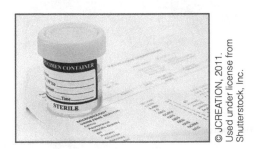

5. Requirement to seek and maintain employment
6. May not possess any weapons

7. Must inform the probation or parole department of his current address and cannot change residence without prior approval of their officer
8. Not to associate with other convicted persons
9. Pay supervision fees
10. Not violate any laws
11. No drinking of any alcoholic beverages (or not to drink to excess)

SPECIAL CONDITIONS

Special conditions of probation and parole are those which are specially tailored to the offender based on the type of offense committed and/or needs of the offender. These conditions are specifically ordered by the sentencing judge or the parole board. An offender convicted of burglary may have a special condition not to possess burglary tools, an offender convicted of uttering a forged instrument may have a special condition not to open a bank account or possess bank checks. Some of the other more common special conditions are:

© Rawpixel.com/Shutterstock.com

1. Restitution to reimburse a victim for damage done or property stolen by the offender
2. Mental health counseling

© ESB Professional/Shutterstock.com

3. Alcohol and/or substance abuse counseling

4. Community service

© dragon_fang, 2011.
Used under license from
Shutterstock, Inc.

5. Electronic monitoring
6. Intensive supervision
7. Pay a fine
8. Obtain a GED

© jcjgphotography, 2011.
Used under license from
Shutterstock, Inc.

9. Not associate with the victim

THE ROLE OF THE PROBATION/PAROLE OFFICER

The ultimate goal of both probation and parole officers is to work with offenders to help them successfully complete their sentence and become productive citizens within their communities. The officers must also supervise their offenders to ensure compliance with all of the terms and conditions of their standard and special conditions. Probation and parole officers must wear several hats in order to successfully fulfill these goals. Officers must be able to perform the duties of counselors, police officers, referral brokers, and court officers. The officers must be able to counsel the offenders they supervise. Offenders, whether they are a probationer or a parolee, will often have personal, family, employment, and other problems that the officer must be able to address in a professional and unbiased manner.

When the offender violates the law, or violates one or more of the conditions of their supervision, the officers must take on the role of police officer. In jurisdictions where the officer is a law enforcement officer, they will make arrests on their own and book the offender into the appropriate facilities to await revocation proceedings. If they are not law enforcement officers, they will have to request the assistance of local police to make the arrest for them.

Many of the offenders under supervision will require the services of counselors, social workers, or other private or governmental agencies to meet a host of issues and compliance requirements. This is where the officer must put on the hat of referral broker. The officer must be familiar with and have a working relationship with the social and other agencies within their jurisdiction so that they can make the proper referrals to meet the needs of the offenders under their supervision.

Finally, the officers are required to be officers of the court and/or representatives of the parole board. The initial order for probation comes from the court and the officer will usually keep the court informed of the progress of the probationer. The same holds true for parolees who have been granted release by parole boards. The officer will also represent their respective departments during revocation proceedings, and if they have to return to the granting authority for modification of the terms and conditions of the offender's probation/parolee agreement. The officer may also have to file new criminal charges in court if an offender is caught committing new criminal acts.

*R*EVOCATION PROCEEDINGS

Revocation Proceedings

When an offender violates any of the terms and conditions of their supervision agreement, they may be arrested and brought back before the granting authority (the court or the parole board) for revocation proceedings.

Technical Violation

A technical violation is a failure to comply with one of the conditions of supervision (either a standard condition or a special condition) that does not amount to a criminal violation.

When an offender violates any of the terms and conditions of their supervision agreement, they may be arrested and brought back before the granting authority (the court or the parole board) for **revocation proceedings**. There are two types of violations that an offender can commit which can result in revocation: technical violations and new charges. A **technical violation** is a failure to comply with one of the conditions of supervision (either a standard condition or a special condition) that does not amount to a criminal violation. If a probationer fails to notify their officer that they moved to a new residence, or fails to report when requested to do so by the officer, that would be a technical violation. There is no requirement for a person who is not under supervision to comply with either of those conditions, but an offender under supervision is required to do both. Failure to comply could result in the offender being arrested and brought back to the granting authority for revocation. If an offender under supervision commits a

© ilya Andriyanov, 2011. Used under license from Shutterstock, Inc.

new criminal offense, they will normally be arrested and brought back to face revocation. In this case, there may also be **new charges** filed with the prosecutor and the offender may also be brought to trial.

PRELIMINARY INQUIRY HEARING

Offenders who are incarcerated prior to the revocation hearing are given the opportunity to have a **Preliminary Inquiry Hearing**. This is an administrative hearing to determine if there is probable cause to hold the defendant in custody pending their revocation hearing before the court or parole board. Because it is an administrative hearing, the offender is not entitled to an attorney. The offender must be given notice of the date and time of the hearing and afforded the opportunity to present witnesses who can give relevant information concerning the violation; however, character witnesses are not permitted. Neither the offender nor the charging officer has subpoena power for the hearing. The Preliminary Inquiry Hearing is conducted by a hearing officer who is usually a probation or parole officer who is not directly involved in the supervision of the offender. If the hearing officer finds probable cause does not exist to continue detention, the offender will be released from custody pending his appearance before the court or parole board. If the hearing officer determines that probable cause does exist, the offender remains in custody. In either instance, the hearing officer must produce a written report explaining his determination. The right to this hearing was established for parolees in 1972 by the United States Supreme Court case of *Morrissey v. Brewer*,[9] and for probationers in the 1973 case of *Gagnon v. Scarpelli*.[10] This hearing is often waived by offenders who chose to proceed directly to the revocation hearing.

REVOCATION HEARING

Revocation hearings are held before the judge who originally sentenced the offender to probation, or in cases of parolees they are held before the parole board. Since this is a hearing and not a trial the level of evidence to determine guilt is much lower. A preponderance of the evidence, rather than guilty beyond a reasonable doubt, is the standard used in these hearings. At the revocation hearing the offender has the following rights:

© Rafa Irusta, 2011. Used under license from Shutterstock, Inc.

1. To present his own testimony regarding the violation and may present documents, evidence, or mitigating circumstances which may affect the violation.
2. To present witnesses who have relevant information concerning the violation.
3. To cross-examine any adverse witnesses.
4. To have legal counsel, and if indigent to have legal counsel provided for them.

The judge or parole board has several decision options after hearing all of the evidence and testimony at a revocation hearing. If the offender is found to have not violated the terms and conditions of their release, they will be released from custody and reinstated to their probation or parole. If the offender is found to be in violation, the judge or the parole board may:

1. Revoke the offender and, in the case of probationers, have the offender start serving the suspended sentence that was originally given to them. Parolees will be sent back to prison to complete the remaining time of their sentence.
2. Reprimand the offender and allow them to continue their supervision.
3. Modify the probation or parole agreement by adding special conditions and then release them to continue supervision with new conditions.
4. Discharge the offender from probation or parole with a less than honorable discharge.

RECIDIVISM

Recidivism

Recidivism is measured by new criminal acts conducted by an offender under supervision that result in the re-arrest, reconviction, or return to prison with or without a new sentence being imposed during a three-year period following the prisoner's release.

Recidivism is measured by new criminal acts conducted by an offender under supervision that result in the re-arrest, reconviction, or return to prison with or without a new sentence being imposed during a three-year period following the prisoner's release. A study was conducted that followed 300,000 prisoners released on parole in 1994 in fifteen states. At the end of 1997, 67.5 percent were rearrested for a felony or serious misdemeanor, 46.9 percent were reconvicted and 25.4 percent were resentenced to prison for a new crime.[11]

A more recent study completed in 2014, followed the release from prison of 404,638 prisoners from 30 states. The study found that 67.8% of those prisoners were arrested within 3 years of release, and 76.6% were arrested within 5 years of release. The study found that crimes with the highest recidivism rates are property offenders (82.1%), drug offenders (76.9%), public order offenders (73.6%), and violent offenders (71.3%).

ADDITIONAL INTERMEDIATE SANCTIONS

Intermediate sanctions are alternative sentencing options that are available to judges in most jurisdictions. Intermediate sanctions allow the courts to sentence offenders to other than just a term of incarceration. While there are many types of intermediate sanctions, some of the more popular include:

1. Drug courts
2. Split sentencing
3. Intensive supervision
4. Electronic monitoring
5. Veterans court

DRUG COURT

Drug courts were first implemented in the late 1980s and have had a continued growth to where there are now over 2,000 such courts in the United States. The purpose of drug courts is to stop the abuse of alcohol and other drugs and related criminal activity. In drug court, the judge heads a team of court staff, attorneys, probation officers, substance abuse evaluators, and treatment professionals who all work together to support and monitor a participant's recovery. Drug court programs are extremely demanding and require intensive supervision that is based on frequent drug testing and court appearances, and a tightly structured regiment of treatment and recovery services.[13] Upon successful completion of most drug court programs, the offender will have his criminal charges reduced or dropped.

Drug court programs are characterized by:

- Collaborative links between the courts, prosecutors, public defenders, law enforcement, treatment providers, Social Service Agencies, and Community-Based Non-Profit organizations.
- A standardized assessment process is utilized to identify eligible non-violent offenders.
- Drug court teams are staffed with individuals trained in substance abuse and recovery issues who operate in a non-adversarial atmosphere.
- Drug courts utilize a system of graduated sanctions and incentives to encourage recovery goals and hold offenders accountable for non-compliant behaviors.
- Drug court professionals are encouraged to remain current in the field by participating in training and education efforts on a state and national level.
- Drug courts emphasize on-going program evaluation efforts to continually assess the effectiveness of program interventions and to update and improve program design when warranted.

SPLIT SENTENCING

Judges will occasionally sentence offenders to a short period of time in jail, typically thirty, sixty, or ninety days, before they are released on probation. **Split sentencing**

Drug Courts

Drug courts were first implemented in the late 1980s and are designed to stop the abuse of alcohol and other drugs and related criminal activity.

Split Sentencing

Judges will occasionally sentence offenders to a short period of time in jail, typically thirty, sixty, or ninety days, before they are released on probation.

is a form of "shock probation" that judges use, hoping that this brief time of incarceration will "shock" the offender into changing their criminal behavior. This type of sentencing is only effective for offenders who have never served a sentence of incarceration in the past. When the offender completes the term of incarceration they do not have to return to court because they have already been put under a sentence of probation.

INTENSIVE SUPERVISION PROGRAM

© Ar T ono, 2011. Used under license from Shutterstock, Inc.

When a judge sentences an offender to an **intensive supervision** program (ISP), they are giving a sentence of probation with very strict supervision. Offenders who are assigned to intensive supervision are required to adhere to very stringent conditions. The number of face-to-face contacts with their probation officers is significantly higher than for those offenders under normal supervision. The increased contacts will normally include those in the probation office, as well as in the offender's home and their work. Additional conditions may also be imposed which could include a curfew, increased drug testing, house arrest, and electronic monitoring (see below).

Intensive Supervision

A sentence of probation with very strict supervision.

ELECTRONIC MONITORING

Electronic Monitoring

Electronic monitoring is part of a system of house arrest, or home confinement, that utilizes an electronic device which is attached to the ankle (typically) of the offender that tells the supervising officer when the offender is at home.

Electronic monitoring is part of a system of house arrest, or home confinement, that utilizes an electronic device that is attached to the ankle (typically) of the offender. Typically there is also another devise that is attached to the offender's home telephone line. When the offender is at home, the device will randomly notify the probation office or an independent monitoring company that the offender is at home. When the offender leaves the home, the monitoring service is notified, which in turn notifies the probation officer assigned to the case. This type of system can only tell when the offender is actually home so offenders under this system must give their probation officer a daily schedule of where they will be at any given time when they are away from their home. The schedule must be approved in advance by the probation officer.

There are also systems available that will do random drug and alcohol testing of the offender right through the device that is attached to their ankle. Other systems will randomly call the offender while they are at home to blow into a breathalyzer that is attached to their telephone line. These monitors take a picture of the offender when they blow into the machine to insure that it is actually the offender who is taking the test.

GPS ELECTRONIC MONITORING

GPS Monitoring

A more sophisticated type of electronic monitoring incorporates global positioning technology (GPS). GPS monitoring allows probation officers to know exactly where their offender is at any given time.

A more sophisticated type of electronic monitoring incorporates global positioning technology (GPS). **GPS monitoring** allows probation officers to know exactly where their offender is at any given time. The officer can find the location of their offenders by logging on to a laptop computer. The GPS can be preprogramed to set off an alarm if an offender enters an area that they are not allowed to go, such as near the victim's residence or work. Alarms can be programed to prevent sex offenders who are on GPS monitoring from going near schools, victims, parks, or any other places they may be forbidden to frequent.

Tampering with any of the monitoring equipment would be a violation of probation, and the offender can be brought back for revocation proceedings.

VETERANS COURT

One of the newest categories of intermediate sanctions is that of **veterans courts**. It is estimated that 10 percent of all adults who are arrested in the United States every year are U.S. Military veterans. "State court judges are joining with local prosecutors, public defenders, U.S. Department of Veterans Affairs officials, and local lawyer volunteers to create courts with veterans-only case proceedings, because they have seen a common thread of post-traumatic stress disorder (PTSD), substance abuse, head injuries, and mental illness underlying the veterans' crimes."[14]

These courts are designed to assist these veterans who have committed misdemeanor and nonviolent felony crimes and were created to assess and assist veterans who may have underlying military-related problems that could be the cause of their criminal activity. Veterans courts have become accepted throughout the United States and have seen tremendous growth in just the last several years.

© Stuart Monk/Shutterstock.com

Veterans Courts
These courts are designed to assist these veterans who have committed misdemeanor and nonviolent felony crimes and were created to assess and assist veterans who may have underlying military-related problems that could be the cause of their criminal activity.

REVIEW QUESTIONS:

1. The "Father of Probation" is _____ _____.

2. The most common form of sentencing in the United States today is _____.

3. _____ refers to criminal offenders who are conditionally released from prison to serve the remaining portion of their sentence in the community while being supervised.

4. The _____ _____ is a panel of individuals who decide whether an inmate should be released from prison after serving a portion of their sentence.

5. A requirement that an offender maintain contact with, and report to, the probation or parole authority at designated times, would be an example of a _____ condition.

6. The requirement that an offender under supervision of probation or parole complete twenty hours of community service, would be an example of a _____ condition.

7. The two types of violations that an offender can commit that can result in revocation are _____ violations and _____ charges.

8. Offenders who are incarcerated prior to the revocation hearing are given the opportunity to have a _____ _____ hearing.

9. The Supreme Court case of _____ gives probationers the right to a preliminary inquiry hearing.

10. Parolees who have the highest recidivism rate are those who have been convicted of the crime of _____.

11. When a judge sentences an offender to a short period of jail time before being released on probation, it is called a _____ sentence.

12. It is estimated that _____ percent of all adults who are arrested every year in the United States are U.S. Military veterans. It is for this reason that the newest category of intermediate sanctions is that of _____ courts.

CRITICAL THINKING QUESTIONS:

1. Discuss, in your own words, how John Augustus became known as the "Father of Probation."

2. Explain why probation has become the most common form of sentencing in the United States today.

3. Describe the various structures of probation departments in the United States. Why do you think there is so much variance between jurisdictions?

4. Explain, in some detail, the difference between parole and probation.

5. Discuss the reason probation and parole violators are afforded the opportunity to have a preliminary inquiry hearing. What is the legal basis for the hearing?

6. Select at least two of the intermediate sanctions that are discussed in this chapter and give your reasons why they are (or are not) valid alternatives to incarceration.

———————————— NOTES ————————————

CHAPTER 12

[1] Howard Abadinsky, *Probation and Parole, theory and practice—9ᵗʰ Edition* (Upper Saddle, New Jersey: Pearson, Prentice Hall, 2006).

[2] New York City Department of Probation website, *History of Probation,* accessed June, 2011 at http://www.nyc.gov/html/prob/html/about/history. shtml.

[3] Ibid.

[4] Danielle Kaeble and Thomas P. Bonczar, *Probation and Parole in the United States, 2015* (U.S. Department of Justice, Office of Justice Programs, Bureau of Justice Statistics, December, 2016).

[5] Probation and pretrial services for the District of the Northern Mariana Islands are provided by the District of Guam.

[6] United States Courts, *Probation and Pretrial Services—Mission,* accessed June, 2011 at http://www.uscourts.gov/FederalCourts/ ProbationPretrialServices/Mission.aspx.

[7] Sarah Hockenberry and Charles Puzzanchera, *Juvenile Court Statistics 2013*, National Center for Juvenile Justice, July, 2015

[8] Kaeble and Thomas, *Probation and Parole in the United States.*

[9] Morrissey v. Brewer, 408 U.S. 471 (1972).

[10] Gagnon v. Scarpelli, 411 U.S. 778 (1973).

[11] Mathew R. Durose, Alexia Cooper, and Howard N. Snyder, *Recidivism of Prisoners Released in 30 States in 2005: Patterns from 2005 to 2010*, Bureau of Justice Statistics, April, 2014.

[12] Ibid.

[13] New Jersey Courts website, *Adult Drug Court Programs,* accessed June, 2011 at http://www.judiciary. state.nj.us/criminal/crdrgct.htm.

[14] The National Law Journal, *Courts for Veterans Spreading Across U.S.,* December 22, 2008.

CHAPTER OVERVIEW

© Sascha Burkard, 2011. Used under license from Shutterstock, Inc.

The first twelve chapters of this textbook have dealt with the adult criminal justice system in the United States. We have looked at the three primary components of the justice system (police, courts, and corrections) and have seen how each of them deals with the adult offender. In this chapter we will take a brief look at the juvenile justice system and explore how justice is administered to our youthful offenders.

The juvenile justice system is much younger than its adult counterpart since it was not established in this country until the mid-1800s. Prior to that time, children had very few rights and when they committed criminal acts, they were treated just like adults. Since the juvenile justice system was loosely based on the one used for adults, there are many similarities between the two and while this is true, there still remain many important and significant differences.

*C*HAPTER LEARNING OBJECTIVES

After reading this chapter you will be able to:

1. Describe the current trends in the juvenile population.
2. Understand the concept of *parens patriae.*
3. Explain the jurisdiction of the juvenile court.
4. Recognize the difference between delinquent and status offenses.
5. Understand the differences between informally and formally processed cases.
6. Describe the concept of judicial waiver.
7. Identify the landmark United States Supreme Court cases that deal with the rights of juveniles.
8. Understand the differences between the juvenile and the adult justice systems.

KEYWORDS

Juvenile	Chattel
Houses of Refuge	*Parens Patriae*
Delinquency	Abuse
Status Offense	Intake
Informally Processed Cases	Dependent Child
Judicial Waiver	Formally Processed Cases
Kent v. United States	*In re Gault*
In re Winship	*Breed v. Jones*
Schall v. Martin	*Roper v. Simmons*
Miller v. Alabama	Residential Placement Facilities

© kaarsten, 2011. Used under license from Shutterstock, Inc.

*J*UVENILE—DEFINITION AND TRENDS

The general accepted definition of a **juvenile** is a person under the age of eighteen. A more accurate definition would be a youth who is at or below the upper age limit of the original jurisdiction of the state of residence (see the Juvenile Court Jurisdiction later in this chapter). In 2010, 75.2 million Americans were under the age of eighteen. This represents about 25 percent of the population of the United States.[1] It is important to note that the population of the United States is currently getting older resulting in the juvenile population increasing less than any other segment of the United States. Over the next twenty years, the population of persons under the age of eighteen is expected to increase 17 percent while the population of persons ages sixty-five and older will increase 65 percent.[2]

The United States will see a tremendous increase in the population of juvenile minorities over the next twenty years. The number of black juveniles is expected to increase by about 6 percent and the number of juveniles of Hispanic ethnicity is expected to increase by 59 percent during this period of time. The population of white juveniles is expected to actually decline by 2 percent over the same period.[3]

Juvenile

The general accepted definition of a juvenile is a person under the age of eighteen.

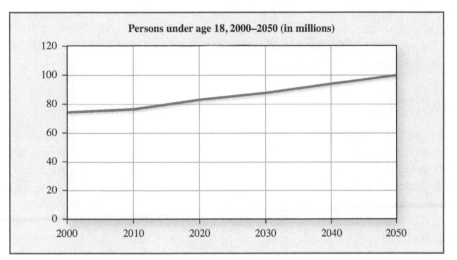

OJJDP Statistical Briefing Book. http://www.ojjdp.gov/ojstatbb/population/qa01101. asp?qaDate=2012 (accessed April 14, 2012).

A Brief History of Juvenile Justice in the United States

Up until the early nineteenth century, children in the United States (and other countries) were generally considered to be **chattel** (property), and as such had very little (if any) rights. Throughout the eighteenth century, only children under the age of reason (traditionally age seven) were protected from criminal prosecution because they were presumed to be incapable of forming the criminal intent *(mens rea)* and therefore were exempt from prosecution and punishment. Once a child reached the age of seven, they could stand trial in an adult criminal court, and if found guilty could be sentenced to jail or prison and serve their time with adult criminals. Children could also even be sentenced to death.[4]

In the early nineteenth century, the first "**houses of refuge**" were established. These houses were designed to deal with children who were not considered to be hardcore criminals and with proper guidance and education could be saved from a life of crime and poverty.[5]

Chattel

Chattel means the personal property of another.

Houses of Refuge

Established in the early nineteenth century, these houses were designed to deal with children who were not considered to be hardcore criminals and with proper guidance and education could be saved from a life of crime and poverty.

In 1825, the Society for the Prevention of Juvenile Delinquency began a movement for separate correctional facilities for juveniles and adults. While the children were still subject to the jurisdiction of the adult criminal court system, this campaign led to the establishment of privately run "youth" prisons in most major cities in America. These prisons soon became highly criticized for committing a variety of abuses on the juveniles who were housed in them, which forced many States to take over the responsibility of operating the juvenile facilities.[6]

The new role of the State taking over control of the juvenile facilities eventually led to the formation of the first juvenile court. The State of Illinois passed the Juvenile Court Act of 1899 which established the first court in the United States with original jurisdiction over juveniles in Cook County, Illinois. By 1910, thirty-two States had established their own juvenile courts, and by 1925, all but two States had established them.

PARENS PATRIAE

parens patriae

The state takes on the role of the parent.

The rationale for the States to be able to get involved directly in the lives of children was based on the British doctrine of **parens patriae** which means that the State takes on the role of the parent (the State as parent). This doctrine has been "interpreted to mean that, because children were not of full legal capacity, the State had the inherent power and responsibility to provide protection for children whose natural parents were not providing appropriate care or supervision. Thus, the delinquent child was also seen as in need of the court's benevolent intervention."[7]

THE JUVENILE JUSTICE SYSTEM FROM THE 1950s TO TODAY

The philosophy of the juvenile justice system during the first half of the twentieth century was centered on the individualized justice that allowed for the rehabilitation of the delinquent youths who were brought into the system. By the 1950s and 1960s, the effectiveness of the rehabilitation efforts began to come into question. Juveniles were receiving very lengthy terms of confinement in the name of treatment and rehabilitation and the success of these efforts was questionable at best. In the 1970s, the focus of treatment for delinquent youths shifted towards community-based programs, diversion, and deinstitutionalization.[8]

The 1980s saw a growing public perception that serious juvenile crime was increasing, and that this increase was the result of the juvenile system becoming too lenient in the way it handled juvenile offenders. In reality, there was a considerable amount of misperception as to the reasons for the increases in juvenile crime rates. The misperceptions did not stop many States from implementing new laws that called for more punitive sanctions to be used against juvenile offenders. Many States also required the juvenile justice system to become more like the adult system as far as court procedures and made it easier to move certain classes of juvenile offenders into the adult court system (see The Juvenile Court System later in this chapter). The 1980s and 1990s continued the trend of treating an increasing number of juvenile offenders as criminals. Many States have adopted laws that hold juveniles more accountable for criminal behavior and now impose punishments more consistent with the seriousness of the crime.[9]

*L*AW ENFORCEMENT AND JUVENILE CRIME

In 2014, law enforcement agencies in the United States made over 1 million juvenile arrests. While this is a very unacceptable number, there have been very significant declines juvenile arrests in both violent and property crimes (see following charts). Following a steady decline since 2006 , and an even more significant decline since the mid 1990's, the juvenile violent crime index arrest rate reached a new historic low in 2014. The juvenile property crime index showed an even larger decline hitting its lowest point in more than 30 years.[10]

The juvenile arrest rate for all crimes decreased substantially for both males and females since the peak in 1996, and at the lowest level for both genders since 1980.[11]

Arrests per 100,000 juveniles ages 10–17, 1980–2014

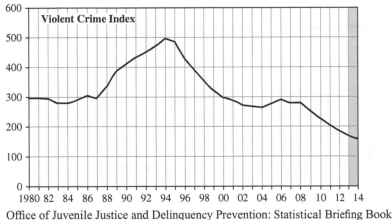

Office of Juvenile Justice and Delinquency Prevention: Statistical Briefing Book

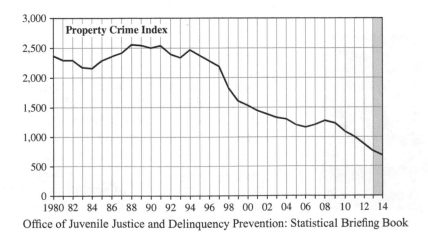

Office of Juvenile Justice and Delinquency Prevention: Statistical Briefing Book

Arrests per 100,000 males ages 10–17, 1980–2014

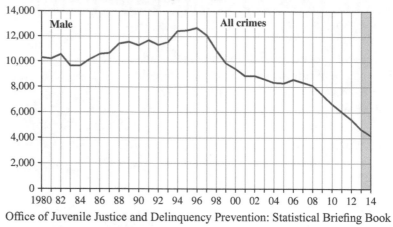

Office of Juvenile Justice and Delinquency Prevention: Statistical Briefing Book

Arrests per 100,000 females ages 10–17, 1980–2014

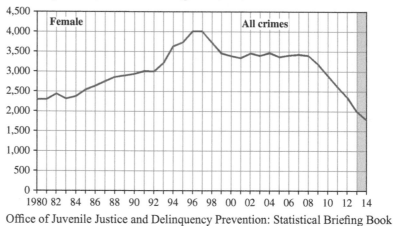

Office of Juvenile Justice and Delinquency Prevention: Statistical Briefing Book

𝒯HE JUVENILE COURT SYSTEM

JURISDICTION

Juvenile courts in the United States, as a general rule, have jurisdiction over all offenses committed by all persons under the age of eighteen. Three States (Connecticut, New York, and North Carolina) have limited the juvenile court jurisdiction to persons under the age of sixteen. Ten other states have set the limit to persons under the age of seventeen.[12] Many States have set the upper age limit higher (typically twenty) for jurisdiction over certain status offenses, abuse, neglect, and dependency matters (see below for definitions of these offenses).

Many States have also extended the upper age limits in juvenile court in order to retain jurisdiction so that it may provide sanctions and services to juveniles who committed offenses while still under the upper age limit of the court. While the age does vary by State, four States (California, Montana, Oregon, and Wisconsin) have extended the age over which the court may retain jurisdiction in delinquency matters to twenty-four.[13]

Juvenile courts also maintain jurisdiction over children who have been victims of abuse (physical, sexual, and emotional), who have been neglected, and who are dependent. Dependent children are those who have no parents or legal guardians, or their parents or guardians are unable to care for them.

DELINQUENCY AND STATUS OFFENSES

Juveniles can be charged with two basic types of offenses: **delinquency** and status. Delinquency is an offense that if committed by an adult, would be a criminal act. A juvenile who commits the crime of burglary would be charged in juvenile court with delinquency. This would be the case unless the juvenile court waives jurisdiction and transfers the case to adult court (see the following).

© sonya etchison, 2011. Used under license from Shutterstock, Inc.

Delinquency
Delinquency is an offense that if committed by an adult, would be a criminal act.

Status offenses are violations that if committed by an adult would not be a criminal act. Examples of status offenses would be: truancy, running away from home, violating curfew, and being incorrigible.

Status Offenses
Status offenses are violations that if committed by an adult would not be a criminal act.

THE JUVENILE COURT PROCESS

Cases can be referred to the juvenile court system in one of several ways depending upon the jurisdiction. Generally, cases are referred by law enforcement, parents, victims, schools, and probation officers. Law enforcement referrals account for 83 percent of all cases entering the juvenile court system in 2009.[14]

INTAKE

Cases that are referred to juvenile court are first screened by the intake department. In most jurisdictions, the intake process is usually conducted by the juvenile probation department. The intake officer will first review the case to make sure that there is sufficient evidence to justify the allegation. If there is not enough evidence, the case will be dismissed at this time. If there is enough evidence, the intake

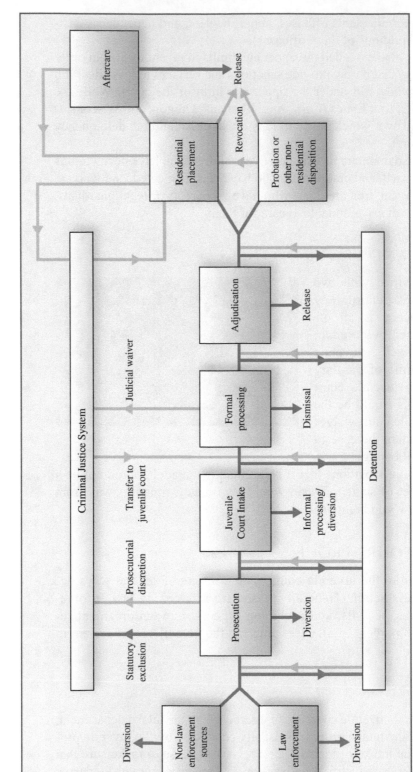

OJJDP Statistical Briefing Book, http://www.ojjdp.gov/ojstatbb/structure_process/case.html

officer will determine if the case should be handled formally or informally. About half of all juvenile cases are handled informally.[15]

INFORMALLY PROCESSED CASES

The majority of informally processed cases will eventually be dismissed. In the other informally handled cases, the juvenile will agree to specific conditions that must be followed during a specified period of time. These conditions can include such things as attending school, abiding by a curfew, attending drug or other counseling, or any other sanction that would be deemed appropriate for the particular case. These conditions are usually monitored by a juvenile probation officer for compliance. This is generally referred to as informal probation. If the juvenile successfully completes the term of informal probation, the case will be dismissed.

FORMALLY PROCESSED CASES

If the intake decision is to formally handle the case, a petition is filed and the case is put on the court calendar. The petition will request that the court formally adjudicate the juvenile as a delinquent, status offender, or dependent child. The adjudication process is almost always conducted by a judge since only a handful of states allow for a jury trial in juvenile court. In some more serious cases, the petition may request that the court waive jurisdiction and transfer the case to adult court.[16]

© Lisa F. Young, 2011. Used under license from Shutterstock, Inc.

JUDICIAL DISPOSITIONS

The juvenile court has a variety of dispositions that it may hand down in formally processed cases. The most serious disposition would be to remove the juvenile from their home and place them in a residential facility. The most common disposition would be to place the child on formal/court-ordered supervision by the juvenile probation department. Other dispositions can include such things as payment of a fine, community service, restitution, or referral to social or other agencies.

TRIED AS AN ADULT

Every State has laws that allow for juveniles to be tried as adults in criminal court under certain circumstances. The process of transferring cases from the jurisdiction of the juvenile court to the jurisdiction of the adult criminal court is called **judicial waiver**. In some jurisdictions the judicial waiver is referred to as certifying the juvenile as an adult. The minimum age that a juvenile may be tried as an adult varies from State to State, and also varies by the type of crime committed. Some States do not specify a minimum age for judicial waiver; it is left up to prosecutorial discretion. In thirty-one States, juveniles who have been tried as adults must then be prosecuted in all future cases as an adult.[17]

Judicial Waiver

The process of transferring cases from the jurisdiction of the juvenile court to the jurisdiction of the adult criminal court is called judicial waiver.

Between 1985 and 1994, the number of cases that were judicially waived increased by 91 percent. This coincided with and was a result of the public perception that the juvenile court system was becoming too lenient in their dispositions (as discussed in a previous section). The number of judicially waived delinquency cases remained relatively stable between 2001 and 2007 and then fell 41% between 2007 and 2013. As a result, the number of cases judicially waived in 2013 was 31% less than in 1985.[18]

The number of cases judicially waived to criminal court peaked in 1994

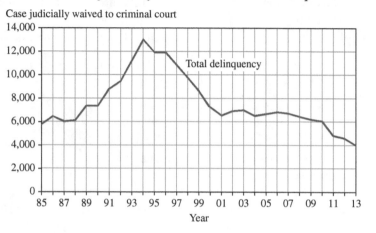

In 1985, more property offense cases were judicially waived than cases in any other offense category; in 2013, more person offense cases were waived than cases in any other category

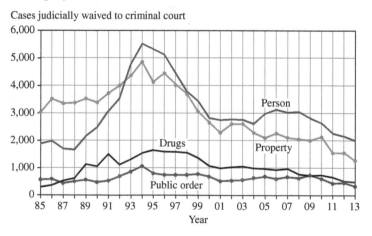

RIGHTS OF THE JUVENILE OFFENDER

Prior to the 1960s, the United States Supreme Court rarely heard any cases dealing with the rights of juveniles within the criminal justice system. These issues were left up to the individual States to deal with. Starting in the mid-1960s, the Supreme Court ruled on several landmark cases that dealt with the rights of juveniles.

SUPREME COURT CASES

KENT V. UNITED STATES (1966)

The first major decision by the United States Supreme Court addressing the issue of juvenile rights was decided in 1966 in the case of **Kent v. United States**.[19] This case dealt with Morris Kent who was a sixteen year old who was charged with rape and robbery and was tried and convicted as an adult in criminal court. Kent's attorney successfully argued that Morris was not given a hearing in juvenile court prior to the waiving of jurisdiction and trying him in the criminal court. The United States Supreme Court agreed with the defense and ruled that juveniles are entitled to a juvenile court hearing prior to judicial waiver.

Kent v. United States

In this case the United States Supreme Court ruled that juveniles are entitled to a juvenile court hearing prior to judicial waiver.

IN RE GAULT (1967)

The next major ruling came the next year, 1967, in the case of **In re Gault**.[20] In this case, Gerald Gault, age fifteen, was on juvenile probation when he and a friend made a crank phone call to their adult neighbor. Gerald was arrested and subsequently adjudicated and committed to training school until he reached the age of majority. After the trial, an attorney was obtained and appealed the verdict. The case was eventually heard by the United States Supreme Court. The issue raised by the defense attorney was that Gault's constitutional rights were violated; specifically, no notice of charges, no counsel present, no ability to confront witnesses, the right to protection against self-incrimination, no right to a transcript of the trial proceedings, and no right to an appeal of the verdict. The Supreme Court ruled that in any hearing that could result in a juvenile being committed to an institution, the juvenile has the following rights:

In re Gault

In this case the Supreme Court ruled that in any hearing that could result in a juvenile being committed to an institution, the juvenile has several enumerated rights equal to the rights of an adult.

1. Right to notice

© Lisa F. Young, 2011.
Used under license from
Shutterstock, Inc.

2. The right to counsel
3. The right to confront any witness against them
4. Protection against self-incrimination

© Lisa F. Young, 2011.
Used under license from
Shutterstock, Inc.

5. Right to a court transcript
6. Right to an appeal

IN RE WINSHIP (1970)

Samuel Winship was a twelve year old who was adjudicated as a delinquent and committed to a training school for stealing $112 from a woman's purse in a store. Following the accepted procedure up until this time, the New York juvenile court adjudicated based on the civil standard of a preponderance of the evidence. The case was appealed to the United States Supreme Court and the ruling in this case, *In re Winship*,[21] was that the same standard of beyond a reasonable doubt that is used in adult criminal cases must also be used in juvenile proceedings.

ADDITIONAL RULINGS

The United States Supreme Court has also ruled on several other important issues that have had an impact on the juvenile justice system. In the 1975 case of ***Breed v. Jones***,[22] the court ruled that if a juvenile is adjudicated for a case in juvenile court, it is double jeopardy if they are tried again for the same offense in adult court. In 1984, in the case of ***Schall v. Martin***,[23] the court ruled that the "pretrial" detention of juveniles is allowable if there was a serious risk that the juvenile would commit another crime if released. In the 2005 case of ***Roper v. Simmons***,[24] the court ruled that the minimum age for imposing the death penalty is eighteen. Finally, in the recent case of ***Miller v. Alabama***, decided on June 25, 2012,[25] the United States Supreme Court ruled that it is a violation of the Eighth Amendment's prohibition of cruel and unusual punishment to have a law that mandates life in prison without the possibility of parole for juvenile homicide offenders.

In re Winship

In this case the United States Supreme Court ruled that the same standard of beyond a reasonable doubt that is used in adult criminal cases must also be used in juvenile proceedings.

Breed v. Jones

The court ruled that if a juvenile is adjudicated for a case in juvenile court, it is double jeopardy if they are tried again for the same offense in adult court.

Schall v. Martin

The court ruled that the "pretrial" detention of juveniles is allowable if there was a serious risk that the juvenile would commit another crime if released.

Roper v. Simmons

The court ruled that the minimum age for imposing the death penalty is eighteen.

Miller v. Alabama

The United States Supreme Court ruled that it is a violation of the Eighth Amendment's prohibition of cruel and unusual punishment to have a law that mandates life in prison without the possibility of parole for juvenile homicide offenders.

*J*UVENILE CORRECTIONS

Juvenile correction facilities, the equivalent of an adult prison, are generally called **residential placement facilities**. Placing a juvenile in one of these facilities is usually the last option that juvenile judges will consider. Only those youths that pose the most serious threat to society are considered for this sanction. Juvenile judges will typically consider less stringent alternatives before resorting to confinement of the juvenile. In 2013, there were 78,700 juveniles who were adjudicated delinquent and placed in residential confinement.[26]

Just like in the adult justice system, probation is the most common form of sanctioning in the juvenile system. In 2013, an estimated 205,000 delinquency cases resulted in a term of probation.[27] There are a variety of other sanctions that can be imposed by the juvenile court system which were discussed earlier in this chapter.

Residential Placement Facilities

Juvenile correction facilities, the equivalent of an adult prison, are generally called residential placement facilities.

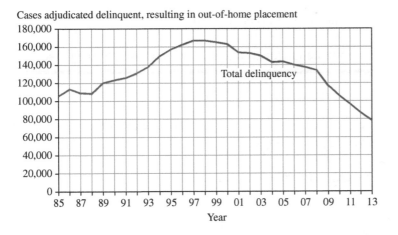

Cases adjudicated delinquent, resulting in out-of-home placement

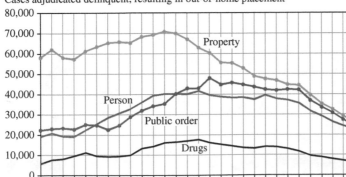

Cases adjudicated delinquent, resulting in out-of-home placement

REVIEW QUESTIONS:

1. The traditionally accepted age of reason during the eighteenth century was _____ years old.

2. The first juvenile court in the United States was established in the State of _____.

3. The term that means "the State as parent" is _____.

4. Juveniles under the age of fifteen account for about _____ of all juvenile arrests.

5. If a juvenile commits an offense that would be a criminal act if committed by an adult, it is called _____.

6. Truancy, running away from home, and violating curfew, are all examples of _____ offenses.

7. In most jurisdictions, the juvenile intake process is conducted by _____.

8. The process of transferring cases from the jurisdiction of the juvenile court to the jurisdiction of the adult criminal court is called _____.

9. The 1970 United States Supreme Court case of _____ established that the standard of beyond a reasonable doubt be used in juvenile proceedings.

10. Juvenile correctional facilities are generally called _____.

CRITICAL THINKING QUESTIONS:

1. Explain the concept of *parens patriae* and how is used to rationalize the modern concept of the juvenile court system.

2. Discuss, in some detail, what you believe are the reasons for the significant decline in juvenile crime rates since the mid 1990's.

3. Describe the jurisdiction of juvenile courts in America and include in your discussion why you think that different States use different ages when defining juveniles.

4. Discuss the difference between informally processed cases and formally processed cases as used in the juvenile justice system.

5. Explain the concept of judicial waiver and discuss your opinion about trying juveniles in adult criminal court.

6. Select one of the United States Supreme Court cases mentioned in the chapter and explain the significance of the Court's decision as it relates to Juvenile justice.

————————— NOTES —————————

CHAPTER 12

[1] OJJDP Statistical Briefing Book, accessed April, 2012 at http://www.ojjdp.gov/ojstatbb/population/qa01101.asp?qaDate=2012.

[2] U.S. Bureau of the Census. "Projected Population by Single Year of Age, Sex, Race, and Hispanic Origin for the United States: July 1, 2000 to July 1, 2050." Released August 14, 2008.

[3] OJJDP Statistical Briefing Book.

[4] Office of Juvenile Justice and Delinquency Prevention, 1999 National Report Series, Juvenile Justice: A Century of Change, December 1999.

[5] Sanford Fox, "Juvenile Justice Reform: An Historical Perspective," Modern Juvenile Justice: Cases and Materials
(St. Paul, MN: 1972).

[6] Juvenile Justice: A Century of Change.

[7] Ibid, page 2

[8] Ibid

[9] Ibid

[10] Office of Juvenile Justice and Delinquency Prevention, Statistical Briefing Book, accessed March, 2017 at https://www.ojjdp.gov/index.html.

[11] Ibid

[12] Georgia, Illinois, Louisiana, Massachusetts, Michigan, Missouri, New Hampshire, South Carolina, Texas, and Wisconsin.

[13] Juvenile Justice: A Century of Change.

[14] OJJDP Statistical Briefing Book, accessed May, 2012 at http://www.ojjdp.gov/ojstatbb/structure_process/case.html.

[15] Ibid

[16] Ibid

[17] Juvenile Justice: A Century of Change.

[18] Sarah Hockenberry and Charles Puzzanchera, *Juvenile Court Statistics 2013*, National Center for Juvenile Justice, July, 2015.

[19] Kent v. United States, 383 U.S. 541, 86 S.Ct. 1045 (1966).

[20] In re Gault, 387 U.S. 1, 87 S.Ct. 1428 (1967).

[21] In re Winship, 397 U.S. 358, 99 S. Ct. 1068 (1970).

[22] Breed v. Jones, 421 U.S. 519, 95 S.Ct. 1779 (1975).

[23] Schall v. Martin, 467 U.S. 253, 104 S.Ct. 2403 (1984).

[24] Roper v. Simmons, 543 U.S. 551 (2005).

[25] Miller v. Alabama 567 U.S. _____ (2012).

[26] Hockenberry and Puzzanchera, 2015.

[27] Ibid.

CHAPTER OVERVIEW

© 3D creation/Shutterstock.com

Ethics is the foundation of all criminal justice agencies and the professionals who are employed by them. Criminal justice professionals are public servants, and as such, are in the public eye more than most other professions. They are under constant scrutiny by the public and the media.

In this chapter, we will examine the ethical issues that confront our police and correctional officers as well as judges, prosecutors, and defense attorneys. This examination will begin with a brief look at the competing views of ethical systems and how individuals develop their own moral and ethical values.

All of the branches of the criminal justice system will be scrutinized from the viewpoint of what ethical considerations are unique to each and where the common areas of misconduct are located. We will also look at how the media has influenced how the public views the criminal justice system in terms of ethics and professionalism.

CHAPTER LEARNING OBJECTIVES

After reading this chapter, you will be able to:

1. Understand the difference between ethics and morals.
2. Explain the difference between deontological and teleological ethics.
3. Understand the importance of an agency's Code of Ethics.
4. Understand the concept of discretion within each branches of the criminal justice system
5. Explain the importance of ethics training in criminal justice.
6. Describe how the media has influenced ethics within the criminal justice system.

--------------------------------- KEYWORDS ---------------------------------

Ethics	Morals
Values	Golden Rule
Deontological Ethics	Teleological Ethics
Utilitarianism	Code of Ethics
Police Discretion	Blue Curtain
Integrity	Impropriety
Exculpatory Evidence	

WHAT IS ETHICS?

Golden Rule

Do unto others as you would have them do unto you

"When most people think of ethics (or morals), they think of rules for distinguishing between right and wrong, such as the **Golden Rule** ("Do unto others as you would have them do unto you"), a code of professional conduct such as the Hippocratic Oath ("First of all, do no harm"), a religious creed such as the Ten Commandments ("Thou Shalt not kill . . ."), or a wise aphorism such as the sayings of Confucius."[1]

© Ionut Catalin Parvu/Shutterstock.com

We must distinguish between the two commonly interchangeable, yet fundamentally different, terms of ethics and morals, both of which deal with the concept of what is right and what is wrong. **Ethics** can be defined as the rules of conduct established

and recognized to determine what is right or wrong by a specific group, culture, or class of people. To put simply, ethics establishes the moral values of an organization or defined group. **Morals**, or moral values, relate to an individual's standards and beliefs as to what is right and wrong. **Values** are a set of common beliefs held by a person that has an emotional component that serves as a guide to enable that person to apply their moral beliefs to decide what is right and wrong in specific situations.[2]

People begin learning their moral values early in life and they continue to be refined throughout their life as they mature. Families, peers, schools, church, and other social interactions all contribute to an individual's beliefs and concepts of what is right and what is wrong. Some of the perceptions of moral values seem to be universal. Most people agree that the index offenses listed in Part I of the Uniform Crime Reports (UCR) of murder, rape, robbery, aggravated assault, burglary, larceny, auto theft, and arson are all inherently wrong. It would seem, with so many universal truths, that moral and ethical decisions would be simple to make and all we would have to do is apply common sense to all of our ethical dilemmas. If this were true, how can we explain so many ethical disputes and issues in our society?

Dr. David B. Resnick, in an article written in 2015, gives a good example as to why this is not true. "One plausible explanation of these disagreements is that all people recognize some common ethical norms but interpret, apply, and balance them in different ways in light of their own values and life experiences. For example, two people could agree that murder is wrong but disagree about the morality of abortion because they have different understandings of what it means to be a human being."[3]

It is important to realize that ethical and moral values vary among different cultures and can change within individual cultures over time. Polygamy, having more than one wife, is an accepted practice in several countries in the world, yet is considered to be an immoral act in the United States. The legal age for drinking alcohol varies around the world from having no minimum age in 19 countries to a complete ban of the consumption of alcohol at any age in 16 countries.[4] Slavery was legal in the United States until 1865.[5] Today, slavery is considered to be completely outdated and immoral.

Morals

Relate to an individual's standards and beliefs as to what is right and wrong

Values

A set of common beliefs held by a person that has an emotional component that serves as a guide to enable that person to apply their moral beliefs to decide what is right and wrong.

*C*OMPETING VIEWS OF ETHICAL SYSTEMS

Emmanuel Kant
(1724–1804)

John Stewart Mill
(1806–1873)

The German philosopher Immanuel Kant (1724–1804) wrote extensively on what is now referred to as deontological or duty-based ethics. **Deontological ethics** looks at the rightness or wrongness of an action or a decision itself rather than the resulting consequences of that action.[6] People have a duty to do the right thing, even if that thing produces more harm than doing the right thing. Kant would have thought that it would be wrong (unethical) to tell a lie even if it meant saving a friend from a murderer.[7] Simply stated, deontological (duty based) ethics is concerned with what people do, not with the consequences of their actions.[8] The act of giving money to a homeless person on the street is a good act. It would not matter that the homeless person used that money to buy illegal drugs. Deontological ethics says the act itself was good.

While deontological ethics looks at the act itself, a different and competing ethical approach looks at the consequences of the act. **Teleological ethics**, one version of which, utilitarianism, was created by Jeremy Bentham (1748–1832) (see Chapter 4) and John Stewart Mill (1806–1873). **Utilitarianism** says that the right course of action is the one that maximizes happiness and reduces suffering.[9] It believes in the concept of the "end justifies the means." Teleological ethics judges the consequences of the act to determine whether the act was good. It is for this reason that teleological ethics is often referred to as consequentialism. Using the given example of giving money to a homeless person, teleological ethics would say that the act was not good because the consequences of the act, buying illegal drugs with the money, was a bad thing.

Deontological Ethics

Looks at the rightness or wrongness of an action or a decision itself rather than the resulting consequences of that action.

Teleological Ethics

Judges the consequences of the act to determine whether the act was good.

Utilitarianism

The right course of action is the one that maximizes happiness and reduces suffering.

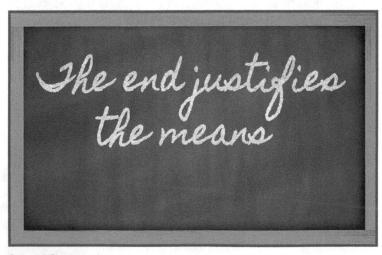

© vepar5/Shutterstock.com

Ethics and The Criminal Justice System

Ethics is the foundation of our criminal justice system. Criminal justice professionals are public servants, and as such, are in the public eye more than most other professions. They are under constant scrutiny by the public and the media.

Most professions have developed a **Code of Ethics**, which can be defined as "the guideline that sets acceptable behaviors for a given group of people or profession."[10] Almost without exception, professional organizations in every field have a Code of Ethics developed specifically for their profession. The National Association of Social Workers, National Society of Professional Engineers, the American Counseling Association, the Association of American Educators, the American Medical Association, just to name a few, all have developed ethical standards for their professions.

Each component of the criminal justice profession has developed its own Code of Ethics which has been adapted, in whole or part, by virtually all of the individual departments and agencies. Some of the professional organizations within the criminal justice system, each of which has established its own standards of professional conduct are as follows:

Code of Ethics
The guideline that sets acceptable behaviors for a given group or profession.

The American Correctional Association[11]
The American Probation and Parole Association[12]
National District Attorneys Association[13]
Criminal Justice Standards for the Defense Function (ABA)[14]
American Bar Association Canons of Professional Ethics[15]
International Association of Chiefs of Police Code of Ethics[16]

© Gustavo Frazao/Shutterstock.com

LAW ENFORCEMENT CODE OF ETHICS[17][18]

As a law enforcement officer, my fundamental duty is to serve the community; to safeguard lives and property; to protect the innocent against deception, the weak against oppression or intimidation and the peaceful against violence or disorder; and to respect the constitutional rights of all to liberty, equality and justice.

I will keep my private life unsullied as an example to all and will behave in a manner that does not bring discredit to me or to my agency. I will maintain courageous calm in the face of danger, scorn or ridicule; develop self-restraint; and be constantly mindful of the welfare of others. Honest in thought and deed both in my personal and official life, I will be exemplary in obeying the law and the regulations of my department. Whatever I see or hear of a confidential nature or that is confided to me in my official capacity will be kept ever secret unless revelation is necessary in the performance of my duty.

I will never act officiously or permit personal feelings, prejudices, political beliefs, aspirations, animosities or friendships to influence my decisions. With no compromise for crime and with relentless prosecution of criminals, I will enforce the law courteously and appropriately without fear or favor, malice or ill will, never employing unnecessary force or violence and never accepting gratuities.

I recognize the badge of my office as a symbol of public faith, and I accept it as a public trust to be held so long as I am true to the ethics of police service. I will never engage in acts of corruption or bribery, nor will I condone such acts by other police officers. I will cooperate with all legally authorized agencies and their representatives in the pursuit of justice.

I know that I alone am responsible for my own standard of professional performance and will take every reasonable opportunity to enhance and improve my level of knowledge and competence.

I will constantly strive to achieve these objectives and ideals, dedicating myself before God to my chosen profession . . . law enforcement.

𝒫OLICE ETHICAL CONSIDERATIONS

Police are the most visible component of the criminal justice system in America. They are in marked vehicles on our streets and highways, answer calls for service wearing uniforms, and interact with the public in excess of 40 million times every year.[19] With all of this exposure, it is essential that they perform their job in a professional and ethical manner at all times. Failure to do so can, in some extreme cases, result in national headlines, public debate, and negative perceptions by citizens that can produce a damaging stereotyping image of the entire profession.

POLICE DISCRETION

Police are given a wide range of discretion to perform their duties. Discretion is authority that police officers have to use their individual judgment concerning decisions that they must make on a daily basis. The decision whether to stop a vehicle for a minor violation, or to issue a warning or a ticket if they do stop the vehicle, is all part of the discretion that most police officers have. Since police officers routinely work without direct supervision, police discretion is a widely accepted and almost universal practice that allows police officers to make decisions based upon their knowledge, experience, training, professionalism, and individual backgrounds.

It is imperative that all discretional decisions be, first and foremost, based on good ethical reasoning. Officers must be fair and nondiscriminatory when applying discretion. Treating any class of citizens differently would be an abuse of discretion. Ticketing only minorities would be a gross violation of discretionary authority. Male officers who routinely issue warnings to female violators while issuing tickets to male violators is another example of discriminatory discretion and would be an abuse of power.

One of the most important decision-making factors that police use is their individual background experiences. Police officer A stops a vehicle for running a red light. Assuming there was no accident or danger to other vehicles; the

© Michael Dechev/Shutterstock.com

© michaeljung/Shutterstock.com

officer decides not to issue a citation and just issues a warning to the driver. Police officer B observes a similar situation and stops the vehicle. Officer B has had a family member seriously injured by a driver who had run a red light several months earlier. Because of this personal experience, officer B has determined that he or she will write a ticket for all traffic light violations that he or she observes and issues a citation to the driver. Both officers would be acting properly within the guidelines of police discretion.

Police discretion can be limited by departmental policies and can also be limited by statute. A police department may decide that there are too many traffic accidents taking place at a specific intersection within its jurisdiction. The department could issue a directive to all police officers that they are to write tickets for all traffic violations observed at that location, thus removing officer discretion. There are also laws that have been enacted that limit police discretion. These types of laws usually require some form of mandatory arrest for specific crimes. Domestic battery laws in many jurisdictions fall into this category of crime in that it takes away the officer's ability to use discretion when there is physical evidence that a battery has taken place.

BLUE CURTAIN

Blue Curtain

A code of silence among police officers where officers refuse to testify or disclose information concerning the corrupt activity of fellow officers.

The **blue curtain**, also referred to as the blue wall of silence, is a code of silence among police officers where officers refuse to testify or disclose information concerning the corrupt activity of fellow officers. Unfortunately, this practice remains widespread among police agencies throughout the country. Fortunately, as we see, there are solutions to this problem that an increasing number of agencies are employing to combat this very serious ethical dilemma.

An extensive study focusing on the issues surrounding the blue curtain was conducted between 1999 and 2000 by the National Institute of Ethics in conjunction with the International Association of Chiefs of Police.[20] The study consisted of surveying 3714 officers and academy recruits from 42 states. Among the recruits surveyed, the study found:[21]

- 79% said that a law enforcement Code of Silence exists and is fairly common throughout the nation
- 52% said that the fact the code exists doesn't really bother them
- 24% said the code is more justified when excessive force involved a citizen who was abusive

Among current officers, the study found:[22]

- 46% said they witnessed misconduct by another employee but concealed what they knew
- The top five reasons officers gave for not reporting misconduct were:
  - They would be ostracized
  - The officer who committed the misconduct would be punished or fired
  - They would be fired
  - They would be "blackballed"
  - The administration would not do anything even if reported

SOLUTIONS: LEADERSHIP AND TRAINING

The same study by The National Institute of Ethics surveyed the same current officers and asked them to offer solutions for controlling the blue curtain or Code of Silence. The five most frequently offered solutions from officers were (in order of frequency):[23]

- Conduct good ethics training
- More consistent accountability
- Ensure open communication between officers and leaders
- Provide an anonymous reporting system
- Protect whistleblowers

There is a consensus amongst law enforcement professionals that the solution to the problem of misconduct, and the subculture of the blue curtain that supports it, requires a three-prong approach.

1. Improve hiring practices
2. Ethics training
3. Leadership

IMPROVE HIRING PRACTICES

While most police agencies conduct rigorous background investigations on potential recruits, there is still room for improvement. The weeding out of unethical individuals who apply can be a very difficult endeavor. Hiring only the most conscientious candidates is important because these are the ones who have a higher degree of **integrity,** which is an adherence to moral and ethical principles.[24]

Integrity
The adherence to moral and ethical principles.

ETHICS TRAINING

Prior to the 1990s, ethics training for law enforcement, with very few meaningful exceptions, was either nonexistent or cursory at best. Police departments have

come to realize that ethics training is essential for all officers and recruits. Departments now recognize that "demand exists for expanded training hours, more quality training resources, and greater involvement with ethics training at all levels of the organization, but the number of hours dedicated to this training remains rather insignificant in the face of such need."[25]

The training must start with a comprehensive educational program in the police academy dealing with ethical decision-making and integrity training. Police recruits must be taught to understand the consequences of unethical behavior and that doing the right thing is essential. Everyone makes mistakes but it is important that officers realize that owning up to mistakes is much better than attempting to cover them up and it is the right thing to do. When cover-ups are later discovered, the consequences are usually much worse because the original problem is now compounded by lies, filing of false reports, perjury, and loss of trust. Covering up for other officers can result in losing their job, their pension, their reputation, and even result in possible jail or prison time. Lying can cost an officer his or her job. There is no circumstance where lying to protect another is important enough to rob an officer of his or her freedom, career, or dignity. Being honest is simply a choice to do the right thing or not.

Ethics training must not end in the academy. It is important that agencies reinforce the initial ethics and integrity training by providing regular, usually yearly, in-service update training.

LEADERSHIP

Good ethics training sets the foundation for a trusted, professional, and respected police agency. In order to build on this foundation, everyone within the agency must be onboard and fully support the principles of ethical behavior. This must start with the top leadership of the agency and include all levels within the chain of command. The best ethics training in the world soon becomes meaningless and rendered ineffective if not fully supported by the leadership.

"Leadership that allows for mediocrity to first exist and then remain, rather than demand the highest level of conduct within the department, can create a climate ripe for misconduct."[26] Leading by providing a positive example is one of the most effective ways to establish an environment of integrity and honesty in any agency. "While ethical supervisors help maintain an ethical workplace, uncaring and incompetent officials can promote misconduct."[27] When officers know that their supervisors demonstrate and demand ethical behavior, it makes it much easier to follow their example and do the right thing. When all leaders in an agency demonstrate consistency concerning ethical behavior and promote integrity among their officers, the negative subculture can be reversed and transformed into a culture of professionalism.

Judicial Ethical Considerations

The judiciary is an independent branch of government that is responsible for interpreting and fairly applying the laws. The criminal sector of the judiciary consists of judges, prosecutors, and defense attorneys, each of which has its own unique ethical considerations.

JUDGES

Judges, depending on the jurisdiction, are elected or appointed to render impartial and fair decisions in all hearings, trials, and appeals. The law is not "black and white," there is a lot of gray area. Because of this gray area, judges are given some latitude in how they rule on legal issues provided that they stay within the legal parameters established by precedent, the rule of law, and the U.S. and State Constitutions. Canon 2 of the Code of Conduct for the U.S. Judges state that "A judge should avoid impropriety and the appearance of impropriety in all activities."[28] **Impropriety** is the failure to observe standards of honesty.

© bikeriderlondon/Shutterstock.com

Impropriety
The failure to observe standards of honesty.

Judges also have considerable discretion, particularly in the areas of sentencing and in many of the ruling that are made, both pre-trial and during the trial.

MISCONDUCT ISSUES

Judges, like all other criminal justice professionals, have an obligation to make ethical decisions at all times. When they don't, they are subject to disciplinary sanctions by their Judicial Review Board, the American Bar Association, as well as possible criminal actions for serious illegal decisions.

Examples of judicial misconduct include:[29]

- Special treatment to friends and relatives
- Special treatment to business associates
- Accepting bribes
- Improperly discussing a case with an attorney
- Lying under oath (note: a judge is always under oath in the courtroom)
- Citing outdated laws or precedents
- Ignoring the law

PROSECUTORS

The role of the prosecutor is to represent the citizens of their respective jurisdiction in all criminal matters that come to the courts. The responsibility of the prosecutor is to not just seek convictions, but to seek justice. The American Bar Association states that "it is the duty of the prosecutor to know and be guided by the standards of professional conduct as defined by applicable professional traditions, ethical codes, and law in the prosecutor's jurisdiction."[30]

PROSECUTORIAL DISCRETION

Within the entire criminal justice system, prosecutors have by far the most discretion to make decisions. Prosecutorial discretion includes:

- Whether or not to actually charge a defendant with a crime, even after arrest.
- What cases will go to trial
- What cases will be offered a plea bargain, and what that bargain will include in terms of reducing the original charge and sentencing considerations.
- Preparing witnesses for trial

PROSECUTORIAL MISCONDUCT

With such broad discretionary authority, comes great responsibility. Prosecutors must be above reproach in everything they do concerning a criminal case, like all attorneys, they must avoid the appearance of impropriety. Four of the more common types of prosecutorial misconduct are:[31]

Exculpatory Evidence

Evidence which tends to show that the defendant is not guilty or has no criminal intent.

- Misusing pretrial publicity
- Withholding **exculpatory evidence** which is evidence which tends to show that the defendant is not guilty or has no criminal intent
- Using preemptory challenges to exclude jurors in a discriminatory manner (see Chapter 9)
- Using false evidence in court

DEFENSE ATTORNEYS

The Sixth Amendment to the U.S. Constitution guarantees that all persons accused of a crime are entitled to assistance of counsel for their defense, and if the accused is indigent, then the government is obligated to pay for their defense. The function of defense attorneys is to provide this counsel and to protect all of the due process rights of the accused. Defense attorneys can come from private practice paid for by the defendant or appointed by the court, or can be public defenders. Public defenders are usually full-time government attorneys whose sole job is to defend indigent defendants.

One of the most important functions of defense attorneys is to provide a zealous and effective defense for their client. They must do this within the bounds of professional ethics and individual morality.

DEFENSE COUNSEL MISCONDUCT

Ethical standards and rules forbid certain actions by defense attorneys. The following conduct is forbidden and would constitute unethical misconduct:[32]

- Engage in motions or actions to intentionally and maliciously harm others
- Knowingly advance unwarranted claims or defenses
- Conceal or fail to disclose that which he or she is required by law to reveal
- Knowingly use perjured or false evidence
- Knowingly make a false statement of law or fact
- Participate in the creation or preservation of evidence when he or she knows or it is obvious that the evidence is false
- Counsel the client in conduct that is illegal
- Engage in any other illegal conduct

*C*ORRECTIONAL ETHICAL CONSIDERATIONS

The function of correction officers is to supervise convicted offenders, or those awaiting trial, when they are in jail, in prison, or in the community on probation or parole. Correctional officers make sure that the facilities that hold offenders are secure and safe, and oversee the day-to-day custody of inmates.[33]

DUTIES OF CORRECTIONAL OFFICERS AND POTENTIAL MISCONDUCT ISSUES

Due to the confined environment of jails and prisons, correctional officers are in constant close proximity with the inmates. This presents several unique ethical issues. Correctional officers get to know the inmates and vice versa. It is essential, from an ethical as well as personal standpoint, that correctional officers act in an ethical and professional manner at all times. Typically, correctional officers are responsible for the following job duties. Overlooking or violating any of these raises ethical concerns.[34]

- Enforce rules and keep order
- Supervise the activities of inmates
- Search for contraband items
- Inspect facilities to ensure that they meet standards
- Report on inmate conduct
- Aid in rehabilitation and counseling of offenders

INMATE RIGHTS

It is also important that correctional officers be constantly aware and knowledgeable of the rights that inmates possess. Any violation of these rights raises serious ethical and legal issues.[35]

© Jospeh Sohm/Shutterstock.com

- Right to be treated fairly, with dignity and respect
- Right to privacy, due process, and initiate a grievance procedure
- Right to be informed of policy in the corrections facility
- Right to healthcare and personal-development training

PROBATION AND PAROLE OFFICERS

The majority of offenders, who are under sentence within the correctional system in the United States, are under the supervision of a probation and/or parole officer. Probation and parole officers serve as a liaison between the offender, victims, and the courts or parole board. Like all other members of the criminal justice system, these officers are expected and required to adhere to strict ethical and professional standards.

ETHICAL ISSUES

Ethical issues for probation and parole officers, like other criminal justice professionals, can arise from an abuse of discretion in managing their caseloads such as accepting gratuities, overlooking violations, giving special favors, and improper relationships with their offenders.

The Media

It would be difficult to write about criminal justice ethics without at least a brief discussion of how the media is shaping the opinions and beliefs of the public in this area. Police officers, correctional officers, judges, prosecutors, and defense attorneys are all under increasing scrutiny by traditional and social media outlets. The police, because they are the most visible of these professionals, seem to be the primary target. Almost everyone has a cell phone with a video camera. It has become standard practice to video any confrontation observed between the police and the public with the hope it will escalate to a newsworthy story.

A news story on CNN brought up an interesting perspective on the increased news coverage of police shootings. "It feels like every week, a name is added to the list: another man, often black and unarmed, has died at the hands of police. Michael Brown, Eric Garner, Tamir Rice, Jason Harrison, Walter Scott, Eric Harris, Freddie Gray, to name a few. The headlines make it feel as if the country is experiencing an unprecedented wave of police violence, but experts say that isn't the case. We're just seeing more mainstream coverage . . ."[36]

There are some positive and encouraging changes that are taking place as a result of this increased exposure. Police Departments are increasing the training of officers, the use and employment of vehicle and body cams is increasing at unprecedented rates, and possibly the most important outcome, is the increased awareness and implementation of community outreach by the police.

On the negative side, too many people formulate negative opinions based on initial news reporting before all of the facts are investigated and finalized. Partial videos often do not show the initial confrontation, only the end results, but they make dramatic news. They also show only one angle or perspective of the incident, which is different from what the officer sees.

It is important to understand that policing is a dangerous profession. Police officers are often called upon to make split second decisions; sometimes these are life and death decisions. They must make these instantaneous decisions based upon their training and experience since they frequently do not have time to make a comprehensive analysis because their life, or the life of another, may well depend on their instantaneous decision.

To use a sports analogy, the officer is like the referee in an NFL football game. The referee sees a play in real time. Did the player drop the ball before or after he or she had control of it and before or after his or her knee touched the ground while surrounded by a pile of players? The referee must make his or her decision immediately based on his or her perspective and position on the field. The referee's decision can now be reviewed by neutral officials who have the luxury of having the time to review the play from many different angles, in slow motion, and in conjunction with several experts. Interestingly, according to the NFL, the referees on the field are correct 95.9% of the time.[37] Just like the referees, police officers must make these split-second decisions in real time. Investigators, the media, the public, and the courts, have the luxury of analyzing these decisions from every angle after interviewing witnesses, viewing every radio call and video, and doing so taking as much time, sometimes months, as is required. It is only then that a final determination is made determining whether or not that split-second decision was the right one.

REVIEW QUESTIONS

1. The _____ _____ says "do unto other as you would have them do unto you."

2. _____ are the rules of conduct established and recognized to determine what is right or wrong by a specific group

3. An individual's standards and beliefs as to what is right and wrong, defines _____.

4. _____ ethics looks at the rightness or wrongness of an action or decision itself rather than the resulting consequences of that action.

5. _____ ethics judges the consequences of an act to determine whether the act was good.

6. A _____ __ _____ is the guideline that sets acceptable behavior for a given group of people or profession.

7. The authority that criminal justice professionals have to use their individual judgment concerning decisions that they must make on a daily basis is referred to as _____.

8. The code of silence among police officers is often referred to as the _____ _____.

9. _____ is the failure to observe standards of honesty.

10. _____ is evidence which tends to show that a defendant is not guilty or has no criminal intent.

CRITICAL THINKING QUESTIONS

1. Explain the difference between ethics and morals.

2. Discuss the difference between deontological ethics and teleological ethics.

3. Discuss the Law Enforcement Code of Ethics. How difficult would it be for a police officer to follow it on a daily basis?

4. Explain how discretion is used in each branch of criminal justice and why it is an important tool.

5. Explain what the blue curtain is and how it can be overcome.

6. Discuss the importance of ethics training in the criminal justice profession.

7. How has the media influenced the criminal justice profession?

─────────── NOTES ───────────

CHAPTER 13

[1] David B. Resnick, J. D., Ph.D. 2015. "What Is Ethics in Research & Why Is it Important?" *National Institutes of Health, U.S. Department of Health and Human Services,* National Institute of Environmental Health Sciences, accessed February, 2017 at https://www.niehs.nih.gov/research/resources/bioethics/whatis/.

[2] "How Are Morals and Values Different", Reference.com, accessed March, 2017 at https://www.reference.com/world-view/morals-values-different-713a71452ef-cfd9?qo=contentSimilarQuestions.

[3] David Resnick, Op.Cit.

[4] "Minimum Legal Drinking Age (MLDA) in 190 Countries", ProCon.org, accessed March, 2017 at http://drinkingage.procon.org/view.resource.php?resourceID=004294.

[5] When the 13th Amendment to the United States Constitution was ratified on December 6, 1865.

[6] Ethics Guide, "Duty Based Ethics", bbc.com, accessed March, 2017 at http://www.bbc.co.uk/ethics/introduction/duty_1.shtml.

[7] Ibid.

[8] Ibid.

[9] New World Encyclopedia, accessed March 2017 at http://www.newworldencyclopedia.org/entry/Utilitarianism.

[10] "What Is a Code of Ethics", Reference.com, accessed March, 2017 at https://www.reference.com/world-view/code-ethics-a6ff5e735318c932.

[11] Can be found at http://www.aca.org/ACA_Prod_IMIS/ACA_Member/About_Us/Code_of_Ethics/ACA_Member/AboutUs/Code_of_Ethics.aspx?hkey=61577ed2-c0c3-4529-bc01-36a248f79eba.

[12] Can be found at https://www.appa-net.org/eweb/DynamicPage.aspx?WebCode=IA_CodeEthics.

[13] Can be found at http://www.ndaa.org/pdf/NDAA%20NPS%203rd%20Ed.%20w%20Revised%20Commentary.pdf.

[14] Can be found at http://www.american-bar.org/groups/criminal_justice/standards/DefenseFunctionFourthEdition.html.

[15] Can be found at http://www.americanbar.org/content/dam/aba/migrated/cpr/mrpc/Canons_Ethics.authcheck-dam.pdf.

[16] Can be found at http://www.iacp.org/codeofethics.

[17] Ibid.

[18] The IACP adopted the Law Enforcement Code of Ethics at the 64th Annual IACP Conference and Exposition in October 1957. The Code of Ethics stands as a preface to the mission and commitment law enforcement agencies make to the public they serve.

[19] Matthew R. Durose, *Contacts Between Police and the Public, 2008*, U.S. Department of Justice, Office of Justice Programs, Bureau of Justice Statistics, October 2011.

[20] Neal Trautman, "*Police Code of Silence Facts Revealed*", The National Institute of Ethics, accessed March, 2017 at http://www.aele.org/loscode2000.html.

[21] Ibid.

[22] Ibid.

[23] Ibid.

[24] Dictionary.com, accessed March, 2017 at http://www.dictionary.com/browse/integrity.

[25] Ibid.

[26] Rick Martin, "*Police Corruption: An Analytical Look into Police Ethics*", FBI Law Enforcement Bulletin, May, 2011, accessed February, 2017, at https://leb.fbi.gov/2011/may/police-corruption-an-analytical-look-into-police-ethics.

[27] Ibid.

[28] United States Courts, Code of Conduct for United States Judges, uscourts.gov., accessed March 2017 at http://www.uscourts.gov/judges-judgeships/code-conduct-united-states-judges.

[29] B. Scott Burton, *Professionalism, Integrity, and Ethics in Criminal Justice*, Great River Learning, 2016.

[30] American Bar Association, Prosecution Function, General Standards, Standard 3–1.2 The Function of the Prosecutor, accessed March 2017, at http://www.americanbar.org/publications/criminal_justice_section_archive/crimjust_standards_pfunc_blk.html.

[31] Joycelyn M. Pollock, *Ethical Dilemmas and Decisions in Criminal Justice, 8th ed.*, Wadsworth Cengage Learning, Belmont, CA, 2014.

[32] Ibid.

[33] The National Center for Victims of Crime, *The Criminal Justice System*, accessed March, 2017 at https://victimsofcrime.org/help-for-crime-victims/get-help-bulletins-for-crime-victims/the-criminal-justice-system.

[34] Correctionalofficer.org, *Correctional Officers Duties*, accessed March 2017 at http://www.correctionalofficer.org/faq/correctional-officer-job-description.

[35] Ibid at http://www.correctionalofficer.org/professional-conduct.

[36] Eliott C. McLaughlin, *"We're not seeing more police shootings, just more news coverage"*, CNN.com, April 21, 2015, accessed March, 2017, at http://www.cnn.com/2015/04/20/us/police-brutality-video-social-media-attitudes/.

[37] NFL Football Operations, accessed March, 2017, at http://operations.nfl.com/the-officials/these-officials-are-really-good.

$\mathscr{U}$NITED STATES CONSTITUTION

We the People of the United States, in Order to form a more perfect Union, establish Justice, insure domestic Tranquility, provide for the common defence, promote the general Welfare, and secure the Blessings of Liberty to ourselves and our Posterity, do ordain and establish this Constitution for the United States of America.

ARTICLE. I.

SECTION. 1.

All legislative Powers herein granted shall be vested in a Congress of the United States, which shall consist of a Senate and House of Representatives.

SECTION. 2.

The House of Representatives shall be composed of Members chosen every second Year by the People of the several States, and the Electors in each State shall have the Qualifications requisite for Electors of the most numerous Branch of the State Legislature.

No Person shall be a Representative who shall not have attained to the Age of twenty five Years, and been seven Years a Citizen of the United States, and who shall not, when elected, be an Inhabitant of that State in which he shall be chosen.

Representatives and direct Taxes shall be apportioned among the several States which may be included within this Union, according to their respective Numbers, which shall be determined by adding to the whole Number of free Persons, including those bound to Service for a Term of Years, and excluding Indians not taxed, three fifths of all other Persons. The actual Enumeration shall be made within three Years after the first Meeting of the Congress of the United States, and within every subsequent Term of ten Years, in such Manner as they shall by Law direct. The Number of Representatives shall not exceed one for every thirty Thousand, but each State shall have at Least one Representative; and until such enumeration shall be made, the State of New Hampshire shall be entitled to chuse three, Massachusetts eight, Rhode-Island and Providence Plantations one, Connecticut five, New-York six, New Jersey four, Pennsylvania eight, Delaware one, Maryland six, Virginia ten, North Carolina five, South Carolina five, and Georgia three.

When vacancies happen in the Representation from any State, the Executive Authority thereof shall issue Writs of Election to fill such Vacancies.

The House of Representatives shall chuse their Speaker and other Officers; and shall have the sole Power of Impeachment.

SECTION. 3.

The Senate of the United States shall be composed of two Senators from each State, chosen by the Legislature thereof for six Years; and each Senator shall have one Vote.

Immediately after they shall be assembled in Consequence of the first Election, they shall be divided as equally as may be into three Classes. The Seats of the Senators of the first Class shall be vacated at the Expiration of the second Year, of the second Class at the Expiration of the fourth Year, and of the third Class at the Expiration of the sixth Year, so that one third may be chosen every second Year; and if Vacancies happen by Resignation, or otherwise, during the Recess of the Legislature of any State, the Executive thereof may make temporary Appointments until the next Meeting of the Legislature, which shall then fill such Vacancies.

No Person shall be a Senator who shall not have attained to the Age of thirty Years, and been nine Years a Citizen of the United States, and who shall not, when elected, be an Inhabitant of that State for which he shall be chosen.

The Vice President of the United States shall be President of the Senate, but shall have no Vote, unless they be equally divided.

The Senate shall chuse their other Officers, and also a President pro tempore, in the Absence of the Vice President, or when he shall exercise the Office of President of the United States.

The Senate shall have the sole Power to try all Impeachments. When sitting for that Purpose, they shall be on Oath or Affirmation. When the President of the United States is tried, the Chief Justice shall preside: And no Person shall be convicted without the Concurrence of two thirds of the Members present.

Judgment in Cases of Impeachment shall not extend further than to removal from Office, and disqualification to hold and enjoy any Office of honor, Trust or Profit under the United States: but the Party convicted shall nevertheless be liable and subject to Indictment, Trial, Judgment and Punishment, according to Law.

SECTION. 4.

The Times, Places and Manner of holding Elections for Senators and Representatives, shall be prescribed in each State by the Legislature thereof; but the Congress may at any time by Law make or alter such Regulations, except as to the Places of chusing Senators.

The Congress shall assemble at least once in every Year, and such Meeting shall be on the first Monday in December, unless they shall by Law appoint a different Day.

SECTION. 5.

Each House shall be the Judge of the Elections, Returns and Qualifications of its own Members, and a Majority of each shall constitute a Quorum to do Business; but a smaller Number may adjourn from day to day, and may be authorized to compel the Attendance of absent Members, in such Manner, and under such Penalties as each House may provide.

Each House may determine the Rules of its Proceedings, punish its Members for disorderly Behaviour, and, with the Concurrence of two thirds, expel a Member.

Each House shall keep a Journal of its Proceedings, and from time to time publish the same, excepting such Parts as may in their Judgment require Secrecy; and the Yeas and Nays of the Members of either House on any question shall, at the Desire of one fifth of those Present, be entered on the Journal.

Neither House, during the Session of Congress, shall, without the Consent of the other, adjourn for more than three days, nor to any other Place than that in which the two Houses shall be sitting.

SECTION. 6.

The Senators and Representatives shall receive a Compensation for their Services, to be ascertained by Law, and paid out of the Treasury of the United States. They shall in all Cases, except Treason, Felony and Breach of the Peace, be privileged from Arrest during their Attendance at the Session of their respective Houses, and in going to and returning from the same; and for any Speech or Debate in either House, they shall not be questioned in any other Place.

No Senator or Representative shall, during the Time for which he was elected, be appointed to any civil Office under the Authority of the United States, which shall have been created, or the Emoluments whereof shall have been encreased during such time; and no Person holding any Office under the United States, shall be a Member of either House during his Continuance in Office.

Section. 7.

All Bills for raising Revenue shall originate in the House of Representatives; but the Senate may propose or concur with Amendments as on other Bills.

Every Bill which shall have passed the House of Representatives and the Senate, shall, before it become a Law, be presented to the President of the United States: If he approve he shall sign it, but if not he shall return it, with his Objections to that House in which it shall have originated, who shall enter the Objections at large on their Journal, and proceed to reconsider it. If after such Reconsideration two thirds of that House shall agree to pass the Bill, it shall be sent, together with the Objections, to the other House, by which it shall likewise be reconsidered, and if approved by two thirds of that House, it shall become a Law. But in all such Cases the Votes of both Houses shall be determined by yeas and Nays, and the Names of the Persons voting for and against the Bill shall be entered on the Journal of each House respectively. If any Bill shall not be returned by the President within ten Days (Sundays excepted) after it shall have been presented to him, the Same shall be a Law, in like Manner as if he had signed it, unless the Congress by their Adjournment prevent its Return, in which Case it shall not be a Law.

Every Order, Resolution, or Vote to which the Concurrence of the Senate and House of Representatives may be necessary (except on a question of Adjournment) shall be presented to the President of the United States; and before the Same shall take Effect, shall be approved by him, or being disapproved by him, shall be repassed by two thirds of the Senate and House of Representatives, according to the Rules and Limitations prescribed in the Case of a Bill.

Section. 8.

The Congress shall have Power To lay and collect Taxes, Duties, Imposts and Excises, to pay the Debts and provide for the common Defence and general Welfare of the United States; but all Duties, Imposts and Excises shall be uniform throughout the United States;

To borrow Money on the credit of the United States;

To regulate Commerce with foreign Nations, and among the several States, and with the Indian Tribes;

To establish an uniform Rule of Naturalization, and uniform Laws on the subject of Bankruptcies throughout the United States;

To coin Money, regulate the Value thereof, and of foreign Coin, and fix the Standard of Weights and Measures;

To provide for the Punishment of counterfeiting the Securities and current Coin of the United States;

To establish Post Offices and post Roads;

To promote the Progress of Science and useful Arts, by securing for limited Times to Authors and Inventors the exclusive Right to their respective Writings and Discoveries;

To constitute Tribunals inferior to the supreme Court;

To define and punish Piracies and Felonies committed on the high Seas, and Offences against the Law of Nations;

To declare War, grant Letters of Marque and Reprisal, and make Rules concerning Captures on Land and Water;

To raise and support Armies, but no Appropriation of Money to that Use shall be for a longer Term than two Years;

To provide and maintain a Navy;

To make Rules for the Government and Regulation of the land and naval Forces;

To provide for calling forth the Militia to execute the Laws of the Union, suppress Insurrections and repel Invasions;

To provide for organizing, arming, and disciplining, the Militia, and for governing such Part of them as may be employed in the Service of the United States, reserving to the States respectively, the Appointment of the Officers, and the Authority of training the Militia according to the discipline prescribed by Congress;

To exercise exclusive Legislation in all Cases whatsoever, over such District (not exceeding ten Miles square) as may, by Cession of particular States, and the Acceptance of Congress, become the Seat of the Government of the United States, and to exercise like Authority over all Places purchased by the Consent of the Legislature of the State in which the Same shall be, for the Erection of Forts, Magazines, Arsenals, dock-Yards, and other needful Buildings;—And

To make all Laws which shall be necessary and proper for carrying into Execution the foregoing Powers, and all other Powers vested by this Constitution in the Government of the United States, or in any Department or Officer thereof.

SECTION. 9.

The Migration or Importation of such Persons as any of the States now existing shall think proper to admit, shall not be prohibited by the Congress prior to the Year one thousand eight hundred and eight, but a Tax or duty may be imposed on such Importation, not exceeding ten dollars for each Person.

The Privilege of the Writ of Habeas Corpus shall not be suspended, unless when in Cases of Rebellion or Invasion the public Safety may require it.

No Bill of Attainder or ex post facto Law shall be passed.

No Capitation, or other direct, Tax shall be laid, unless in Proportion to the Census or enumeration herein before directed to be taken.

No Tax or Duty shall be laid on Articles exported from any State.

No Preference shall be given by any Regulation of Commerce or Revenue to the Ports of one State over those of another; nor shall Vessels bound to, or from, one State, be obliged to enter, clear, or pay Duties in another.

No Money shall be drawn from the Treasury, but in Consequence of Appropriations made by Law; and a regular Statement and Account of the Receipts and Expenditures of all public Money shall be published from time to time.

No Title of Nobility shall be granted by the United States: And no Person holding any Office of Profit or Trust under them, shall, without the Consent of the Congress, accept of any present, Emolument, Office, or Title, of any kind whatever, from any King, Prince, or foreign State.

SECTION. 10.

No State shall enter into any Treaty, Alliance, or Confederation; grant Letters of Marque and Reprisal; coin Money; emit Bills of Credit; make any Thing but gold and silver Coin a Tender in Payment of Debts; pass any Bill of Attainder, ex post facto Law, or Law impairing the Obligation of Contracts, or grant any Title of Nobility.

No State shall, without the Consent of the Congress, lay any Imposts or Duties on Imports or Exports, except what may be absolutely necessary for executing it's inspection Laws: and the net Produce of all Duties and Imposts, laid by any State on Imports or Exports, shall be for the Use of the Treasury of the United States; and all such Laws shall be subject to the Revision and Controul of the Congress.

No State shall, without the Consent of Congress, lay any Duty of Tonnage, keep Troops, or Ships of War in time of Peace, enter into any Agreement or Compact with another State, or with a foreign Power, or engage in War, unless actually invaded, or in such imminent Danger as will not admit of delay.

ARTICLE. II.

SECTION. 1.

The executive Power shall be vested in a President of the United States of America. He shall hold his Office during the Term of four Years, and, together with the Vice President, chosen for the same Term, be elected, as follows:

Each State shall appoint, in such Manner as the Legislature thereof may direct, a Number of Electors, equal to the whole Number of Senators and Representatives to which the State may be entitled in the Congress: but no Senator or Representative, or Person holding an Office of Trust or Profit under the United States, shall be appointed an Elector.

The Electors shall meet in their respective States, and vote by Ballot for two Persons, of whom one at least shall not be an Inhabitant of the same State with themselves. And they shall make a List of all the Persons voted for, and of the Number of Votes for each; which List they shall sign and certify, and transmit sealed to the Seat of the Government of the United States, directed to the President of the Senate. The President of the Senate shall, in the Presence of the Senate and House of Representatives, open all the Certificates, and the Votes shall then be counted. The Person having the greatest Number of Votes shall be the President, if such Number be a Majority of the whole Number of Electors appointed; and if there be more than one who have such Majority, and have an equal Number of Votes, then the House of Representatives shall immediately chuse by Ballot one of them for President; and if no Person have a Majority, then from the five highest on the List the said House shall in like Manner chuse the President. But in chusing the President, the Votes shall be taken by States, the Representation from each State having one Vote; A quorum for this purpose shall consist of a Member or Members from two thirds of the States, and a Majority of all the States shall be necessary to a Choice. In every Case, after the Choice of the President, the Person having the greatest Number of Votes of the Electors shall be the Vice President. But if there should remain two or more who have equal Votes, the Senate shall chuse from them by Ballot the Vice President.

The Congress may determine the Time of chusing the Electors, and the Day on which they shall give their Votes; which Day shall be the same throughout the United States.

No Person except a natural born Citizen, or a Citizen of the United States, at the time of the Adoption of this Constitution, shall be eligible to the Office of President; neither shall any Person be eligible to that Office who shall not have attained to the Age of thirty five Years, and been fourteen Years a Resident within the United States.

In Case of the Removal of the President from Office, or of his Death, Resignation, or Inability to discharge the Powers and Duties of the said Office, the Same shall devolve on the Vice President, and the Congress may by Law provide for the Case of Removal, Death, Resignation or Inability, both of the President and Vice President, declaring what Officer shall then act as President, and such Officer shall act accordingly, until the Disability be removed, or a President shall be elected.

The President shall, at stated Times, receive for his Services, a Compensation, which shall neither be increased nor diminished during the Period for which he shall have been elected, and he shall not receive within that Period any other Emolument from the United States, or any of them.

Before he enter on the Execution of his Office, he shall take the following Oath or Affirmation:—"I do solemnly swear (or affirm) that I will faithfully execute the Office of President of the United States, and will to the best of my Ability, preserve, protect and defend the Constitution of the United States."

SECTION. 2.

The President shall be Commander in Chief of the Army and Navy of the United States, and of the Militia of the several States, when called into the actual Service of the United States; he may require the Opinion, in writing, of the principal Officer in each of the executive Departments, upon any Subject relating to the Duties of their respective Offices, and he shall have Power to grant Reprieves and Pardons for Offences against the United States, except in Cases of Impeachment.

He shall have Power, by and with the Advice and Consent of the Senate, to make Treaties, provided two thirds of the Senators present concur; and he shall nominate, and by and with the Advice and Consent of the Senate, shall appoint Ambassadors, other public Ministers and Consuls, Judges of the supreme Court, and all other Officers of the United States, whose Appointments are not herein otherwise provided for, and which shall be established by Law: but the Congress may by Law vest the Appointment of such inferior Officers, as they think proper, in the President alone, in the Courts of Law, or in the Heads of Departments.

The President shall have Power to fill up all Vacancies that may happen during the Recess of the Senate, by granting Commissions which shall expire at the End of their next Session.

SECTION. 3.

He shall from time to time give to the Congress Information of the State of the Union, and recommend to their Consideration such Measures as he shall judge necessary and expedient; he may, on extraordinary Occasions, convene both Houses, or either of them, and in Case of Disagreement between them, with Respect to the Time of Adjournment, he may adjourn them to such Time as he shall think proper; he shall receive Ambassadors and other public Ministers; he shall take Care that the Laws be faithfully executed, and shall Commission all the Officers of the United States.

SECTION. 4.

The President, Vice President and all civil Officers of the United States, shall be removed from Office on Impeachment for, and Conviction of, Treason, Bribery, or other high Crimes and Misdemeanors.

ARTICLE III.

SECTION. 1.

The judicial Power of the United States shall be vested in one supreme Court, and in such inferior Courts as the Congress may from time to time ordain and establish. The Judges, both of the supreme and inferior Courts, shall hold their Offices during good Behaviour, and shall, at stated Times, receive for their Services a Compensation, which shall not be diminished during their Continuance in Office.

SECTION. 2.

The judicial Power shall extend to all Cases, in Law and Equity, arising under this Constitution, the Laws of the United States, and Treaties made, or which shall be made, under their Authority;—to all Cases affecting Ambassadors, other public Ministers and Consuls;—to all Cases of admiralty and maritime Jurisdiction;—to Controversies to which the United States shall be a Party;—to Controversies between two or more States;—between a State and Citizens of another State,—between Citizens of different States,—between Citizens of the same State claiming Lands under Grants of different States, and between a State, or the Citizens thereof, and foreign States, Citizens or Subjects.

In all Cases affecting Ambassadors, other public Ministers and Consuls, and those in which a State shall be Party, the supreme Court shall have original Jurisdiction. In all the other Cases before mentioned, the supreme Court shall have appellate Jurisdiction, both as to Law and Fact, with such Exceptions, and under such Regulations as the Congress shall make.

The Trial of all Crimes, except in Cases of Impeachment, shall be by Jury; and such Trial shall be held in the State where the said Crimes shall have been committed;

but when not committed within any State, the Trial shall be at such Place or Places as the Congress may by Law have directed.

SECTION. 3.

Treason against the United States, shall consist only in levying War against them, or in adhering to their Enemies, giving them Aid and Comfort. No Person shall be convicted of Treason unless on the Testimony of two Witnesses to the same overt Act, or on Confession in open Court.

The Congress shall have Power to declare the Punishment of Treason, but no Attainder of Treason shall work Corruption of Blood, or Forfeiture except during the Life of the Person attainted.

ARTICLE. IV.

SECTION. 1.

Full Faith and Credit shall be given in each State to the public Acts, Records, and judicial Proceedings of every other State. And the Congress may by general Laws prescribe the Manner in which such Acts, Records and Proceedings shall be proved, and the Effect thereof.

SECTION. 2.

The Citizens of each State shall be entitled to all Privileges and Immunities of Citizens in the several States.

A Person charged in any State with Treason, Felony, or other Crime, who shall flee from Justice, and be found in another State, shall on Demand of the executive Authority of the State from which he fled, be delivered up, to be removed to the State having Jurisdiction of the Crime.

No Person held to Service or Labour in one State, under the Laws thereof, escaping into another, shall, in Consequence of any Law or Regulation therein, be discharged from such Service or Labour, but shall be delivered up on Claim of the Party to whom such Service or Labour may be due.

SECTION. 3.

New States may be admitted by the Congress into this Union; but no new State shall be formed or erected within the Jurisdiction of any other State; nor any State be formed by the Junction of two or more States, or Parts of States, without the Consent of the Legislatures of the States concerned as well as of the Congress.

The Congress shall have Power to dispose of and make all needful Rules and Regulations respecting the Territory or other Property belonging to the United States; and nothing in this Constitution shall be so construed as to Prejudice any Claims of the United States, or of any particular State.

SECTION. 4.

The United States shall guarantee to every State in this Union a Republican Form of Government, and shall protect each of them against Invasion; and on Application of the Legislature, or of the Executive (when the Legislature cannot be convened), against domestic Violence.

ARTICLE. V.

The Congress, whenever two thirds of both Houses shall deem it necessary, shall propose Amendments to this Constitution, or, on the Application of the Legislatures of two thirds of the several States, shall call a Convention for proposing Amendments, which, in either Case, shall be valid to all Intents and Purposes, as Part of this Constitution, when ratified by the Legislatures of three fourths of the several States, or by Conventions in three fourths thereof, as the one or the other Mode of Ratification may be proposed by the Congress; Provided that no Amendment which may be made prior to the Year One thousand eight hundred and eight shall in any Manner affect the first and fourth Clauses in the Ninth Section of the first Article; and that no State, without its Consent, shall be deprived of its equal Suffrage in the Senate.

ARTICLE. VI.

All Debts contracted and Engagements entered into, before the Adoption of this Constitution, shall be as valid against the United States under this Constitution, as under the Confederation.

This Constitution, and the Laws of the United States which shall be made in Pursuance thereof; and all Treaties made, or which shall be made, under the Authority of the United States, shall be the supreme Law of the Land; and the Judges in every State shall be bound thereby, any Thing in the Constitution or Laws of any State to the Contrary notwithstanding.

The Senators and Representatives before mentioned, and the Members of the several State Legislatures, and all executive and judicial Officers, both of the United States and of the several States, shall be bound by Oath or Affirmation, to support this Constitution; but no religious Test shall ever be required as a Qualification to any Office or public Trust under the United States.

ARTICLE. VII.

The Ratification of the Conventions of nine States, shall be sufficient for the Establishment of this Constitution between the States so ratifying the Same.

The Word, "the," being interlined between the seventh and eighth Lines of the first Page, the Word "Thirty" being partly written on an Erazure in the fifteenth Line of the first Page, The Words "is tried" being interlined between the thirty second and thirty third Lines of the first Page and the Word "the" being interlined between the forty third and forty fourth Lines of the second Page.

Attest William Jackson Secretary

done in Convention by the Unanimous Consent of the States present the Seventeenth Day of September in the Year of our Lord one thousand seven hundred and Eighty seven and of the Independance of the United States of America the Twelfth In witness whereof We have hereunto subscribed our Names,

G°. Washington
Presidt and deputy from Virginia

Delaware
Geo: Read
Gunning Bedford jun
John Dickinson
Richard Bassett
Jaco: Broom

Maryland
James McHenry
Dan of St Thos. Jenifer
Danl. Carroll

Virginia
John Blair
James Madison Jr.

North Carolina
Wm. Blount
Richd. Dobbs Spaight
Hu Williamson

South Carolina
J. Rutledge
Charles Cotesworth Pinckney
Charles Pinckney
Pierce Butler

Georgia
William Few
Abr Baldwin

New Hampshire
John Langdon
Nicholas Gilman

Massachusetts
Nathaniel Gorham
Rufus King

Connecticut
Wm. Saml. Johnson
Roger Sherman

New York
Alexander Hamilton

New Jersey
Wil: Livingston
David Brearley
Wm. Paterson
Jona: Dayton

Pennsylvania
B Franklin
Thomas Mifflin
Robt. Morris
Geo. Clymer
Thos. FitzSimons
Jared Ingersoll
James Wilson
Gouv Morris

The Preamble to The Bill of Rights

Congress of the United States
begun and held at the City of New-York, on
Wednesday the fourth of March, one thousand seven hundred and eighty nine.

THE Conventions of a number of the States, having at the time of their adopting the Constitution, expressed a desire, in order to prevent misconstruction or abuse of its powers, that further declaratory and restrictive clauses should be added: And as extending the ground of public confidence in the Government, will best ensure the beneficent ends of its institution.

RESOLVED by the Senate and House of Representatives of the United States of America, in Congress assembled, two thirds of both Houses concurring, that the following Articles be proposed to the Legislatures of the several States, as amendments to the Constitution of the United States, all, or any of which Articles, when ratified by three fourths of the said Legislatures, to be valid to all intents and purposes, as part of the said Constitution; viz.

ARTICLES in addition to, and Amendment of the Constitution of the United States of America, proposed by Congress, and ratified by the Legislatures of the several States, pursuant to the fifth Article of the original Constitution.

Note: The following text is a transcription of the first ten amendments to the Constitution in their original form. These amendments were ratified December 15, 1791, and form what is known as the "Bill of Rights."

AMENDMENT I

Congress shall make no law respecting an establishment of religion, or prohibiting the free exercise thereof; or abridging the freedom of speech, or of the press; or the right of the people peaceably to assemble, and to petition the Government for a redress of grievances.

AMENDMENT II

A well regulated Militia, being necessary to the security of a free State, the right of the people to keep and bear Arms, shall not be infringed.

AMENDMENT III

No Soldier shall, in time of peace be quartered in any house, without the consent of the Owner, nor in time of war, but in a manner to be prescribed by law.

AMENDMENT IV

The right of the people to be secure in their persons, houses, papers, and effects, against unreasonable searches and seizures, shall not be violated, and no Warrants shall issue, but upon probable cause, supported by Oath or affirmation, and particularly describing the place to be searched, and the persons or things to be seized.

AMENDMENT V

No person shall be held to answer for a capital, or otherwise infamous crime, unless on a presentment or indictment of a Grand Jury, except in cases arising in the land or naval forces, or in the Militia, when in actual service in time of War or public danger; nor shall any person be subject for the same offence to be twice put in jeopardy of life or limb; nor shall be compelled in any criminal case to be a witness against himself, nor be deprived of life, liberty, or property, without due process of law; nor shall private property be taken for public use, without just compensation.

AMENDMENT VI

In all criminal prosecutions, the accused shall enjoy the right to a speedy and public trial, by an impartial jury of the State and district wherein the crime shall have been committed, which district shall have been previously ascertained by law, and to be informed of the nature and cause of the accusation; to be confronted with the witnesses against him; to have compulsory process for obtaining witnesses in his favor, and to have the Assistance of Counsel for his defence.

AMENDMENT VII

In Suits at common law, where the value in controversy shall exceed twenty dollars, the right of trial by jury shall be preserved, and no fact tried by a jury, shall be otherwise re-examined in any Court of the United States, than according to the rules of the common law.

AMENDMENT VIII

Excessive bail shall not be required, nor excessive fines imposed, nor cruel and unusual punishments inflicted.

AMENDMENT IX

The enumeration in the Constitution, of certain rights, shall not be construed to deny or disparage others retained by the people.

AMENDMENT X

The powers not delegated to the United States by the Constitution, nor prohibited by it to the States, are reserved to the States respectively, or to the people

AMENDMENT XI

Passed by Congress March 4, 1794. Ratified February 7, 1795.

Note: Article III, section 2, of the Constitution was modified by amendment 11.

The Judicial power of the United States shall not be construed to extend to any suit in law or equity, commenced or prosecuted against one of the United States by Citizens of another State, or by Citizens or Subjects of any Foreign State.

AMENDMENT XII

Passed by Congress December 9, 1803. Ratified June 15, 1804.

Note: A portion of Article II, section 1 of the Constitution was superseded by the 12th amendment.

The Electors shall meet in their respective states and vote by ballot for President and Vice-President, one of whom, at least, shall not be an inhabitant of the same state with themselves; they shall name in their ballots the person voted for as President, and in distinct ballots the person voted for as Vice-President, and they shall make distinct lists of all persons voted for as President, and of all persons voted for as Vice-President, and of the number of votes for each, which lists they shall sign and certify, and transmit sealed to the seat of the government of the United States, directed to the President of the Senate;—the President of the Senate shall, in the presence of the Senate and House of Representatives, open all the certificates and the votes shall then be counted;—The person having the greatest number of votes for President, shall be the President, if such number be a majority of the whole number of Electors appointed; and if no person have such majority, then from the persons having the highest numbers not exceeding three on the list of those voted for as President, the House of Representatives shall choose immediately, by ballot, the President. But in choosing the President, the votes shall be taken by states, the representation from each state having one vote; a quorum for this purpose shall consist of a member or members from two-thirds of the states, and a majority of all the states shall be necessary to a choice. [And if the House of Representatives shall not choose a President whenever the right of choice shall devolve upon them, before the fourth day of March next following, then the Vice-President shall act as President, as in case of the death or other constitutional disability of the President. —]* The person having the greatest number of votes as Vice-President, shall be the Vice-President, if such number be a majority of the whole number of Electors appointed, and if no person have a majority, then from the two highest numbers on the list, the Senate shall choose the Vice-President; a quorum for the purpose shall consist of two-thirds of the whole number of Senators, and a majority of the whole number shall be necessary to a choice. But no person constitutionally ineligible to the office of President shall be eligible to that of Vice-President of the United States.

*Superseded by section 3 of the 20th amendment.

AMENDMENT XIII

Passed by Congress January 31, 1865. Ratified December 6, 1865.

Note: A portion of Article IV, section 2, of the Constitution was superseded by the 13th amendment.

SECTION 1.

Neither slavery nor involuntary servitude, except as a punishment for crime whereof the party shall have been duly convicted, shall exist within the United States, or any place subject to their jurisdiction.

SECTION 2.

Congress shall have power to enforce this article by appropriate legislation.

AMENDMENT XIV

Passed by Congress June 13, 1866. Ratified July 9, 1868.

Note: Article I, section 2, of the Constitution was modified by section 2 of the 14th amendment.

SECTION 1.

All persons born or naturalized in the United States, and subject to the jurisdiction thereof, are citizens of the United States and of the State wherein they reside. No State shall make or enforce any law which shall abridge the privileges or immunities of citizens of the United States; nor shall any State deprive any person of life, liberty, or property, without due process of law; nor deny to any person within its jurisdiction the equal protection of the laws.

SECTION 2.

Representatives shall be apportioned among the several States according to their respective numbers, counting the whole number of persons in each State, excluding Indians not taxed. But when the right to vote at any election for the choice of electors for President and Vice-President of the United States, Representatives in Congress, the Executive and Judicial officers of a State, or the members of the Legislature thereof, is denied to any of the male inhabitants of such State, being twenty-one years of age,* and citizens of the United States, or in any way abridged, except for participation in rebellion, or other crime, the basis of representation therein shall be reduced in the proportion which the number of such male citizens shall bear to the whole number of male citizens twenty-one years of age in such State.

SECTION 3.

No person shall be a Senator or Representative in Congress, or elector of President and Vice-President, or hold any office, civil or military, under the United States, or under any State, who, having previously taken an oath, as a member of Congress, or as an officer of the United States, or as a member of any State legislature, or as an executive or judicial officer of any State, to support the Constitution of the United States, shall have engaged in insurrection or rebellion against the same, or given aid or comfort to the enemies thereof. But Congress may by a vote of two-thirds of each House, remove such disability.

SECTION 4.

The validity of the public debt of the United States, authorized by law, including debts incurred for payment of pensions and bounties for services in suppressing insurrection or rebellion, shall not be questioned. But neither the United States nor any State shall assume or pay any debt or obligation incurred in aid of insurrection or rebellion against the United States, or any claim for the loss or emancipation of any slave; but all such debts, obligations and claims shall be held illegal and void.

SECTION 5.

The Congress shall have the power to enforce, by appropriate legislation, the provisions of this article.

Changed by section 1 of the 26th amendment.

AMENDMENT XV

Passed by Congress February 26, 1869. Ratified February 3, 1870.

SECTION 1.

The right of citizens of the United States to vote shall not be denied or abridged by the United States or by any State on account of race, color, or previous condition of servitude—

SECTION 2.

The Congress shall have the power to enforce this article by appropriate legislation.

AMENDMENT XVI

Passed by Congress July 2, 1909. Ratified February 3, 1913.

Note: Article I, section 9, of the Constitution was modified by amendment 16.

The Congress shall have power to lay and collect taxes on incomes, from whatever source derived, without apportionment among the several States, and without regard to any census or enumeration.

AMENDMENT XVII

Passed by Congress May 13, 1912. Ratified April 8, 1913.

Note: Article I, section 3, of the Constitution was modified by the 17th amendment.

The Senate of the United States shall be composed of two Senators from each State, elected by the people thereof, for six years; and each Senator shall have one vote. The electors in each State shall have the qualifications requisite for electors of the most numerous branch of the State legislatures.

When vacancies happen in the representation of any State in the Senate, the executive authority of such State shall issue writs of election to fill such vacancies: *Provided,* That the legislature of any State may empower the executive thereof to make temporary appointments until the people fill the vacancies by election as the legislature may direct.

This amendment shall not be so construed as to affect the election or term of any Senator chosen before it becomes valid as part of the Constitution.

AMENDMENT XVIII

Passed by Congress December 18, 1917. Ratified January 16, 1919. Repealed by amendment 21.

SECTION 1.

After one year from the ratification of this article the manufacture, sale, or transportation of intoxicating liquors within, the importation thereof into, or the exportation thereof from the United States and all territory subject to the jurisdiction thereof for beverage purposes is hereby prohibited.

SECTION 2.

The Congress and the several States shall have concurrent power to enforce this article by appropriate legislation.

SECTION 3.

This article shall be inoperative unless it shall have been ratified as an amendment to the Constitution by the legislatures of the several States, as provided in the Constitution, within seven years from the date of the submission hereof to the States by the Congress.

AMENDMENT XIX

Passed by Congress June 4, 1919. Ratified August 18, 1920.

The right of citizens of the United States to vote shall not be denied or abridged by the United States or by any State on account of sex.

Congress shall have power to enforce this article by appropriate legislation.

AMENDMENT XX

Passed by Congress March 2, 1932. Ratified January 23, 1933.

Note: Article I, section 4, of the Constitution was modified by section 2 of this amendment. In addition, a portion of the 12th amendment was superseded by section 3.

SECTION 1.

The terms of the President and the Vice President shall end at noon on the 20th day of January, and the terms of Senators and Representatives at noon on the 3d day of January, of the years in which such terms would have ended if this article had not been ratified; and the terms of their successors shall then begin.

SECTION 2.

The Congress shall assemble at least once in every year, and such meeting shall begin at noon on the 3d day of January, unless they shall by law appoint a different day.

SECTION 3.

If, at the time fixed for the beginning of the term of the President, the President elect shall have died, the Vice President elect shall become President. If a President shall not have been chosen before the time fixed for the beginning of his term, or if the President elect shall have failed to qualify, then the Vice President elect shall act as President until a President shall have qualified; and the Congress may by law provide for the case wherein neither a President elect nor a Vice President shall have qualified, declaring who shall then act as President, or the manner in which one who is to act shall be selected, and such person shall act accordingly until a President or Vice President shall have qualified.

SECTION 4.

The Congress may by law provide for the case of the death of any of the persons from whom the House of Representatives may choose a President whenever the right of choice shall have devolved upon them, and for the case of the death of any of the persons from whom the Senate may choose a Vice President whenever the right of choice shall have devolved upon them.

SECTION 5.

Sections 1 and 2 shall take effect on the 15th day of October following the ratification of this article.

SECTION 6.

This article shall be inoperative unless it shall have been ratified as an amendment to the Constitution by the legislatures of three-fourths of the several States within seven years from the date of its submission.

AMENDMENT XXI

Passed by Congress February 20, 1933. Ratified December 5, 1933.

SECTION 1.

The eighteenth article of amendment to the Constitution of the United States is hereby repealed.

SECTION 2.

The transportation or importation into any State, Territory, or Possession of the United States for delivery or use therein of intoxicating liquors, in violation of the laws thereof, is hereby prohibited.

SECTION 3.

This article shall be inoperative unless it shall have been ratified as an amendment to the Constitution by conventions in the several States, as provided in the Constitution, within seven years from the date of the submission hereof to the States by the Congress.

AMENDMENT XXII

Passed by Congress March 21, 1947. Ratified February 27, 1951.

SECTION 1.

No person shall be elected to the office of the President more than twice, and no person who has held the office of President, or acted as President, for more than two years of a term to which some other person was elected President shall be elected to the office of President more than once. But this Article shall not apply to any person holding the office of President when this Article was proposed by Congress, and shall not prevent any person who may be holding the office of President, or acting as President, during the term within which this Article becomes operative from holding the office of President or acting as President during the remainder of such term.

SECTION 2.

This article shall be inoperative unless it shall have been ratified as an amendment to the Constitution by the legislatures of three-fourths of the several States within seven years from the date of its submission to the States by the Congress.

AMENDMENT XXIII

Passed by Congress June 16, 1960. Ratified March 29, 1961.

SECTION 1.

The District constituting the seat of Government of the United States shall appoint in such manner as Congress may direct:

A number of electors of President and Vice President equal to the whole number of Senators and Representatives in Congress to which the District would be entitled if it were a State, but in no event more than the least populous State; they shall be in addition to those appointed by the States, but they shall be considered, for the purposes of the election of President and Vice President, to be electors appointed by a State; and they shall meet in the District and perform such duties as provided by the twelfth article of amendment.

SECTION 2.

The Congress shall have power to enforce this article by appropriate legislation.

AMENDMENT XXIV

Passed by Congress August 27, 1962. Ratified January 23, 1964.

SECTION 1.

The right of citizens of the United States to vote in any primary or other election for President or Vice President, for electors for President or Vice President, or for Senator or Representative in Congress, shall not be denied or abridged by the United States or any State by reason of failure to pay poll tax or other tax.

SECTION 2.

The Congress shall have power to enforce this article by appropriate legislation.

AMENDMENT XXV

Passed by Congress July 6, 1965. Ratified February 10, 1967.

Note: Article II, section 1, of the Constitution was affected by the 25th amendment.

SECTION 1.

In case of the removal of the President from office or of his death or resignation, the Vice President shall become President.

SECTION 2.

Whenever there is a vacancy in the office of the Vice President, the President shall nominate a Vice President who shall take office upon confirmation by a majority vote of both Houses of Congress.

SECTION 3.

Whenever the President transmits to the President pro tempore of the Senate and the Speaker of the House of Representatives his written declaration that he is unable to discharge the powers and duties of his office, and until he transmits to them a written declaration to the contrary, such powers and duties shall be discharged by the Vice President as Acting President.

SECTION 4.

Whenever the Vice President and a majority of either the principal officers of the executive departments or of such other body as Congress may by law provide, transmit to the President pro tempore of the Senate and the Speaker of the House of Representatives their written declaration that the President is unable to discharge the powers and duties of his office, the Vice President shall immediately assume the powers and duties of the office as Acting President.

Thereafter, when the President transmits to the President pro tempore of the Senate and the Speaker of the House of Representatives his written declaration that no inability exists, he shall resume the powers and duties of his office unless the Vice President and a majority of either the principal officers of the executive department or of such other body as Congress may by law provide, transmit within four days to the President pro tempore of the Senate and the Speaker of the House of Representatives their written declaration that the President is unable to discharge the powers and duties of his office. Thereupon Congress shall decide the issue, assembling within forty-eight hours for that purpose if not in session. If the Congress, within twenty-one days after receipt of the latter written declaration, or, if Congress is not in session, within twenty-one days after Congress is required to assemble, determines by two-thirds vote of both Houses that the President is unable to discharge the powers and duties of his office, the Vice President shall continue to discharge the same as Acting President; otherwise, the President shall resume the powers and duties of his office.

AMENDMENT XXVI

Passed by Congress March 23, 1971. Ratified July 1, 1971.

Note: Amendment 14, section 2, of the Constitution was modified by section 1 of the 26th amendment.

SECTION 1.

The right of citizens of the United States, who are eighteen years of age or older, to vote shall not be denied or abridged by the United States or by any State on account of age.

SECTION 2.

The Congress shall have power to enforce this article by appropriate legislation.

AMENDMENT XXVII

Originally proposed Sept. 25, 1789. Ratified May 7, 1992.

No law, varying the compensation for the services of the Senators and Representatives, shall take effect, until an election of representatives shall have intervened.

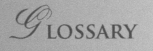

GLOSSARY

Actus reus   The guilty act.

Administrative Law   Laws related to the various regulatory agencies of the United States and the various states.

Adolphe Quetelet   Adolphe Quetelet (1796–1874) was the first person to find a strong relationship between crime rates and such factors as climate, gender, and age.

Aggravating Circumstances   Aggravating circumstances are factors that relate to the commission of a specific crime that cause its severity to be greater than that of a typical instance of the same type of offense.

Alibi   An alibi is a defense that establishes the accused could not have committed the crime because they can offer evidence that they were in another place at the time the crime was committed.

Allen Charge   An *Allen* charge allows the judge to tell the jurors who are in the minority in a hung jury to reconsider their decision and see if they can change their mind and vote with the majority.

Amendment process   The amendment process is the procedure used to modify or add to the United States Constitution. The Constitution has been amended -twenty--seven times since its inception.

Anomie   Emile Durkheim and Robert Merton looked at a person's reason for developing criminal behavior in terms of anomie. Anomie literally means "normlessness."

Arraignment   The arraignment is the first time the defendant is brought before the court that has the jurisdiction to actually conduct the trial.

Arrest   An arrest is the legal detention of a person to answer for criminal charges. An arrest must be based on probable cause.

Atavism   Atavism states that some people are born criminals because they are throwbacks to a more primitive stage of development.

ATF   Alcohol, Tobacco, Firearms, and Explosives

Auburn System   This new prison system emphasized putting the prisoners to work at hard labor and reintroduced corporal punishment. This system is still in use in Europe.

Bail   Bail is a way for an accused individual to be released from custody prior to trial by posting money or some other form of collateral.

Bill of Rights   The Bill of Rights is the common name given to the first ten amendments of the United States Constitution. The Bill of Rights was ratified on December 15, 1791, three years after the Constitution was ratified.

Biological Theories   The followers of these theories believe that some criminal behavior could be attributed to a lack of evolutionary development.

Blue Curtain   A code of silence among police officers where officers refuse to testify or disclose information concerning the corrupt activity of fellow officers.

Bobbies   Named after Sir Robert "Bobbie" Peel, this is the nickname given to the police officers of the London Metropolitan Police.

Breach of Contract   Failing to fulfill a contractual obligation that can result in a civil lawsuit.

Breed v. Jones   The court ruled that if a juvenile is adjudicated for a case in juvenile court, it is double jeopardy if they are tried again for the same offense in adult court.

Burden of Proof   The burden of proof is always on the prosecution to prove their case beyond a reasonable doubt. The prosecution always presents their case first.

Carroll Doctrine   The Supreme Court as early as 1925 in the case of *Carroll v. U.S.* recognized that vehicles are highly mobile and police officers often do not have time to obtain search warrants.

Case Law   Law that is generated by the courts.

Cesare Beccaria   Cesare Beccaria (1738–1794) was an Italian economist and jurist. Beccaria wrote an essay "On Crimes and Punishment" that became the foundation of the classical school of criminology.

Cesare Lombroso   Cesare Lombroso (1835–1909) is considered by many to be the "father of criminology and developed the theory of atavism.

Challenge for Cause   A challenge for cause is a challenge where the attorney (either prosecution or defense) must state a reason why they feel that juror should not serve on the jury.

Charles Darwin   Charles Darwin (1809–1882) influenced many of the early biological theorists with his famous writing of the *Theory of Evolution*.

Chattel   Chattel means the personal property of another.

Checks and balances   Checks and balances is the system set up by the United States Constitution to ensure that none of the branches becomes too powerful. Each branch holds certain powers that can keep each of the other two branches in check.

City (Municipal) Police   City police are the largest and most visible segment of law enforcement in the United States.

Civil Laws   Regulate the relationship between people and/or other parties.

Classical School of Criminology   Founded by Cesare Beccaria, the Classical School of Criminology is based on the notion that all decisions, including those that involve criminal activity, are the result of free will.

Classification   Classification is an assessment of a new prisoner's risks and needs.

Closing Arguments   Closing arguments are a summary of all of the evidence that has been presented during the trial. Closing arguments are not evidence and are given by both the prosecutor and the defense attorney.

Code of Ethics   The guideline that sets acceptable behaviors for a given group or profession.

Community Policing   Community policing is a strategy that involves a working relationship between police and the community to deter and prevent crime.

Compensatory Damages   Recovery of actual -out--of--pocket expenses for injury sustained by another party.

Concurrence   The joining of the guilty act (*actus reus*) and the requisite mental state (*mens rea*).

Concurrent Sentence   Concurrent sentencing that means the defendant will serve each of the separate sentences at the same time.

Conflict Theories   Conflict theories are based on the premise that the fundamental causes of crime are the social and economic forces operating within society.

Consecutive Sentencing   Consecutive sentencing means that the defendant will serve the first sentence and only then will the second sentence start.

Consent   A person may waive their Fourth Amendment rights and voluntarily allow the police to search their property (or themselves) without a warrant by giving their consent to do so.

Corpus delicti   The facts that prove that a crime has actually taken place—"the body of the crime."

Corrections   The correctional component of the criminal justice system is responsible for overseeing those individuals who have been arrested and are awaiting trial, as well as those who have been convicted of a crime and are sentenced to serve time. Corrections include both jails and prisons.

Court   The court system in the United States (part of the judicial system), is comprised of many different types of courts: criminal, civil, administrative, and a variety of specialized courts, as well as our appellate courts.

Crime Clock   The UCR Crime Clock is a way of showing the frequency of crime in the United States.

Crime Control Model   This model is based on the proposition that crime must be controlled at all cost in order to have a safe society. In this model the rights of the many (society) outweigh the rights of the few (those who are accused of crime).

Criminal Law   The branch of law that deals with crimes and their punishments.

Dark Figure of Crime   The dark figure of crime represents those crimes that are not reported to the police.

DEA   Drug Enforcement Administration

Deadly Force   Any force that could reasonably be expected to cause death.

Deadly Force   Deadly force is that force that could be reasonably expected to cause death or serious bodily harm.

Delinquency   Delinquency is an offense that if committed by an adult, would be a criminal act.

Deontological Ethics   Looks at the rightness or wrongness of an action or a decision itself rather than the resulting consequences of that action.

Determinate Sentencing   Determinate sentencing is a fixed term of incarceration.

Deterrence   Deterrence is a philosophy that says we should punish criminals in order to deter others from committing crimes.

Differential Association   Differential association states that crime is learned in the same way that lawful activities are learned.

Drug Courts   Drug courts were first implemented in the late 1980s and are designed to stop the abuse of alcohol and other drugs and related criminal activity.

Dual Court System   The United States of America has a dual court system which is comprised of the federal court system and the courts of the individual states.

Due Process Model   This model is designed to protect the rights of the individual who is accused of a crime and make sure that all legal resources and protections are available and utilized. In this model the rights of the accused outweigh the rights of the many (society).

Duress   Making a person do something they do not want to do by the use of force or the threat of force.

Edwin H. Sutherland   Edwin H. Sutherland (1883–1950) developed a social learning theory that he called differential association theory.

Electronic Monitoring   Electronic monitoring is part of a system of house arrest, or home confinement, that utilizes an electronic device which is attached to the ankle (typically) of the offender that tells the supervising officer when the offender is at home.

Entrapment   Entrapment is inducing a person to commit a crime that he or she would not have committed without such inducement.

Exceptions and limitations   The rights afforded all Americans by the Bill of Rights are not absolute. Over the past 220 years, the United States Supreme Court has recognized the need to apply exceptions and impose certain limitations on the constitutional rights granted by amendments to the United States Constitution. The court has the power to do this through its use of judicial review and its authority to interpret the Constitution.

Exclusionary Rule The exclusionary rule states that any evidence that is illegally seized by the police will be inadmissible in a criminal trial.

Exculpatory Evidence Evidence which tends to show that the defendant is not guilty or has no criminal intent.

Executive branch The executive branch of government is responsible for carrying out or enforcing the laws that have been passed by the legislative branch. Each level of government (federal, state, and local) has an executive branch. The President of the United States heads the executive branch of the federal government. Governors run the executive branch of the states, and mayors run the executive branch of cities.

Exigent (emergency) Circumstances Exigent (emergency) circumstances necessitate that police officers enter a home or other building, or extend the parameters of a search, without obtaining a warrant.

FBI Federal Bureau of Investigation

Federal Bureau of Prisons The federal correctional system is overseen by the Federal Bureau of Prisons.

Federal Circuit Courts of Appeals The Federal Circuit Courts of Appeals consists of the -ninety--four United States judicial districts which are or-ga-nized into twelve regional circuits (plus the Federal Circuit), each of which has a United States court of appeals.

Federal Court System The federal court system is a three tiered system that was originally set up by Article III of the U.S. Constitution.

Federal District Courts Federal district courts are the trial courts of the federal government.

Federal Law Enforcement Federal law enforcement includes all law enforcement agencies within the federal government.

Felony A criminal offense that is punishable by death or incarceration in a prison facility for at least one year.

First Appearance If an arrested person is unable to make bail, they must be brought before a judge or magistrate "without unnecessary delay" for their first appearance in court.

Furman v. Georgia A 1972 U.S. Supreme Court case that suspended all executions in the United States because the death penalty was often used arbitrarily and disproportionally used based on the race of the defendant.

Gagnon v. Scarpelli The right to the Preliminary Inquiry Hearing was established for probationers in 1973 by the United States Supreme Court case of *Gagnon v. Scarpelli*.

Georgia v. Gregg A 1976 U.S. Supreme Court case that reinstated the death penalty in all states that use a bifurcated -(two--stage) process for deciding if a defendant qualified for the death penalty.

Golden Rule "Do unto others as you would have them do unto you"

Good Faith Exception In the 1984 U.S. Supreme Court case of *United States v. Leon* the court allowed for the admission of evidence that would normally not be admissible under the exclusionary rule, if the officers acted in good faith.

GPS Monitoring A more sophisticated type of electronic monitoring incorporates global positioning technology (GPS). GPS monitoring allows probation officers to know exactly where their offender is at any given time.

Grand Jury The grand Jury serves the same purpose as the preliminary hearing except that this is not a trial type setting. Instead the evidence is heard by a jury of -twenty--three (usually) citizens.

Great Law of the Quakers The Great Law was the body of laws in Pennsylvania that saw hard labor as a more effective punishment than corporal punishment and death for crimes, and also demanded compensation to the victims.

Herbert L. Packer Herbert L. Packer (1925–1972) was a Professor of Law at Stanford University who wrote the paper "Two Models of the Criminal Process" in 1964.

Hierarchy Rule The Hierarchy Rule counts only the most serious offense and ignores all others that may have occurred at the same time.

Houses of Refuge Established in the early nineteenth century, these houses were designed to deal with children who were not considered to be hardcore criminals and with proper guidance and education could be saved from a life of crime and poverty.

Hung Jury If the jury cannot come to a unanimous verdict then they are a hung jury.

Impropriety The failure to observe standards of honesty.

In re Gault In this case the Supreme Court ruled that in any hearing that could result in a juvenile being committed to an institution, the juvenile has several enumerated rights equal to the rights of an adult.

In re Winship In this case the United States Supreme Court ruled that the same standard of beyond a reasonable doubt that is used in adult criminal cases must also be used in juvenile proceedings.

Incapacitation The modern implication of incapacitation is putting criminals in prison with the ultimate goal of removing them as a threat to society so that they cannot commit any additional crimes.

Indeterminate Sentencing This is a sentence that that provides for a range of time and includes a minimum time that the person must serve before becoming eligible for parole consideration, and a maximum amount of time that indicates the completion or discharge date.

Inevitable Discovery Exception In the 1984 case of *Nix v. Leon*, the court established an exception to the exclusionary rule stating that if illegally seized evidence would have been found legally in the normal course of an investigation (it would have been inevitably discovered), it can be admitted into court.

Infancy A person under a certain age (determined by law) cannot be charged with a criminal offense.

Information The information is a formal accusation submitted to the court by a prosecutor and alleges that a specific person(s) has committed a specific offense(s).

Insanity Plea A legal excuse that says a person is not responsible for their illegal actions because of a mental disease or defect.

Integrity The adherence to moral and ethical principles.

Intensive Supervision A sentence of probation with very strict supervision.

Involuntary Intoxication   A person would have a possible legal excuse if they ingest an intoxicating substance without their knowledge and as a consequence of the intoxication commits an act that would constitute a crime.

Ivan Petrovich Pavlov   Ivan Petrovich Pavlov (1849–1936) experimented with behavior modification the he called "classical conditioning."

Jails   Jails are short term facilities where those who have been convicted of crimes serve a sentence that is generally for a term of less than one year. Jails also hold a host of other persons who have not yet been convicted of a crime.

Jails   Jails are usually local facilities that serve several different functions including housing people who have been arrested and awaiting trial and those who are serving time for misdemeanor crimes.

John Augustus   John Augustus (1785–1859) is known as the "Father of Probation" based on his work with the Boston courts in the mid 1800s.

John G. Roberts Jr.   The current Chief Justice of the United states Supreme Court.

Judicial branch   The judicial branch of government consists of the courts at each governmental level. The court systems of the federal, state, and local governments are responsible for interpreting the laws passed by the legislative branch and enforced by the executive branch. The United States Supreme Court is the highest court in the country.

Judicial Reprieve   The earliest form of probation was the English courts practice of judicial reprieve.

Judicial Waiver   The process of transferring cases from the jurisdiction of the juvenile court to the jurisdiction of the adult criminal court is called judicial waiver.

Just Deserts   Just deserts incorporates the idea that criminals are responsible for their own actions and their decisions, and that punishment is the natural consequence of those actions.

Justice   While the term justice can have a variety of meanings, for criminal justice it is best described as fundamental fairness.

Justification Defenses   This is a legal defense that states even though the accused person admits to committing a crime, they had a legal justification for doing so and should not be found guilty of the crime. Legal justifications include -self--defense and necessity.

Juvenile   The general accepted definition of a juvenile is a person under the age of eighteen.

Kansas City Experiment   Conducted during 1972 and 1973, the Kansas City experiment attempted to show that crime could be curtailed and citizens would feel safer if there was more police visibility. The experiment failed to prove either hypothesis.

Karl Marx   Many of the conflict theories are based on the writings of Karl Marx (1818–1883).

Kent v. United States   In this case the United States Supreme Court ruled that juveniles are entitled to a juvenile court hearing prior to judicial waiver.

Law Enforcement   Law enforcement is a term that describes the individuals and agencies responsible for enforcing laws and maintaining public order and public safety.

Legal Excuses   A legal excuse is applied when a defendant can show that they should not be held criminally liable for a crime because there was no *mens rea* present.

Legislative branch   The legislative branch of government is responsible for writing and passing all laws. Each level of government (federal, state, and local) has a legislative branch. The United States Congress makes the laws on the federal level. Each state has a legislature that makes the laws for each state. Local governments have a legislative process which is typically comprised of a city council or county commission.

Levels of Security   Prisons are divided into different levels of security: minimum, medium, maximum, and "supermax." The type of prison is based on the types of security features that are included in the construction of the facility as well as the type of prisoner that is housed there.

Lex talionis   The concept of *lex talionis* or "an eye for an eye," was an early philosophy based on the idea that the punishment should equal the crime.

Mala in se   Crimes that are immoral or wrong on their face.

Mala prohibita   Crimes that are only illegal because the government says they are.

Mandatory Sentences   Mandatory sentences require that a certain penalty will be set and carried out in all cases upon conviction for a specified offense (e.g., all persons convicted of burglary would get the same sentence).

Mapp v. Ohio   This is the 1961 landmark U.S. Supreme Court case that applied the exclusionary rule to the states.

Mens rea   The guilty mind.

Metropolitan Police Act   This act was passed in 1829 in England and established the London Metropolitan Police.

Miller v. Alabama   The United States Supreme Court ruled that it is a violation of the Eighth Amendment's prohibition of cruel and unusual punishment to have a law that mandates life in prison without the possibility of parole for juvenile homicide offenders.

Miranda v. Arizona   This 1966 United States Supreme Court case established the rights that must be given to a suspect who is in custody and being questioned by the police.

Misdemeanor   An offense that is punishable by incarceration, usually in a jail facility, for a period of time less than one year.

Mistake of Fact   This a legal excuse for committing an act that would constitute a crime but the person did so without the requisite *mens rea*.

Mistake of Law   This is a legal excuse for committing an act that would constitute a crime when the law is vague or was not properly published.

Mitigating Circumstances   Mitigating circumstances are those that favor the defendant and tend to reduce some of the blame for the crime.

Morals   Relate to an individual's standards and beliefs as to what is right and wrong

Morrissey v. Brewer   The right to the Preliminary Inquiry Hearing was established for parolees in 1972 by the United States Supreme Court case of *Morrissey v. Brewer.*

NCVS   The National Crime Victimization Survey (NCVS) is a statistical survey that attempts to find out how much crime is not reported to the police.

Necessity   A legal justification for when a person commits a crime for the sole reason of preventing a more serious crime.

New Charges   If a person who is on probation or parole commits a new crime they can be bought back before the judge or parole board for revocation proceedings.

NIBRS   The National -Incident--Based Reporting System is an enhanced version of the UCR that collects much more detailed information about each reported crime.

Offenses and Infractions   An offense for which the penalty is usually a fine or some other form of -non--incarceration punishment; however, limited jail time is an option in most jurisdictions.8

Opening Statement   The first part of the trial is the opening state-ments. The opening statements are made by both the prosecution and the defense. These statements are a brief outline of the case that each side will present.

parens patriae   the state takes on the role of the parent.

Parole Board   The parole board is a panel of individuals who decide whether an inmate should be released from prison on parole after serving a portion of their sentence.

Parole   Parole refers to criminal offenders who are conditionally released from prison to serve the remaining portion of their sentence in the community under the supervision of a parole officer or agent.

Part I Crimes   Part I crimes include the eight most serious crimes: murder, rape, robbery, and aggravated assault.

Part II Crimes   The UCR compiles data on -twenty--one additional crimes not included in Part I. These crimes are only counted when an actual arrest is made.

Pat--down Search   A -pat--down search is a cursory search of the outer clothing for the purpose of determining if the suspect has a weapon.

Patrol   Patrol is considered to be the backbone of police work at the local and state levels of law enforcement. Patrol is also the most expensive item in police department budgets.

Penitentiary   The Quakers developed the concept of a "penitentiary," a place where prisoners could reflect on their crime in silence and repent over their -wrong--doing.

Pennsylvania System   The Walnut Street Jail became a model for what became known as the "Pennsylvania System" of prison design and philosophy.

Peremptory Challenge   Peremptory challenges are also made by both the prosecution and the defense; however the attorneys do not have to state a reason for wanting a juror removed from the jury pool.

Phrenology   Phrenology is the studying of the skull to determine personality traits.

Plain View Doctrine   The "plain view doctrine" states that if a police officer is lawfully at a location and he sees contraband within his view, he may seize it without a warrant.

Plea Bargaining   Plea bargaining is the negotiation between the prosecutor and the defendant (usually the defendants attorney) which results in the defendant entering a plea of guilty in exchange for a reduction of charges or sentence.

Police   Police departments (at all levels) are the largest and most visible component of the Criminal Justice System and operate under the Executive Branch of government. Police are tasked with the job of enforcing the criminal laws within their jurisdiction.

Positivist School   The positivist school of thought believed that crime could be eliminated through the systematic application of the scientific method.

Precedent   Prior case law that is used as the basis of new court decisions.

Preliminary Hearing   The preliminary or probable cause hearing is a formal court preceding that is used to determine if there is probable cause to justify the arrest and to send the case over to the grand jury (in some jurisdictions) or to the trial court.

Preliminary Inquiry Hearing   This is an administrative hearing to de-termine if there is probable cause to hold the defendant in custody pending their revocation hearing before the court or parole board.

Preponderance of the Evidence   This is the level of evidence used to determine the outcome of a civil case. The winner of a civil case is deter-mined by which party has the most impressive or convincing evidence.

Presumptive Sentencing   Presumptive sentencing is a model that combines the use of indiscriminate sentencing with that of determinate sentencing.

Prisons   Prisons are long term facilities that are operated by state and federal governments and hold prisoners who have been convicted of felony crimes.

Prisons   Prisons are long term facilities that are run by the state or the federal government. Prisons generally house those who have been convicted of felonies and are serving sentences that are typically one year or longer in length.

Private Prisons   Private prisons in the United States are run by private corporations under the supervision of government correctional agencies.

Probable Cause   A simplified working definition (not a legal definition) of probable cause for an arrest is: *It is more likely than not that the person being arrested committed the crime that they are being arrested for.*

Probation Officer   Probation officers are responsible for the supervision of those offenders who have been placed on court ordered probation.

Probation   Probation is a form of sentencing where the offender is given a jail or prison sentence that is suspended, and is then placed on community supervision in lieu of actually serving time.

Property Crimes   Property crimes (crimes against property) include: burglary, larceny (theft), motor vehicle theft, and arson.

PSI   The presentence investigation (PSI) is a detailed background investigation that is conducted on the defendant to assist the judge in determining what sentence should be imposed.

Psychological Theories   Psychological theories look at the individual as the focus of study.

Punitive Damages   Money awarded in a civil court intended to punish the party who is at fault and caused the injury.

Rate of Crime   Rates of crime are generally expressed as "*x* number of offenses per 100,000 people." This provides a crime rate that can be compared over time, and from one geographic location to another.

Reasonable Suspicion   Reasonable suspicion can be defined as the level of evidence that a police officer needs in order to justify the detention of an individual who is suspected of engaging in criminal activity.

Recidivism   Recidivism is mea-sured by new criminal acts conducted by an offender under supervision that result in the -re--arrest, reconviction, or return to prison with or without a new sentence being imposed during a -three--year period following the prisoner's release.

Rehabilitation   Rehabilitation is the philosophy premised on the idea that criminals can be "cured" and made to change their criminal ways.

Residential Placement Facilities   Juvenile correction facilities, the equivalent of an adult prison, are generally called residential placement facilities.

Restorative Justice   The concept of restorative justice focuses on the needs of the victim and society, as well as the offender.

Retribution   A more modern philosophy based on the concept of *lex talionis* that states the actual punishment should match the crime as closely as possible so that the offender can feel the same pain as they caused the victim.

Revocation Hearings   Revocation hearings are held before the judge who originally sentenced the offender to probation, or in cases of parolees they are held before the parole board.

Revocation Proceedings   When an offender violates any of the terms and conditions of their supervision agreement, they may be arrested and brought back before the granting authority (the court or the parole board) for revocation proceedings.

Roper v. Simmons   The court ruled that the minimum age for imposing the death penalty is eighteen.

ROR   Release on recognizance (ROR) allows a person to be released from jail prior to trial on their promise to refrain from criminal activity and to return to court at the date and time specified without having to post collateral.

Rule of Four   In order for a case to be accepted for review, at least four of the Justices must agree to hear the case.

SARA   Scanning, Analysis, Response, and Assessment

Schall v. Martin   The court ruled that the "pretrial" detention of juveniles is allowable if there was a serious risk that the juvenile would commit another crime if released.

Scientific method: The scientific method uses observation, hypothesis, the testing of the hypothesis, analysis of the data (interpretation), and conclusion as the basis of validating any theory.

Search Incident to a Lawful Arrest   When the police make a lawful arrest, they are allowed to conduct a complete search of the person arrested as well as the area within the immediate control of the arrestee.

Selection of the Jury   The first order of business in a jury trial is the selection of the jury.

Self--Defense Laws   Laws that give a person the right to defend themselves if they are attacked without provocation.

Sentencing Reform Act of 1984   The goal of the Sentencing Reform Act of 1984 was to eliminate sentencing disparity through the use of guidelines that were based on both offense and offender characteristics.

Sheriff   Most commonly the sheriff is considered to be the chief law enforcement officer in a county.

Shire--reeve   The -Shire--reeve was the Sheriff of the County in early England.

Sigmund Freud   Sigmund Freud (1856–1939) developed the psychoanalytic theory in which he tried to explain human behavior in terms of the unconscious.

Sir Robert Peel   Sir Robert Peel (1788–1850) was responsible for getting the Metropolitan Police Act passed in 1829 in England, which established the London Metropolitan Police.

Social Contract   The social contract is an implied agreement between citizens and their government as a way of maintaining social order.

Social Justice   The concept of social justice varies from society to society and deals with the perception of what constitutes right from wrong within that society.

Social Process Theories   The foremost social process theories fall under the broad heading of social learning. Social learning theorists say that crime and criminal behavior is a product of learning the norms and values of criminal behavior.

Social Structure Theories   Social structure theories include social disorganization theory and the strain theory (as well as others). Social disorganization theory ties crime rates to the structure of individual neighborhoods.

Society   A society is a structured group of people with similar traits (traditions, culture, nationality, moral values). We all live in several different societies at the same time.

Special Conditions   Special conditions of probation and parole are those which are specially tailored to the offender based on the type of offense committed and/or needs of the offender.

Specialized Police Agencies   Specialized police departments have limited jurisdiction over specific areas of concern.

Speedy Trial   While the Sixth Amendment of the United States Constitution states that the accused in any criminal prosecution is entitled to a speedy and public trial, the Court has left it up to the states to define the time constraints.

Split Sentencing   Judges will occasionally sentence offenders to a short period of time in jail, typically thirty, sixty, or ninety days, before they are released on probation.

Standard Conditions   Standard conditions of probation/parole are those which are included in all probation and parole agreements and must be followed by all offenders.

Stare decisis   The practice of following precedent when deciding new cases.

State Law Enforcement   State law enforcement consists of all of the law enforcement agencies operating at the state level within individual states.

Status Offenses   Status offenses are violations that if committed by an adult would not be a criminal act.

Statutory Law   These are the laws that are passed and enacted by the legislative branch of government (at all levels) and then codified into written statutes.

Strict Liability Crimes   These are crimes that do not require concurrence between *actus reus* and the *mens rea.*

Structured Sentencing   Structured sentences were designed to reduce judicial discretion when it comes to sentencing. Determinate sentencing, mandatory sentencing, and presumptive sentencing all fall under the heading of structured sentencing.

Supermales   The British geneticist Patricia Jacobs discovered that a small percentage of males have an extra male chromosome (XYY) and were labeled "supermales."

"Supermax" Prisons   These facilities house the worst and most dangerous prisoners. These prisoners are usually sent to these facilities when they have killed other prisoners or have assaulted correctional officers.

Technical Violation   A technical violation is a failure to comply with one of the conditions of supervision (either a standard condition or a special condition) that does not amount to a criminal violation.

Teleological Ethics   Judges the consequences of the act to determine whether the act was good.

Tennessee v. Garner   This is the 1985 U.S. Supreme Court landmark case that set forth the procedures that law enforcement must follow when using deadly force.

Terry v. Ohio   The landmark U.S. Supreme Court case that established the level of evidence of reasonable suspicion.

"Three--Strike" Laws   Some states have enacted mandatory sentencing laws called "three strikes" that mandate long term incarceration for offenders upon conviction of their third felony.

Tort   A civil wrong.

"Truth in Sentencing" Laws   States that have enacted truth in sentencing laws have done so in order to reduce the possibility of early release from incarceration.

Tything   The tything system which was used in early England made all citizens responsible for law and order in each community.

U.S. Marshals Service   The U.S. Marshals Service is the oldest federal law enforcement agency.

UCR   The Uniform Crime Report (UCR) is a nationwide statistical compilation of reported crime data from more than 18,000 city, county, state, tribal, university and college, and federal law enforcement agencies.

United States Constitution   The United States Constitution is the basis of all laws in the United States and was ratified and became the law of the land on June 21, 1788. The Constitution also set up the framework of our government and defined the roles of the three separate branches.

United States Supreme Court   The United States Supreme Court is the highest court in the federal Judiciary and in the United States.

Utilitarianism   The right course of action is the one that maximizes happiness and reduces suffering.

Values   A set of common beliefs held by a person that has an emotional component that serves as a guide to enable that person to apply their moral beliefs to decide what is right and wrong.

Venire   The venire is the group of prospective jurors summoned by the court to report at a specified date and time.

Veterans Courts   These courts are designed to assist these veterans who have committed misdemeanor and nonviolent felony crimes and were created to assess and assist veterans who may have underlying -military--related problems that could be the cause of their criminal activity.

Violent Crimes   Violent crimes (crimes against persons) include: murder, rape, robbery, and aggravated assault.

Voir dire   The questioning of the prospective jurors by the defense attorney, the prosecutor, and the judge is called the *voir dire.*

Walnut Street Jail   The Walnut Street Jail was the first true penitentiary in the United States and was opened in Pennsylvania in the United States in 1790.

Warrant   A warrant is a court order issued by a judge that authorizes a police officer to make an arrest or conduct a search.

Watchmen   The watchmen were citizens who were paid to patrol the streets and guard the gates of the town in 1600 and 1700 England.

William Penn   William Penn (1644–1718) was the founder of Pennsylvania and the leader of the Quakers.

Writ of Certiorari   A *writ of certiorari* is a court order that is issued by an appeals court to a lower court telling them to send up the record of the proceedings of the case.

INDEX